Italian TV Drama and Beyond
Stories from the Soil, Stories from the Sea

by Milly Buonanno

Translated by Jennifer Radice

intellect Bristol, UK / Chicago, USA

First published in the UK in 2012 by
Intellect, The Mill, Parnall Road, Fishponds, Bristol, BS16 3JG, UK

First published in the USA in 2012 by
Intellect, The University of Chicago Press, 1427 E. 60th Street,
Chicago, IL 60637, USA

Copyright © 2012 Intellect Ltd

All rights reserved. No part of this publication may be reproduced, stored in a retrieval system, or transmitted, in any form or by any means, electronic, mechanical, photocopying, recording, or otherwise, without written permission.

A catalogue record for this book is available from the British Library.

Cover designer: Persephone Coelho
Copy-editor: MPS Ltd.
Typesetting: John Teehan
Production manager: Tim Mitchell

ISBN 978-1-84150-459-9

Contents

	Introduction	1
	Invisible Italian TV drama	3
	The structure of the book	7
1.	**Building the Nation: The Origins of Italian TV Drama**	**11**
	The words to say it	13
	The domestic stage	14
	Literary adaptation	16
	Electronic library	17
	The implication approach	19
	The foreign sources of a national genre	22
	Literature and history	24
2.	**The Cinematic Turn and the Americanization of the Television Landscape**	**27**
	Keeping the cinema at bay	29
	The cinematic turn	33
	The rise of the miniseries	37
	The flood of American imports	39
	The Italian response to *Dallas*	42
3.	**The Political Career of a Popular Fiction: *La Piovra (The Octopus: The Power of the Mafia)***	**49**
	A phenomenon of popularity	51
	Bond and beyond	52
	An *intertextual* octopus	53
	The origins of *La Piovra*'s success	55
	Mafia plots	59
	Social melodrama	63
	The fascination of the loser	68
	Italian-style serial	74
	Television event	80
	The Mafia and politics	83

4. *A Place in the Sun*: The First Italian Soap Opera 89
   Escape from fiction 91
   Turning point 93
   The close encounter of local and global 95
   An Italian sense of place 97
   A seminal story 100

5. Mimetic Heroes and Ironic Leaders: The Genesis and Evolution of Italian Police Drama 107
   The season of the detective story 109
   Stories from the sea 110
   Stories from the soil 113
   The funny detective 116
   The hero is 'one of us' 119
   A 'heritage' trilogy 121
   Squads 125
   The girls with a gun 127
   Women on top 130
   The merging of sailor's and peasant's storytelling 134

6. In the Footsteps of *La Piovra*: Twenty years of Mafia stories in Italian TV drama 139
   Mob stories are always hot: a tour d'horizon 141
   A 20-year cycle 145
   The centrality of Cosa Nostra 146
   Facts burst into fiction 149
   Heroes and villains 153
   A male-dominated genre and its exceptions 157
   The Mafia is everywhere 162

7. Life Stories: A Heroic Enclave and the Rise of the Religious Biopic 165
   The rebirth of the biopic 167
   Anti-heroic society 169
   The biography genre and the shifting definition of the fame 172
   A heroic enclave 176
   The Bible Project 179
   A plural catholicism 188

8. **The Re-enactment of the Past and the Politics of Memory and Identity in Contemporary Drama**   **197**
    The temporal turn   199
    Past and present   206
    Television as historian   209
    Divided, denied, shared memory   214
    'We are not like them'   221

Conclusion   **225**
    The convocative power of the mainstream drama   227
    Visibility for what?   231

References   **235**

Index   **253**

*With immense gratitude, I dedicate this book
to the memory of Manuel Alvarado.*

MB

Introduction

Invisible Italian TV drama

Italy is world famous for a number of reasons: fashion and style, good food and wine, Tuscan sun, magnificent landscapes, an enviable historical and artistic patrimony, opera, football teams, Ferrari cars, the strange case of a media tycoon turned prime minister and so forth. But, however much we may extend the list by adding trite stereotypes (pizza, spaghetti and mandolins) and negative clichés (the Mafia), we will never find any mention (for better or for worse) of Italian TV drama.

This is not much of a surprise. In Italy as elsewhere – although there are well-known exceptions to the rule, related but not limited to the usual Anglo-American suspects – the popularity of homegrown television drama remains confined within national boundaries, in sharp contrast with the world renown enjoyed by Italy in the field of cinema.

Although Italian cinema has been languishing since the 1970s, merely surviving, as it were – despite occasional and much-awaited signs of a resurgence of its one-time splendour – it is still in fact widely known, fondly remembered by international filmgoers and cinephiles. And a number of genres, as well as periods of its history, from the epics of the silent era to post-World War II neo-realism, the spaghetti westerns of the 1960s, have, over the years, continued to attract plenty of scholarly attention on the international scene of film studies. Keying 'Italian cinema' or 'Italian film' in the research string of Amazon, Google books, JSTOR, Ingenta Connect and similar search engines results in a legion of publication titles. However, the same test would undoubtedly demonstrate that just the opposite is true with television drama, excepting of course the works published in Italy in the Italian language (and a handful of writings by the present author in other languages).

Is Italian television, in general, deemed much less worthy of academic interest and work with respect to the cinema? However plausible, the affirmative answer to this question does not entirely convince, given the fact that a sizeable body of literature, produced by national and international scholars, exists and circulates in journals and books dealing with different aspects of the Italian broadcasting system, history and programming, such as the deregulated rise of commercial networks, television and politics, television news, prospects of public service, and more than anything else, the 'Berlusconi factor'. In addition, and mostly in relation to the Berlusconi factor, a 'narrative image' (Ellis, 1992) of Italian television has taken shape, which bears the disreputable marks of excess in the provision of trash programmes. I am unable to say to what extent such an image has spread through public opinion and scholarly circles outside Italy – where it prevails in the commonsensical perception of contemporary national television – but it is interesting to note the unusual way it has been received and housed as it were in an international journal. When the authoritative *International Journal of Cultural Studies* embarked on its second decade of existence, it smartened up its cover. Starting with the June 2008 issue, the cover features a magnificent photographic composition by the artist Patrick Nicholas, who likes to reproduce artistic masterworks of the past, reinterpreting them as if modern. The picture was inspired by Johann Heinrich Füssli's most famous painting, the sombre and disturbing *Nightmare* (1781). Like the original, the picture shows a sleeping girl in the foreground whose head and arms are hanging over the edge of a bed, mind and body sunk in deep slumber. Unlike the original, however, the photograph does not have recourse to allegories of monsters to conjure up the oppressive fear of troubled sleep. The body of the sleeping girl stands out against a background of a wall, tilted and encircling her, covered with television screens. Thus, for the artist, the present-day nightmare is television and reality television in particular, as the title of the photo ('Reality') indicates, and as is exemplified by the panoply of images displayed on the screens. And one remarkable detail stands out, illustrating the Gothic horror of reality shows, in that the artist has chosen to use images recognizably taken from Italian television programmes.

I offer this example only in support of the fact that Silvio Berlusconi's media power and trash TV – two elements that are not infrequently regarded as inseparable, tied together in a symbiotic relationship or a causal connection – now seem to constitute the most conspicuous features of the Italian television scene, even more so in the eyes of those who observe it from outside Italy. Undeniably, the rise, on more than one occasion, of a media mogul to the head of Italy's government provides irresistible grounds for curiosity and interest, and prompts questions concerning media power and control that must be asked again and again. And I do not wish to deny or underrate the demeaning vulgarity of a good deal of domestic entertainment programmes. But as far as the Italian television landscape is concerned, there is more than meets the eye: namely, TV drama.

'More than meets the eye' proves particularly appropriate in relation to TV drama, as the fictional forms of homegrown televisual storytelling are practically invisible, simply overlooked outside Italy. I should recall here the useful notion of 'invisible television' that has recently been advanced and explored in the spring 2010 issue of the journal *Critical Studies in Television*; the term is intended to capture the idea that a substantial amount of televisual content hardly ever (or never) enters the sphere of attention and interest of media scholars and thus remains unnoticed – or literally 'unseen within academia' (Mills, 2010: 1). In principle, the notion of invisibility seems to apply more properly to individual programmes, which, their longevity and high ratings notwithstanding, 'are repeatedly ignored by the vast majority of academic work' (Mills, 2010: 1). However, Sue Turnbull's article in the same issue (Turnbull, 2010) looks at the question of disinterest in most Australian television within Anglophone media scholarship, and convincingly demonstrates that the applicability of the notion 'invisible television' can be extended to entire national landscapes or large bodies of televisual texts, which are 'repeatedly ignored' by and unknown to the vast majority of international scholars.

As a clear instance of invisible television, Italian TV drama appears even more flawed than Australian programmes. One fatal flaw is, first and foremost, the language disadvantage, which, by making it unsuitable for export (and more so, to Anglophone countries), precludes *a priori* the very possibility that an Italian drama might enter the horizon of consciousness of foreign audiences and scholars – a necessary but insufficient premise behind the rise, to some degree, of extra-local visibility and interest.

But the truth is that even if such premises existed, or in other words, even if the basic conditions of international circulation were present, Italian TV drama would be an extremely improbable candidate for visibility within the 'taste community' (Hills, 2010: 96) of current television scholarship. Matt Hills, in the above-mentioned issue of *Critical Studies in Television*, acutely identifies and discusses the main requisites of what has come to be considered worthy of attention and a subject for case studies in academia nowadays, among which are novelty, edginess, cult status, narrative complexity, transmediality, technological now-ness, youth following, forensic fandom and the like.

It would be extremely unlikely for TV drama produced in Italy to keep pace with such demanding requirements – which, needless to say, are tailored to fit high-end high-budget American drama, and in any event end up by granting it the highest visibility in the show-case of academic work. A few reminders about Italian society and television will suffice to put the earlier statement into context.

Although it is not a country 'for' old people – does such a thing exist anywhere? – Italy is a country with an increasingly large proportion of elderly people (over 65 years), currently the largest in Europe (20,6), and the second largest in the world after Japan. Although the rejuvenation of audiences is what Italian broadcasters yearn for (and commercial channels boast better results here than their public counterpart), the hard fact remains that the average viewer's age for the largest number (four out of six) of major broadcast channels is over 60, which clearly cannot be disregarded by drama production and programming policies. This is even more so when further factors are taken into account; for example homegrown drama happens to be commissioned and screened almost exclusively by just two networks – Raiuno and Canale 5, flagships respectively of the Rai and Mediaset – and, apart from the soaps, the bulk of production is aired in prime time and is intended for a generalist audience, made up of segments of diverse demographics, among which elderly viewers systematically prevail to a greater (Raiuno) or lesser (Canale 5) extent. Younger viewers have not altogether deserted the broadcast networks – which still gather a combined market share of 75% – when it comes to reality, talent, cabaret and satirical shows. But their interest in domestic fiction is scarce, with the exception of a few family-teen dramas, and they prefer by far the US 'quality' series on offer both on broadcast and niche channels on digital and satellite platforms (but mostly accessed via Internet and free downloading). It has to be added that, contrary to developments in the United States, where innovative products launched by cable outlets have triggered a virtuous circle of competition between broadcasting and narrowcasting television, in Italy no serious challenge or competitive stimulus to mainstream drama on traditional channels has come from the satellite environment, to date. Despite the critical accolades and cult status gained by a handful of dramas that have been produced by niche channels over the last five years, it is clear that domestic fiction is not intended for, or destined to become, a staple of narrowcasting television in Italy.

This nexus of circumstances does not encourage broadcasters to push the envelope of TV drama, venturing into the risky territories of innovation, as far as formulae and genres, concepts and contents, language and style, aesthetics and technology are concerned. In fact, small doses of novelty are indeed being injected, albeit cautiously, into Italian TV drama, which, on the whole, continues to be made in the good (or not always so good) old-fashioned way, i.e., in tune with the tastes and consumption habits of a mostly ageing, viewing audience who – like it or not – are the main determinants of the success of domestic TV drama. To highlight that the latter is much more mainstream than edgy, more narratively linear than multi-strand, simple rather than complex and, moreover, slow-paced, barely hyperdiegetic, wary of generic experimentation – and to make a potentially long list short, lacking the most accredited markers of contemporary quality drama – is the same as saying that it would be a poor competitor in gaining visibility on the international television scholarship scene.

However, this does not prevent Italian TV drama from having either high cultural significance within Italian society (admittedly a rather obvious requisite, and which risks being dismissed as 'too parochial') or being of broader trans-local interest, as I hope to show.

This book is intended to fill the current void of knowledge on the international scholarly scene as regards Italian television storytelling. TV drama in Italy has, from the beginning, displayed distinctive features, which are the hallmarks of its identity and its difference, and which, to the extent that they are related to national history and culture, provide deep insights into past and present Italian society.

However, the book is not aimed at elaborating on the distinctiveness of Italian TV drama as if it were a kind of walled preserve of national culture, untouched by any outer contact and influence. On the contrary, I develop the idea that in many significant instances, the formation of what has come to be considered as peculiarly 'national' storytelling has gone through a process of recombination between domestic and foreign, native and imported, local and global elements and cultural ingredients. In this way, the work joins that stream of studies, which, under the challenge of re-configuration of contemporary television landscapes, acknowledge the need to re-think and re-conceptualize the meaning and genesis of what counts as national and not national in the production and consumption of media cultures.

This work is equally in tune with the historical turn that is now emerging in European television studies. Without being a full rendering of the history of Italian TV drama, this book is engaged in the reconstruction of its crucial stages of development and it privileges, in many chapters, a diachronic perspective which embraces middle to long-term periods. On the other hand, I am also committed to counterbalancing a double and related trend that is well established in current western TV studies, i.e., the almost exclusive focalization on Anglo-American TV drama, more recently boosted by the much-celebrated emergence of new golden ages of (mainly US) television fiction, and the penchant for case studies of individual TV series. As an alternative, this book heralds and adopts a more comprehensive approach to televisual storytelling and a shift of focus outside (albeit in relation to) Anglo-American drama.

The title and the subtitle of the book are intended to pay homage to authors to whom I feel intellectually indebted, as they have been a great inspiration for writing many pages of the manuscript, the two longest Chapters (3 and 5) in particular. I refer to Tony Bennett and Janet Woollacott, whose *Bond and Beyond* (1983) provided the (unattainable) model for the intertextual analysis of the hugely popular Mafia story *La Piovra*; and Walter Benjamin, whose suggestive metaphors of the peasant and the sailor as archaic masters of storytelling I have appropriated to account for the evolution of the Italian police series. Furthermore, the title and subtitle are meant to communicate from the cover onwards the approach I have adopted in dealing with the topic, i.e., a contextualist and relational approach, inasmuch as domestic drama leads the discourse beyond itself into the wider context of Italian history, society and culture, and the process of its identity formation and transformation can be traced back to the interrelationships with different 'others', be it national cinema or international television, springing from the local soil or coming from overseas lands.

The structure of the book

The book is divided into eight chapters, which ideally, though not formally, coalesce into two sections. The first four chapters selectively retrace the history of Italian television drama from mid-1950s to mid-1990s, focusing on the key elements – starting and turning points, groundbreaking narratives and seminal processes – that characterized the domestic dramatic landscape over four decades.

The opening chapter revolves around the *sceneggiato* as a crucial component in the 'nation-building' strategy pursued by early Italian television. Be it literary adaptation or period and biographical drama, the *sceneggiato* re-enacted for the Italians – a culturally diverse and largely illiterate population in the 1950s – the major historical events and the novelistic tradition in which a once fragmented country turned one nation in relatively recent times was encouraged to recognize the roots – and the routes – of a common history and national belonging.

The reshaping of the Italian televisual system, which came about with the genesis and development of commercial broadcasting in the 1970s and 1980s, was accompanied by a process of internationalization, more specifically of Americanization. This process spread to all levels and found striking concretization in a true deluge of imports from the United

States. The second chapter recalls the 'great transformation' of the Italian television landscape, highlighting the instrumental role played by US imports (particularly *Dallas*) in favouring the establishment of commercial television, and the 'internationalization from within' by which domestic TV drama reacted to internationalization from abroad.

The third chapter is dedicated to the case study of *La Piovra* (*The Octopus. Power of the Mafia*), without any doubt the most remarkable in the whole history of Italian TV drama, owing to its unequalled popular appeal and status as an authentic 'media event' that the programme gained after its first appearance in 1984. Acclaimed as the 'Italian response to *Dallas*', *La Piovra* was a melodramatic and visionary Mafia story, a recombinant drama under several respects (genre, content, visual style, narrative structure), a veritable text of Italian identity, yet in many ways influenced by the American competitor it was intended, and proved – impressively – to be able to overcome.

Chapter 4 wishes to illustrate the Italian case as highly representative of the practices of adoption and adaptation, the processes of negotiations and hybridization, through which in contemporary television ecologies the local is produced, reproduced, modified and, as it were, kept alive. After more than a decade of crisis, in the second half of the 1990s, Italian TV drama entered a phase of renaissance. This was also due to long-running serial forms, alien until then to the local tradition, introduced by means of international formats and production practices. The first Italian soap opera *A Place in the Sun* here provides appropriate material for a case study of format adaptation/indigenization.

The successive four chapters are aimed at outlining the contemporary drama scene through the prism of the major genres (police drama, Mafia story, biopic, period drama) that have emerged from the late twentieth century and in the early 2000s.

Using the categorization advanced by Walter Benjamin as regards popular storytelling – stories told by sailors, and those told by peasants, the former, internationally oriented, the latter locally based – Chapter 5 reconsiders the history of Italian police drama in terms of transition from 'foreign' or international to 'domestic' or national/local storytelling: in other words, from the adaptation of foreign classics in the first two decades of Italian television to the establishment and popularity of the now hegemonic formula *all'italiana* (Italian style) from the 1990s onwards. The contemporary police drama is a fully localized genre, yet this doesn't cover the footprints of a trans-nationalization that is still underway, whereby the sailor's and the peasant's voices converge and merge.

The Mafia story as a narrative genre has proved hugely successful on the big (*The Godfather*) and the small (*The Sopranos*) screens. But nowhere in the world as in Italian TV drama has this genre flourished to the point that almost a hundred Mafia stories have been produced and screened over the last two decades. Chapter 6 provides an overview of this peculiar feature of Italian TV drama, pointing out the persistent glorification of 'cosa nostra' as a kind of criminal aristocracy.

We live in a post or anti-heroic era, as a whole body of current literature frequently reminds us. Popular narratives are, to a greater or lesser extent, an exception (or a counterbalance), inasmuch as they continue to be a factory of imaginary or reality-based heroes. In this latter case, we are dealing with the biography genre or biopic. As discussed in Chapter 7, the peculiarity of Italian TV drama resides in a unique propensity to tell the stories of the major figures of Christianity (Popes, Saints, Prophets, the Christ), thus making the religious biopic a mainstay genre in domestic TV drama.

The passage to the third millennium has coincided with a temporal turn in domestic drama, in the sense that an impressive array of stories set in time past have been produced and, in many cases, successfully aired. Thus the last chapter revolves around the vigorous trend of the re-enactment of the past in contemporary drama, bringing into focus the politics of memory and identity reflected in the cluster of the historical fictions that have drawn inspiration from, and re-enacted, the traumatic and controversial events of twentieth-century Italian history.

Integrative comments and conclusive remarks are provided in the few final pages of the book.

Acknowledgements

Parts of Chapters 1, 2, 4, 5, 7 have been previously published in:

Gilles Delavaud and Denis Maréchal (eds) (2010), *Télévision: le moment expérimental*, London: INA-Apogée (*Une nation en construction*, pp. 31–44).

"Critical Studies in Television" (2009), vol. 4, n. 1 (*From Literary to Format Adaptation: Multiple Interactions Between the Foreign and the Domestic in Italian TV Drama*, pp. 65–83).

Albert Moran (ed.) (2010), *TV Formats Worldwide*, Bristol: Intellect (*A Place in the Sun: Global Seriality and the Revival of Domestic Television Drama in Italy*, pp. 255–270).

"Media International Australia" (2005), n. 5 (*The Sailor and the Peasant. The Italian Police Series Between Foreign and Domestic*, pp. 48–59).

Enric Castello, Alexander Dhoest and Hugh O'Donnell (eds.) (2009), *The Nation on Screen*, Newcastle: Cambridge Scholars Publishing (*Religion and History in Contemporary Italian Television Drama*, pp. 13–28).

Chapter 1

Building the Nation: The Origins of Italian Television Drama

The words to say it

In Italy home-grown television drama is now called 'fiction'. This was not always so. The use of the English word, which replaced the original Italian word *sceneggiato* (or *teleromanzo*), began to gain popularity in professional and academic language, and later in common parlance, some 30 years ago. This coincided with a major change in the Italian televisual system and in culture, brought about by the break-up of public television's monopoly and the advent of private networks (see Chapter 2).

In one sense this was a standardization with the vocabulary of other Latin countries. As Jerome Bourdon has pointed out, 'in the field of television, until the 1980s the word fiction was not used; there was a range of different terms, taken from the theatre ("dramatique" in French, "drama" in English, "Fernsehspiel" in German), the radio and the press ("feuilletons")' (Bourdon, 2004a: 177).[1] During the 1980s a general reformulation of television jargon, mainly under Anglo-American influence, occurred across Europe and well beyond Italy. One consequence was that the previous local variants for 'television drama' ended up converging at the same name. Within the Latin countries, the word was 'fiction' in French, 'ficción' in Spanish and 'ficção' in Portuguese. In each of these instances, however, the word used pertains to the vocabulary of the national language, as is testified by both the dictionary and the pronunciation. The Italian case is different: 'fiction' is and remains an English (or Anglo-American) word, pronounced (more or less correctly) in the English way.

Therefore in Italy we have recourse to a *foreign* word to denote just one concept: *indigenous* televisual storytelling. Thus, a national *signified* is associated with a transnational *signifier*, while the familiar domestic drama is made strange by a non-native word and pronunciation.

Not so long ago, when media-cultural imperialism (Schiller, 1969, 1976 and 1991) still served as 'the central myth of the study of trans-national communication' (Miller, 2000: 3), a similar example would be readily advanced to corroborate the belief that the dominance of Anglo-American media culture went so far as to dictate 'the words to say it', to quote Marie Cardinal (2000). I do not deny that there is some substance in this argument, since the invasiveness of English, especially in media jargon, is indisputable; but that is not the point I wish to emphasize. Rather than resurrecting the much-debated issues of cultural imposition and dependence (not necessarily outmoded: they just have not got us very far!), I think that it is more useful to take as my starting point this emblematic case of lexical and semantic contamination and attempt to reconstruct the relationship between the national and the non-national, the native and the non-native, in Italian television drama. We are dealing with long-term relationships to be regarded as recurrent factors in the history of indigenous television drama, albeit in different configurations according to the evolutionary phases of the national television system and its environment. These relationships helped shape domestic television drama in forms and contents that have in turn become part and parcel of its own tradition and identity.

In what follows I shall focus on TV drama at the dawn of Italian broadcasting. There was no 'fiction' in those early times, but rather its precursor or ancestor, namely the *sceneggiato*. The *sceneggiato* – which literally means 'scripted novel' – was the privileged and almost exclusive narrative genre of Italian television for two decades, from the mid-1950s to the mid-1970s. It enjoyed immense popularity and still today remains firmly established in the vocabulary and generational memory (Colombo and Aroldi, 2003) of older viewers, and is, in addition, often nostalgically evoked by those complaining about the worthlessness, as they see it, of contemporary fiction.

My intention here is to argue that the *sceneggiato* has been a crucial component of the strategy of 'nation building' that was pursued at the inception of Italian television. Whether it was literary adaptation or historical drama, the *sceneggiato* re-enacted for the Italians – a culturally diverse and largely uneducated population at that time – the key historical events and the novelistic tradition in which a once fragmented country, that had become one nation in relatively recent times, was encouraged to recognize the roots – and the routes – of a common history and culture. Interestingly enough, however, this effective vehicle for the construction and transmission of national commonalities and national identity, as the *sceneggiato* proved to be, has from the start entertained apparently contradictory relationships with the cultural heritage of foreign nations. Unfortunately, I do not have sufficiently precise comparative evidence to maintain that this was a feature peculiar to Italy; a history of European television is still in its early stages (Bignell and Fickers, 2008) and the historical macro-overviews that are currently available, valuable though they are, need to be supplemented by focused micro-overviews in the future of European television studies (Jacobs, 2000). Since I am well aware of the temptation (often irresistible to researchers) to proclaim national uniqueness or specificity in the absence of a valid basis for comparison, I shall confine myself to reconstructing the origins of domestic television drama, focusing on the short 'experimental moment' (Delavaud and Maréchal, 2011) of the 1950s, which coincides with the first quinquennium (or a little more) of national broadcasting in Italy.

The domestic stage

Italian state television (Rai) came into being in 1954 and was run for more than two decades as a public service monopoly (Buonanno, 2004a). These are the years that some nostalgically consider to be the golden age of Italian television drama, perhaps of television *tout court* (Colombo and Aroldi, 2003). During these years, Rai's production and programming policies were essentially inspired by cultural and educational principles. Television was first and foremost conceived as a means of enlightening a mass audience and broadening its horizons. If such a conception was shared at that time by most European public television companies (Bourdon, 2004b), in Italy it reflected not so much the adoption of a model and an ethos of public service as the deep-rooted convictions of the Rai's board of directors about the unprecedented educational and cultural potential of the new medium. This ruling group was made up of intellectuals and managers who combined a predominant humanist-literary background with a Catholic-political orientation, responsive to liberal and modernizing aspirations, in accordance with the left wing of the Christian Democratic Party then governing Italy (Monteleone, 1992). It is well known that the Catholic forces were much more far-sighted and advanced than the political and cultural forces of the Left (who remained entrenched for years in their positions of unshakeable ideological denial) in understanding the importance of television and the strategic role that it could play in the process of modernizing Italian society (Gundle, 2000). It may be useful to add that in the 1950s the Catholic world played a prominent part in the organization of popular entertainment, thanks to a widespread network of both parish cinemas and amateur dramatics.

As regards the humanistic roots of televisual culture (Bettetini, 1985), Sergio Pugliese, a distinguished founding father and powerful Director of Programmes from 1954 to 1965, was for example an esteemed playwright. Under his direction the weekly appointment with theatre on Friday evenings became one of the cornerstones of the programme schedule; and the start of transmissions on 3 January 1954 received a theatrical imprint from the live broadcast of a comedy by Carlo Goldoni (Grasso, 1992). Hence the features of the 'domestic stage' that were widely attributed to Italian television at its origins.

Theatre was the favourite pastime of intellectuals and the bourgeois class in Italy. The arrival of television on the scene helped to bring about a remarkable increase in audiences for theatrical drama, which became an established feature of the viewing habits of a broad section of middle-class audiences. The attraction of novelty and the public's declared thirst for instruction (De Rita, 1964) – the viewers seemed to share a somewhat scholastic conception of the new medium – served to confer a fair degree of success on stage plays broadcast on television. So much so, indeed, that some observers were prompted to state, with some exaggeration, that television 'had accomplished the miracle of turning Italy into a country of thespian fans' (Lombezzi, 1980: 51). In fact radio had already gone a long way towards opening the gates of the highbrow citadel of the stage theatre to the people; television followed in its footsteps.

It was, however, not thespian art but novels that turned out to be the main vehicle of widespread diffusion of humanistic and literary culture with respect to the Italian public. Rai's educational scheme found one of its most congenial and fertile fields of expression in the popularization of the novelistic narrative. An intensive if somewhat artisanal production of TV drama was almost exclusively devoted to the latter. Therefore the sense of an enlightening mission coupled with the highest regard for classic culture gave rise to a genre that soon became the hallmark and pride of Italian television drama: the *sceneggiato* (or *teleromanzo*: De Fornari, 1990), a word still used to refer to home-grown television drama by elderly people who are not at ease with the foreignness of the word 'fiction'.

Literary adaptation

The *sceneggiato* was in essence a literary adaptation: a story told in instalments and based on an already published work of fiction or, as people preferred to say, 'from the author's work'. The division into instalments, six on average, and the literary source of the story being narrated were distinctive characteristics of the Italian *sceneggiato*, but they were not sufficient to define it. Its specific identity was constructed from an inseparable ensemble of elements which, together with the narrative formula and the literary source, comprised an expressive model and a cultural project.

Shot in interiors using analogue technology and initially broadcast live, the *sceneggiato* chose the stage, not the cinema, as its reference model. The entire production reflected the deliberate construction of the *sceneggiato* as a theatrical performance: the studio fitted out like a stage with wings and a backcloth, the screenplay divided into 'acts', the actors drawn mainly from the theatre world, the preponderance of dialogues and soliloquies on the action. Particularly in the early days, it was a true 'theatricalized novel', completely in tune with the home theatre that television had originally supplied. But even in later years, when it became possible to record on film, eliminate live broadcasting, edit footage and shoot on location, the original 'theatre in the studio' formula was never completely abandoned.

Linking television drama to the theatre was a coherent and strategic policy on the part of the Rai, coherent with the basic humanistic inspiration, which was reinforced by the alliance between theatre and novel; and strategic in relation to the purpose of conferring legitimacy on television drama, placing it under the banner of an established and prestigious cultural asset. At the same time the aim was to protect television drama from possible association with, and contamination by, the cinema. Various reasons that cannot be explored here (see Chapter 2) counselled against any reference to filmic models (Sanguineti, 1980), be they the so-called *auteur cinéma* which in the previous decade had emerged in the famous neo-realism movement, or the lowbrow Italian film industry that had achieved its greatest successes in Italy with social melodrama, comedy and musical genres. Criticism and televisual aesthetics in turn supported the idea of an essential diversity and a necessary separateness of languages and styles between the two media, and constantly deplored those directors who purported to 'make films on television' (Lombezzi, 1980: 48).

Italy did not of course have exclusivity in literary adaptation, which was cherished by European public television because of its strategic capacity to combine two of the three fundamental purposes of the public service: to educate and to entertain. 'The adaptation of classic literature ... has been a characteristic of British television almost since television began' (Caughie, 2000: 207). In particular, the BBC inaugurated its tradition of 'classic serials' – replacing the previous one-off adaptations (Kerr, 1982) – in the early 1950s, a few years before the inception of Italian television. And French television drama, for its part, made wide use of literary sources from the 1960s (Chaniac, 1996). Literature, like the theatre (or history) thus came to be 'mobilized' in order to provide a cultural legitimacy extrinsic to a medium that was suspected of being 'not itself good' (Brundson, 1997: 113), in Italy as elsewhere.

But it was possibly in Italy that literary adaptations achieved – and kept, for some time – a pre-eminent position on the domestic drama scene in terms of production volumes, magnitude of success and reputation for quality. The great flowering of the nineteenth-century novel provided the sources for hundreds of adaptations that were destined to become hugely popular and would generate phenomena of TV personality worship. Up to 1977 there were always literary adaptations, not infrequently more than one title, among the ten most watched programmes of each season (Grasso, 1992). Their repeats have filled up the night-time programming schedules of the terrestrial networks for years, and have become more recently a resource for satellite and terrestrial digital channels, while many titles are being reissued and marketed as DVDs.

The *sceneggiati* of yesteryear remain established in the Italian collective memory and they remain the most remarkable example of 'national popular TV drama' created by Italian television in the first stage of its history.[2]

Electronic library

Even today, despite a flourishing publishing industry that produces over 60,000 titles per year and a fairly high level of schooling (three out of four Italians have attended school for at least eight years), international comparative research into cultural consumption still brings up the historical 'problem' (Forgacs and Gundle, 2007) of reading habits in Italy. It may be excessive to claim irrefutably, as newspapers frequently do, that 'Italians don't read'; but it cannot be denied that they read less assiduously than other nationalities. For example, almost 45 per cent of Italians over fourteen are habitual readers (at least three books per year) as against over 60 per cent of Germans and the English (AIE, 2010).

Obviously in the 1950s the situation was even worse. At the beginning of the decade the illiteracy rate in Italy as a whole was nearly 14 per cent, while in the southern regions and generally the agricultural areas it almost exceeded 25 per cent. Fewer than 60 per cent of Italians had any educational qualifications (De Mauro, 1991). The low level of education was in turn an obstacle to the acquisition of a common language: the numerous regional languages and dialects remained predominant in everyday speech, whereas the habitual use of standard Italian was confined to a small minority of the educated class. Only 17.5 per cent of all Italian families comprised at least one member who read books (Peresson,

2008). By contrast, illustrated magazines, photostories and comic strips had achieved a huge circulation among ordinary people by the end of the 1940s. The fact was that their strong graphic component offered less literate people the opportunity for visual reading that relied upon the eloquence of the pictures, without the effort needed to decipher the written text.

Thus the cultural scene in 1950s Italy was characterized not so much by general backwardness – indeed the conditions for the 'economic miracle' that was to explode in the 1960s were already developing – as by the wide gap between an élite minority that was able and willing to practise and enjoy reading and the less-educated majority, who were wedded to printed material made more accessible by the predominant presence of 'pictures' ('looking at the pictures' was the expression used in Italy to mean reading through images). These two unequal components of Italian society had neither reading nor language in common.

The extremely effective role played by television, in advance of universal schooling, in bringing about the linguistic and therefore cultural unification of Italians is well known. In this connection the *sceneggiato*, along with other televisual genres, participated in the spread of a national language and thus contributed to the recovery of a 'linguistic commonality' (De Mauro, 1991: 459) that still needed to be created a century after the political and governmental unification of Italy. But the specific contribution of the *sceneggiato*, inherent in its nature of adaptation of novels, and its mission, in this respect, was to promote the development of a common literary culture among Italians. In a society in which familiarity with reading books and novels was the privilege of the few, the *sceneggiato* – inspired by the educational ambition of offering the masses access to the resources of humanistic culture – established and increased intensively over the years the televisual version of a well-stocked library. No less than a huge repository of a novelistic patrimony was brought into the reach of all for the first time.

I shall shortly turn to the specific composition of the novelistic patrimony drawn upon by public broadcasting, in its promotion of a 'literary commonality' founded upon a shared repertory of authors and titles. But first I want to address, briefly, a question that in my view has not been sufficiently clarified in the historiography of early broadcasting in Italy.

The aim of the *sceneggiato* was to bring about an encounter between literature and the people – 'the masses who want to learn, know, enjoy themselves, become elated' (Pugliese, 1964: 73). However, unlike (at least in part) the theatre, it was not the instrument of an operation carried out under a cultural élitist banner, with the purpose of imposing the refined intellectual tastes of highbrow circles on the lowbrow masses. Television drama was an integral part of a scheme for the 'cultural improvement' of the nation. But a similar operation, admittedly *dirigiste*, albeit inspired by 'enlightened' *dirigisme*, would not have succeeded if it had been slanted too much in the direction of 'erudite culture'. In fact the *sceneggiato* achieved such a profound popular impact because, in large measure, it was popular – by reason of its structure, language, visual style and content. It was a scaled-down version of the *feuilleton*, in that the story was divided into instalments; the static character of the scenes and the shots were reminiscent of the aesthetics of the photostory (this, together with the cinema, was the biggest phenomenon of popular entertainment in post-World War II Italy), which were used to offer 'costume drama' in nineteenth-century settings. The scriptwriters and directors, while claiming faithful adherence to the original texts, did not hesitate to 'popularize' the plots by adding large doses of sentimentalism and melodrama, and the actors indulged in melodramatic excess in their recitative style.

Furthermore, and perhaps more importantly, the choice of novels to be transformed into *sceneggiati* did not focus solely on the literary classics and the great works of all time, but were also frequently extended to what in Italy is defined as the *romanzo di consumo* (low literature or popular fiction) or stories for the people. Works were also chosen that had gained fame through earlier film or radio adaptations, in such a way that even those who were not directly familiar with the written texts could sense the cogent recall of the 'return of the already known' (Buonanno, 2007; Eco, 1984), a basic working principle of the popular narrative. The most eloquent proof of a production policy that was only partially interested in respecting the canons and celebrating the classics is supplied by the case of *I promessi sposi/The Betrothed*. Alessandro Manzoni's work, universally acknowledged as the greatest novel in Italian literature, was adapted for the small screen in 1967, thirteen years after the arrival of television (see Chapter 2). The long delay can perhaps be attributed to a reverential fear of competing with such a 'giant' but also, and genuinely, to circumspection prompted by evidence that *I promessi sposi* had never been popular with a wide range of Italian readers – and this remains the case. In fact, wanting first and foremost to popularize literature, the *sceneggiato* created its own mixed repertoire, in which high literature and popular fiction, the great writers of the West and the authors of successful but not outstanding works, co-existed side by side.

The effectiveness of the *sceneggiato* in encouraging the Italian public's acquaintance with literature had appreciable reverberations on the book market: television adaptations fostered an upsurge in sales of novels and the publishers often had to reprint them. Thus the *sceneggiato* was not merely a substitute for reading, but also served to activate it – succeeding to a greater or lesser extent in reinforcing the public's links with the humanistic and literary culture that was regarded as a building block of Italian identity.

The implication approach

In the very first phase of its history (1954–1960) Italian television produced 26 *sceneggiati*, all of them broadcast on the only national channel then existing (the second channel was inaugurated in 1961). Who were the authors and novelists in question? It is worth verifying this in order to grasp in what sense the *sceneggiato* can be considered to be a national genre, and what is meant by the claim that it sought to contribute to the unification of Italians within a common national literary culture. The question has something to do with the implicit postulate that everything classified as 'national' must correspond with generative factors and building blocks that are necessarily situated within the boundaries of the nation itself. The case of Italian *sceneggiato* gives the lie to this postulate, even though it is easy for the mythology of the early days of broadcasting, fostered by a misty and nostalgic recollection of the past, to allow literary adaptation to be romanticized as perhaps the most truly indigenous genre of Italian television: the epitome of the halcyon days when the schedules of the only one or two national channels offered a very high proportion of home-produced programmes, and when imports from foreign, European and extra-European markets, had a very marginal role.

It is indeed true that during the era of its monopoly Italian public television could claim credit for having the highest rate of self-production, in every genre, of all television services in Europe. Bought-in foreign products did not make a significant appearance until the mid-1970s. Nevertheless, to support the belief in a genre that was completely contained within the confines of national culture, without significant and influential contacts with foreign cultures, would be to adhere to the myth rather than the reality of the *sceneggiato*. The latter was certainly indigenous at the level of economy and production practices. It drew on a pool of native creative talents and actors, brought into existence a national star system and also helped with nation-building by addressing its viewers in standard Italian intended to promote unification and linguistic improvement in a multi-dialect population. Moreover, as I said above, the *sceneggiato* thrived in a regime that was notably restricted as regards imports; it was thus sheltered from the influences that might have been exerted by foreign products conveyed by international flows of television.

Precisely in this connection, one cannot but agree with Paul Rixon's warning (2006) against the reductionism that has induced television studies, at any rate in the past, to subsume the question of cultural interactions between different televisual systems under the crowded umbrella of international trade in programming. Although the dynamics of relationships between domestic and foreign, local and cross-border televisual cultures are structured to a considerable extent through the 'visible or quantifiable' import and export of programmes (and, more recently, of formats) (Rixon, 2006: 15), yet there is more here than meets the eye, or can be quantified.

In disciplinary and discursive contexts other than media studies, the prominent globalization scholar Saskia Sassen has on several occasions called for 'digging into the shadow' (Sassen, 2007), to discover elements that might otherwise have escaped our notice, since our attention is more easily attracted by things that are brightly lit. Responding to such an appeal allows us, for example, to glimpse unsuspected and unobserved relationships (some of them elusive, some discernible) that were systematically maintained by Italian *sceneggiato* with televisual and literary cultures outside Italy.

First of all, the identity and the very genesis of *sceneggiato* cannot be completely understood without placing it in the context of the comparison afforded by Italian broadcasting, whether overtly or covertly, with other countries' televisual systems and cultures. These countries were essentially the United Kingdom and the United States, which played the opposing and complementary roles respectively of a virtuous model of public service, committed to educating and improving its citizens, and a depraved model of commercial broadcasting, committed to pandering to the coarse tastes of the uncultured masses. It would be far too simplistic to maintain that admiration for British broadcasting automatically translated into emulation; but the BBC in particular certainly stood for an ideal of public television that was an inspiration for Italian broadcasting and provided to some extent a yardstick against which domestic programmes were appraised and judged for quality.

US broadcasting, by contrast, stood for 'other' television – something to be shunned. This attitude prevailed despite Rai, in its early years, acquiring musical shows (such as the *Perry Como Show*) from the United States, producing very successful domestic versions of the games and quiz shows launched on US networks, and allowing a few American anthologies and drama series to slip into the schedules. In many respects the American televisual system and culture appeared (and was perceived as being) poles apart from Italian broadcasting. This had already happened with cinema. The late 1940s and early 1950s had seen intellectual and cinematographic circles engaging furiously in what was being defined as 'a battle of ideas' in favour of Italian art films and against American cinema: the artistic quality, realist aesthetics and social relevance of Italian neo-realism were contrasted with the standardized (such as they were thought) generic products aimed at the masses, created in industrial style in the Hollywood factory (Forgacs, 1990). When transferred to the field of television storytelling, this contrast was recalibrated around an issue that in Italy has long dominated the intellectual debate on élite culture and mass culture: seriality, as the unmistakable epitome of the 'popular', in fact one of the 'ghosts' that have persistently haunted public broadcasters in Europe despite any attempts at exorcism (Bourdon, 2004b). This issue will be addressed in the other chapters of the book.

The absence of a seriality oriented production culture, which was in turn the corollary of a deep-seated aversion to seriality, was for over 40 years a distinct feature of public television in Italy; and from the start this absence served to mark the key difference between the domestic product and the alien American one. In this instance, it would probably be stretching things to maintain that *sceneggiato* was the offspring of a 'logic of distinction' (Bourdieu, 2007) from American commercial broadcasting, consciously pursued by Italian public television. But there is no doubt that a genre that was constructed on the alliance between literary content, the short running formula and the handcrafted and prototypal production mode, incorporated and expressed a difference when compared with American television drama. This difference became one of the fundamental traits of Italian television's identity, which was modelled, among other factors, on the subtle and elusive interplay of similarities and differences with respect to the televisual 'other', European and American.

I shall again cross the boundaries of media and television scholarship to draw from the thought of Barbara Adam the concept of 'implication'. Adam is the proponent of an innovative theoretical approach to the study of time (Adam, 1995) which advocates and practises the abandonment of the dualisms and dichotomies that are so dear to traditional social science in favour of a 'full-scale implication approach' (Adam, 1995: 155); this proves more appropriate if we wish to grasp the complexity of temporal phenomena (and not only this). The principle of implication 'stresses permeation, interpenetration, simultaneity... thus emphasizing the coexistence and unification of phenomena traditionally considered contradictory, incompatible and incommensurable' (Adam, 1995: 153). This clarification convincingly offers us the chance to resort to an identical or analogous conceptual principle in order to call into question the dualism between the domestic and the foreign in televisual cultural space, and to reconsider their inter-relationship on the basis of analytical categories that are more apt to envisage forms of connection, inclusion, conflation and merging, wherever they exist. In the case of *sceneggiato*, for example, the concept of implication captures and restores in an appropriate manner the embedding, as it were, of foreign references within an indigenous televisual genre.

The foreign sources of a national genre

In yet another way foreignness was implicated in the indigenousness of the *sceneggiato*. Here we are dealing with a regular and discernible presence, even if it is largely unacknowledged – as nearly always happens with phenomena that are taken for granted. In fact the *sceneggiato*'s narrative material, the stories taken from literary fiction and adapted for the small screen, were for the most part foreign.

I have already premised that, given the absence of an articulated comparative framework, I do not feel entitled to speak of a possible uniqueness in the Italian situation. But when some comparison is made available, the difference emerges clearly enough between the Italian route to literary adaptation and the practices of other countries, where the genre also flourished in the early days of national broadcasting. Even though, as Bourdon affirms, each national television was inclined to combine 'universal literature (that is European, with scarce American additions) and national literature'[3] (Bourdon, 2004a: 180), the latter prevailed. In France 'French literature unquestionably overcame foreign texts'[4] (Chaniac, 1996: 34). In Britain the BBC's classic serials drew primarily on the heritage of national literature, 'the classic English novel established in the canon of English literature' (Nelson, 2008: 50).

The sources of Italian *sceneggiato*, by contrast, were spread throughout international literature, particularly European. It was not simply a question of making room here and there for what might be called universal literature, so as to add a touch of cosmopolitan flavour to a catalogue that was mainly based on Italian titles and authors. What happened was precisely the opposite: Italian novels provided far less inspirational source material for the *sceneggiato* than foreign novels.

Let us look at the origins of the novels from which the 26 *sceneggiati* drew their material. Only seven were Italian; the remaining nineteen were British (10), American (3), French

(3), Russian (2) and German (1). They included *Little Women* by Louisa May Alcott (1955); *Wuthering Heights* by Emily Brontë (1957); *The Romance of a Poor Young Man* by Octave Feuillet (1957); *Humiliated and Insulted* by Fyodor Dostoevsky (1958); *Little Lord Fauntleroy* by Frances Hodgson Burnett (1960); and *Tom Jones* by Henry Fielding (1960), making up a varied sequence of immortal masterpieces, children's classics, high literature and popular novels.

A large series of adaptations was inspired by the novels of authors from Russia (Dostoevsky, Tolstoy, Turgenev, Pushkin, Gogol), Britain (Dickens, Fielding, Thackeray, Austen, the Brontë sisters, Stevenson), France (Hugo, Balzac, Flaubert, Dumas, Zola) and foreign countries in general. Silj reports that between the 1950s and the 1960s, 'out of 307 adaptations of literary works, over 60% were foreign' (Silj, 1988: 187).

A system of storytelling that feeds only partially on native imagery can raise doubts concerning the prerequisite of 'cultural proximity' (Straubhaar, 1991) with respect to the national public that it serves. Or in other words: how could the fact that most literary adaptations narrated non-Italian stories, stories created and set in other countries, be reconciled with the status of a national genre?

The hypothesis that it was a more or less mandatory choice, given the relatively small patrimony of Italian novels bequeathed to us from the nineteenth and early twentieth centuries, is barely plausible. The preponderance of foreign works, alongside the large number of literary adaptations of major works of Italian literature, is due not so much to the lack of indigenous material as to the 'unusually high degree of openness to non-national cultural goods' (Forgacs, 1990: 28), to be regarded as a typically Italian feature.

In fact – and the paradox is only apparent – it was precisely in the throwing open of the gates to non-Italian literature that the Italianness of *sceneggiato* could be recognized. It must be remembered that the widespread presence, in both supply and demand of cultural goods and materials (including books) of foreign origin, has, since the beginning of the twentieth century, accounted for one of the most specific and distinctive components of Italian cultural space. The predominance of translated fiction over novels by Italian authors – the object, in former times, of critical comments by Antonio Gramsci (1985) on the relationship between Italian intellectuals and the people – was a standard feature of the book market throughout the twentieth century, before and after World War II. Research conducted in the latter half of the 1940s, for example, revealed that thirteen out of the twenty novels most read in Italy were translations (Forgacs and Gundle, 2007). During the 1950s, and well beyond, the striking predilection of Italians for foreign writers and novels remained unchanged, as surveys of reading confirmed. In giving preference to non-national literature, the *sceneggiato* went along with and helped to cultivate and spread throughout Italian society those traits of cosmopolitan culture, or more simply of openness to the culture and cultural goods of other countries, that have deep roots in Italy's history and go back well before television was introduced.

Literature and history

In terms of Italian history, it should not be forgotten that the great flowering of the European novel, the main source of the Italian *sceneggiato*, coincided with the crucial historical period when Italian national unity was forged. Literary adaptations helped to put nation building (the socio-political process known in Italy as the *Risorgimento*) into the context of the wider landscape of other nineteenth-century European societies. In fact the *sceneggiato* did not limit itself to contextualizing national unification through European literature; it made the *Risorgimento* the main subject matter of a series of historical dramas, which in this case drew on Italian literature. As I recalled earlier, seven of the 26 *sceneggiati* produced by Rai between 1954 and 1960 were adaptations of works by Italian authors. With the exception of *Canne al vento/Reeds in the Wind*, Grazia Deledda's masterpiece (Nobel Prize in 1926), the other six works all belong to the peculiarly Italian genre of the '*Risorgimento* novel': a variant of the historical novel, which interweaves heroic and patriotic motives with romantic and sentimental themes in the literary re-evocation – not infrequently autobiographical – of the troubled process of creating a unified Italy.

Although this genre had its heart in the nineteenth century, it has been practised intermittently and has enjoyed renewed popularity in later years. One remarkable example is *Il gattopardo/The Leopard* (Giuseppe Tomasi di Lampedusa, 1958). Two of the *sceneggiati* of the early years (*L'Alfiere/The ensign*,[5] 1956, and *Ottocento/Nineteenth Century*,[6] 1960) were in fact based on novels by contemporary living authors, first published in the early 1940s. The other four adaptations drew on nineteenth-century fiction. Two of them (*Piccolo mondo antico/The Patriot*,[7] 1957; *La Pisana/The Woman of Pisa*,[8] 1960) adapted masterpieces of the *Risorgimento* novel; the others drew upon a very famous children's classic, universally known in Italy as *Il libro cuore/Heart: a Schoolboy's Journal* (*Il romanzo di un maestro/The Novel of a Teacher*,[9] 1959) and a popular novel written by a patriot forced into exile (*Il dottor Antonio/Doctor Antonio*,[10] 1954), ignored by histories of literature but already adapted several times for cinema, radio and opera and destined to be the progenitor of Italian *sceneggiati*. *Il dottor Antonio* was the first literary adaptation produced and broadcast by national television in the year (1954) of its inception. It was not by chance that the Italian *sceneggiato* made its debut by telling the story of a young patriot who renounces love and personal freedom and sacrifices his life fighting for the independence and unity of his country.

Novels of the *Risorgimento* genre gave television drama the opportunity to combine literature (both highbrow and popular) and history and, more importantly, the history of Italy's unification. The imminence of the first centenary of Italian unity, celebrated in 1961, certainly provided a stimulus in this sense; it is well known for example that Sergio Pugliese, director of programming, was firmly determined to have *La Pisana* broadcast before the centenary. The *sceneggiato* adapted *Le confessioni di un italiano/The Castle of Fratta* by Ippolito Nievo, writer and Garibaldian hero. 'I was born a Venetian and through the grace of God will die an Italian' is the resonant opening of the novel. The *sceneggiato*, furthermore, found conditions of authentic elective affinity with its own cultural mission in the peculiarly educational message of the *Risorgimento* historical novel, permeated with the values of the fatherland and patriotic sacrifice and depicting the good citizen who contributes to the birth and development of the nation with his virtuous civic actions. This mission was in turn fully consistent with the spirit of the *Risorgimento*, recalling after a century the ideals and achievements of Italian unification, and reappraising them in the context of national language and culture.

The heritage of international literature and the epic of the *Risorgimento*, mediated through national literature, thus constituted the prime materials used by the *sceneggiato* in the early days of broadcasting to help to give Italians a common language and culture and the shared sense of belonging to the same nation.

Notes

1. My translation from the French original: '*dans le champ télévisuel, jusqu'aux années 1980, on n'utilise pas le mot fiction mais une variété de termes, issus du théâtre (français "dramatique", anglais "drama", allemand "Fernsehspiel"), de la radio et de la presse ("feuilletons")*'.
2. It is worth noting in this connection that the *sceneggiato* seems to have established once and for all the quality standards of Italian television drama. Even today the basic requirements of a programme that is to be regarded as 'good TV drama' are recognized as a combination of short form (very few episodes, preferably between two and four), serious content (literary, historical, biographical) and a story set in the past. These prerequisites also structure the viewer's preferences, as emerges from the ranking of the most watched programmes
3. My translation from the French original: '*littérature universelle (c'est à dire européenne, avec un rare ajout américain) et littérature nationale*'.
4. My translation from the French original '*la littérature française l'emportait sans conteste sur les textes étrangers*'.
5. From the novel of Carlo Alianello, *L'alfiere/The Ensign*, Einaudi: Torino, 1943.
6. From the novel of Salvator Gotta, *Ottocento/The Nineteenth Century*, Baldini & Castoldi: Milano, 1945.
7. From the novel of Antonio Fogazzaro, *Piccolo mondo antico/The Patriot*, Galli: Milano, 1895.
8. From the novel of Ippolito Nievo, *Le confessioni di un italiano/The Castle of Fratta*, Le Monnier: Firenze, 1867.
9. From the novel of Edmondo De Amicis, *Cuore/Heart: a School-boy's Journal*, Treves: Milano, 1886.
10. From the novel of Paolo Ruffini, *Il dottor Antonio/Doctor Antonio*, Tauchnitz: Milano, 1855.

Chapter 2

The Cinematic Turn and the Americanization of the Television Landscape

Keeping the cinema at bay

Taking his cue from H. M. Enzensberger's statement about a hypothetical phylogenesis of the media – 'it is a rule of their evolution that each new medium first of all orientates itself towards an older one, before it discovers its own possibilities' (Enzensberger, 1992: 66) – the Italian television historian Aldo Grasso has nicely defined the transformative aptitude and metamorphic nature of the media in terms of 'a tenacious unfaithfulness' to themselves (Grasso, 2000: 130) and to their contingent principles and reference models. Regardless of its potential for generalization, such an imputation seems to apply unconditionally to Italian TV drama when considered in the second phase of its evolution, that began towards the end of the 1960s. In this chapter, I intend to explain precisely how a twofold 'unfaithfulness' to the original premises should have reconverted both cinema and American TV drama, both of them seriously challenged and ostracized at the beginning, into elements that had a crucial impact (in different times and ways) on the development and shaping of the Italian TV drama scene.

In the previous chapter, I discussed the close relationship, established by early Italian television, between the *sceneggiato* and the theatre; but I have left out an analytical investigation of what caused television to distance itself from the cinema – a stance that contrasted with the preference for thespian art, yet reinforced it. It is worth clarifying first that such a symmetrical opposition of preferences was not typical of Italian broadcasting; rather, it displayed undeniable similarities with British television. In his reconstruction of early drama, for example, John Caughie is at pains to underline the lack of connection with the cinema, speculating that 'it may be one of the specific features of British television' (Caughie, 2000: 41). Clearly it was not, but that does not preclude us from recognizing the situated specificity of the factors that in each country accounted for the same television feature. Caughie emphasizes the prevalence in the British context of an essentialist aesthetics, which, in identifying 'liveness' as the quintessential property of television, put the highest value on the medium's ability to capture and render in real time, as in the theatre, the immediacy of a live drama performance.

Such an explanation was equally valid for Italy, where the advent of television had triggered a long-lasting intellectual debate on the so-called 'televisual specific'; in underlining the technical and linguistic differences between cinema and television, the theoretical analysis acknowledged the idea of a televisual originality constructed on the primacy of 'liveness', the centrality of the studio as a performance space and the naturalness of the pre-eminently slow-paced style in contrast to the faster tempo of the elliptical cinematic narrative.[1] The fact that reclaiming the 'televisual specific' did not prevent the establishment of relations of cultural dependency on other expressive forms – the theatre, in the case of TV drama – did not seem to trouble either the theory or the televisual practice of the era.

But 1950s Italian television had in truth its own reasons – cultural, political and competitive – for wishing to keep the cinema at a due distance, both as an aesthetic and productive reference model and as a programming resource. Concerning the last point, the Rai at its debut used films merely as filler,[2] preferring to offer classics, with incursions here and there into popular Italian film (Monteleone, 1999). Yet even when it inaugurated a new course of greater valourization of the cinema, it maintained its restricted programming to just one film per week on each channel[3] (in 1961 a second channel was launched).

Cultural aversion towards the cinema was first and foremost caused by the shabby behaviour and callous lack of scruples that the refined and cultured leadership of public television attributed, rightly or wrongly, to most of the cinema world. To them it seemed like 'something irredeemably disreputable and shifty; stooping to deals or compromising with cinema was out of the question' (Alessandrini, 1988: 83). Certainly a large number of the films produced at that time – commercial and escapist cinema made up of comedies, melodramas and peplum movies, popular with the public and cold-shouldered by critics in equal measure – did not elude, for its part, an elitist verdict of coarseness and vulgarity. Similarly the rise and establishment in the 1950s of a star system that featured 'bombshells' – shapely Italian beauties (Silvana Mangano, Gina Lollobrigida, Sofia Loren, Marisa Allasio) who quickly became icons and ambassadors to the world of a new ideal of physically flamboyant femininity – was intrinsically tied to a kind of film production that willingly indulged in the 'aggressive exhibition of the [female] body' (Brunetta, 2009: 149). This was hard to reconcile with the moral code of a television where variety show ballerinas were obliged to wear thick leotards.

Furthermore – and just as important for Italian public television, which was then managed by Catholic forces and was aiming at the cultural unification of the nation – the cinema itself had been a fierce battleground between Communists and Catholics in the post-World War II years and the early 1950s (Gundle, 1990 and 2000). This ideological conflict had flared up around the controversial question of defending and reinforcing the Italian film industry against the invasiveness of American films. I shall turn later to considering the presence of American films in Italy; for the moment I will simply recall that Italian cinema after World War II witnessed, in the context of a gradual resumption of productive activity, the emergence of the neo-realism movement, which gave rise to art-house films both stylistically innovative and engaged with social issues.[4] Often drawing on true stories, the neo-realist directors portrayed the tragic realities of a country devastated by war; they chose to narrate, for the first time, the suffering, misery and humiliated yet dignified humanity of ordinary people, men and women in the street, and it was from the streets that the actors were often recruited, instead of professional performers. Neo-realism inspired films, suffused with criticism and social condemnation, became the sympathetic narrator and portrayer of the conditions and aspirations of the humble, and they revisited reality in the light of a secular and progressive vision of history. It is accordingly no surprise that this genre of film should have aroused conflicting reactions from various circles i.e., triumphant welcome from the critics, especially outside Italy; moderate enthusiasm on the part of the Italian public, whose own preferences inclined towards less harsh and more comforting stories. The Christian Democrat ruling class proved hostile and discriminatory towards films that were accused of tarnishing Italy's image abroad; the Communist party was in favour of this socially engaged cinema – the hoped-for creator of the post-war Renaissance of a national film industry – that sympathized with the downtrodden working class. Finally the Catholic world was deeply suspicious about movies appreciated by the Left (and many neo-realist directors were indeed sympathetic, aligned even) considering them a sort of conveyor belt of Marxist ideology and propaganda.

The conflict that set Communist and Catholic parties against each other on the battlefield of the Italian film industry found a further (and related) contentious issue in the large amount of American films that were imported into Italy in the post-World War II period. It is worth emphasizing that the neo-realist movement was an exceptional art phenomenon, which succeeded in leaving an indelible mark on the history of Italian, and also world cinema; but it was a relatively short-lived phenomenon (it lasted for less than ten years) and had little quantitative weight. At its height in the second half of the 1940s, neo-realism accounted for less than 10% of the total number of Italian films released (Wagstaff, 2007: 147). In the same time span, the Italian film industry gradually increased its productive capacity, but nevertheless remained well below the level of 100 titles per year. Yet the total number of films released in Italian cinemas was in excess of 400 and sometimes 500 titles: this was the effect of the massive flow of imports of foreign films, most of them from the United States. 'At a post-war peak in 1948, American films accounted for three-quarters of all new films shown on Italian screens' (Forgacs, 1990: 119).

The post-war overflow of American films was consciously favoured by the Italian government's open gates policy, in agreement with its US counterpart and the influential representatives of the Allied cinema industry; and the influx found favourable and welcoming conditions in a country where the Americans were awaited and greeted as 'the liberators'. But it is equally true that American cinema's hegemony was neither a new occurrence in the Italian market, nor in the experience of the Italian public. During the greater part of the Fascist era[5] it was precisely the Hollywood dreams factory that fed the imagination and created the pantheon of film stars for millions of Italian filmgoers. Most of the major Hollywood studios had been opening offices in Rome from the very beginning of the regime. In this connection, Brunetta speaks of the 'American cinema's march on Rome'[6] (Brunetta, 2009: 60) and Gundle acknowledges that 'Hollywood never enjoyed the sort of domination after the war that it did in the Thirties' (Gundle, 1990: 199), that is to say, in the middle of the Fascist regime.

The Italian public's long-standing familiarity with American movies – part and parcel of the specific openness and inclusivity of Italian cultural space, which I have already addressed in the previous chapter – deserves attention in the present discursive context. On the one hand, this will help us to relativize, if not the undeniably disrupting impact, the historical novelty which is tempting to grant to the invasion of American TV drama that has occurred since the early 1970s (see later). On the other hand, precisely this deep-rooted familiarity with the America of the big screen has managed to convert the 'alien invasion' of American series and serials into a 'return of the already known', thus constituting one potential facilitating factor for the popularity of American television imports.

In the post-World War II years, American films were probably less dominant, in terms of market share and successes, than they were during the Fascist era; but they nevertheless supplied material that generated fierce controversy between Communists and Catholics. The Communists opposed them, fearing the harmful influence on the masses of a film culture that was imbued with banality, violence and the spirit of capitalism, and ran the risk of marginalizing and inhibiting the development of a national film industry that would reflect the specific conditions and tensions of Italian society. By contrast, US films were welcomed and appreciated in Catholic circles; certain aspects in the cinematic portrayal of American society – consumerist tendencies, deviant behaviour, dissolubility of marriage – did not fail to arouse concern, but family values, the rule of law, trust in institutions and the optimistic vision of life that generally permeated American films seemed entirely to accord with the principles that the Catholic Church 'was keen to promote' (Treveri Gennari, 2009: 96) in the reconstruction of Italy. The approval of the Catholic establishment was decisive in enabling the widest possible theatrical distribution of American films, since at that time the Church managed an extensive system of parish cinemas[7] – especially in city suburbs, provincial towns and rural areas – where films that had been approved by the *Centro Cattolico Cinematografico*[8] were shown. Sex and violence were invariably forbidden, but otherwise American movies, especially the comedies and Westerns that 'were deemed eminently suitable for family audiences' (Gundle, 1990: 209), were approved and recommended much more often than Italian films.

At the dawn of Italian television in the mid-1950s, the head-on conflict between Communists and Catholics on the terrain of the cinema was starting to ease off, but the battlefield was still not sufficiently neutralized and cleansed of all grounds for controversy to make it advisable for the new medium to attempt an incursion; at any rate not before finding the right path (the televisual specific) and becoming established by comparison with a predecessor at the peak of its own rise to glory.

A peculiar feature of the history of Italian broadcasting is that the birth of television happened during the phase of cinema's greatest splendour and popularity. In the mid-1950s, when other large European countries were already experiencing a progressive decline in cinema attendance and numbers of screens since the late 1940s (Sorlin, 1991), the Italian film market flourished as never before and was the third largest in the world after the United States and the Soviet Union. Italians enjoyed going to the cinema and used to go more often than any other population in continental Europe; the total number of admissions rose to over 800 million in 1955 and never fell below 700 million in the following seven years. In that same year the number of cinemas reached a maximum of 10,500 and remained more or less constant until 1967 (MEDIA Salles, 1994).

Various factors helped to create this favourable situation, in particular the efficient organization of the exhibition sector, which was in a position 'to exploit films from their first run in city centre cinemas ... (*prima visione*) to suburban cinemas (*seconda visione*) and on to small towns (*terza visione*) and a variety of church halls, political associations, seaside and seasonal venues' (Wood, 2005: 10). Thanks to this widespread distribution of cinemas over national territory, the broad popular and rural component of a society that was still agricultural (though on the verge of industrialization and economic wellbeing) was not excluded from cinema-going – an activity that in other countries had assumed a mainly urban character – and indeed helped largely to reinforce the ranks of Italian filmgoers. The low cost of admission (Sorlin, 1991), despite increases due to the general rise in the cost of living, was a further element of attraction and loyalty maintenance for the general public, for whom the cinema in particular 'represented a channel of inclusion and participation as well as entertainment' (Gundle, 1990: 201) that made it an essential part of daily life in the 1950s.[9]

It should be added that in the same years Italian cinema was creating new and very successful genres – '*neo-realismo rosa*' (pink neo-realism), the launching-pad of the 'curvaceous film star', and Italian-style comedy – that succeeded in entering and winning, with their local appeal, the contest with American films. And the national film industry was experiencing an alliance with the American film industry, putting the *Cinecittà* studios and the gorgeous scenery of Rome at the disposal of Hollywood productions: *Quo Vadis?* (Melvin LeRoy, 1951), *Roman Holiday* (William Wyler, 1953), *Ben Hur* (William Wyler, 1959). Rome attracted a constant flow of producers, directors and international stars and for a while seemed to have become the world capital of the cinema. In any case 'Hollywood on the Tiber', as the press defined the phenomenon at the time, denoted an era of exhilarating vitality in the flourishing Italian film industry.

This era ran its course, and indeed reached its peak, at the birth and in the early years of Italian broadcasting. Just as the cinema was almost indifferent to television and seemed not to fear any immediate competition, so nascent television for its own part preferred – for the reasons stated, including the imbalance of forces – to keep out of the way of the cinema.

The cinematic turn

New Year's Day 1967 fell on a Sunday, the day traditionally dedicated to the *sceneggiato*. That evening at the beginning of the year saw the broadcast of the first of eight weekly episodes of *I promessi sposi/The Betrothed* (hereafter *I promessi sposi*), an adaptation of the greatest modern novel in Italian literature: in fact *the* Italian novel *par excellence*, the loved yet hated work[10] of the nineteenth-century writer Alessandro Manzoni.

Thirteen years had passed since the birth of Italian television in 1954, and three years since the start of the making of *I promessi sposi*. The Rai had waited for a decade (after achieving a firm base of maturity in production) before daring to take on the dramaturgical challenge of adapting Manzoni's masterpiece for television.[11]

The results met the expectations and justified the financial investment, which was unusually high. The press had stirred up and fuelled curiosity about *I promessi sposi* by following each phase, step by step, in the three years of its making; and the adaptation attracted a huge audience of over 18 million viewers, which ranked it in third place among the most-watched programmes of the year. Although the critics were not unanimous in their praise, the *sceneggiato* acquired the aura of a symbolic event and the status – acknowledged to this day – of one of the Rai's cult programmes (Grasso, 1992: 209). But if *I promessi sposi* occupies pride of place in the history of the *sceneggiato*, this is not only because it dared – with almost triumphal results – to compete with a legendary masterpiece of Italian literature, but also because of its significant position at the watershed between the first and second phase of Italian TV drama's evolution.

Scrupulously faithful to its literary origin, divided into acts, like a stage play (and for the most part entrusted to the most illustrious theatrical actors of the time), permeated with that 'sort of obsession with interiors'[12] that was instigated by the search for the 'televisual specific', and therefore shot entirely on tape and in studio, *I promessi sposi* was the most accomplished and perfect embodiment of the cultural and aesthetic conception of the *sceneggiato*, deploying and masterfully exploiting the high level of expressive quality and production skills that had been reached during a decade of intense experimentation. Nevertheless, at the very moment that it marked, with its *cachet* of insuperable model, the top in the art of the *sceneggiato*, *I promessi sposi* decreed the end (or at least the beginning of the end) of the hegemony of the *sceneggiato* itself as a form of television drama, modelled by the privileged relationship with the theatre and literature. It would perhaps be misleading to evoke in this connection the metaphor of the swansong, since *I promessi sposi* was not the last of the traditional *sceneggiati* – more were still to be made, with varying degrees of success, in the years to come. But there is no doubt that the lofty ambitions and outstanding achievements of this adaptation of Manzoni bore the trace of something definitive, a feeling that the traditional form of the *sceneggiato* had now realized its maximum potential of artistic and cultural expression, as well as popular success, reaching a threshold beyond which a change or turning point had become indispensable to assure future growth in Italian TV drama.

A year later *Odissea/The Odyssey*, Italian television's first truly cinematographic *sceneggiato*, made its appearance and I shall have more to say about this later. The good placing of the title, which ranked sixth among the most watched programmes of 1968, testified to the favourable inception of a 'cinematic turn' which, in the field of TV drama production, saw the original alliance with the theatre yield to new forms of cooperation with the cinema.[13]

The Cinematic Turn and the Americanization of the Television Landscape

Television's 'cinematic turn' matured in the 1960s in the context of those processes through which the Rai readjusted its own strategies and redefined its own role in national and international space. The change in the company's top management was decisive in that connection. Ettore Bernabei, the Rai's new director, who was appointed in 1961 (he was to remain in charge until 1974), was close to the Christian Democrat Catholic wing that had brought about the first centre–left government in Italy. He chose to focus on the information component of the Reithian triad (to educate, inform and entertain), wishing to make public television the central information system and opinion leader in a society that was in the grip of major sociopolitical and cultural changes. Italy was then in the midst of the so-called economic miracle, and was witnessing a massive phenomenon of migration from the south to the north of the country, and the spread of new and modern customs and lifestyles. As a result, journalism departments were considerably strengthened; and thanks to the additional schedule made available by the launch of a second channel, new information programmes were created that introduced 'models of the cultural features, social investigation, historical reconstruction, current affairs discussion and science popularization' (Monteleone, 1999: 349).

This type of programmes required the television gaze to range out of doors, breaking with the claustrophobia of the studio; for their part, outdoor shots called for the abandonment of the telecamera in favour of the more manageable cinecamera and the consequent use of rolls of film. The ideational and productive models of television thus began to make room for cinema technology, though without endorsing the language and visual styles of the cinematographic medium. Subsequently the film also made an incursion into the television drama sector, where a tendency developed to insert filmed scenes here and there. In 1964 *Mastro don Gesualdo*[14] was the first *sceneggiato* to be recorded entirely on film, although, as was proved by the case of *I promessi sposi*, the electronic support was not dispensed with.

At the same time, the expansion of cultural programming provided room for presentation and critical appraisal of cinematic products; the films screened on television were now valourized by being framed into cycles, overviews and retrospectives, and were introduced and discussed in accordance with a typical cineclub formula. This was an integral part of a project to promote and spread cinematographic culture.

It is plausible to speculate that none of these small moves – and not even all of them together – would have been able to bridge the gap between cinema and television that was deliberately established and maintained by the latter. Other factors favoured a close encounter: some of these factors were perhaps potentially more binding and in any case could not be ignored by an institution like the Rai, which despite being monopolist and thus sheltered from competition was constantly testing public reactions and taking them into account. And there were indeed signals from the public of a certain weariness with what domestic drama was offering, still dominated by the *sceneggiato*; and, by contrast, indicators of true appreciation of the cinematographic offering, which was always used sparingly but appeared more selective and of better quality than in the past. Assiduous

Italian filmgoers 'by 1968 ... were still making an average of 10.4 visits to the cinema per year, in contrast to the EEC average of 5.7' (Gundle, 1990: 212); but they were beginning to desert the cinemas at an increasing rate (in 1967 cinema attendance fell for the first time below 600 million visits per year) and seemed to be redirecting their cinematic habits, preferences and choices towards the small screen. Indeed the films that were broadcast weekly on television were widely welcomed by the public and many of them entered the ranking of most-watched programmes, frequently achieving the best placings in the top ten.

But in the end, the encounter and indeed the new alliance between television and cinema was to occur by virtue of two fundamental conditions. First, the cinema had almost entirely ceased to be a political and ideological battleground between the Catholics and the Communists. For multiple reasons, and because of the *détente* between Left and Right ushered in by the new political formula of the centre-left government, both parties had toned down the contest to dominate the development of national cinematography. The Catholics were able to make up for this withdrawal thanks to the control they had acquired over television, now a *fait accompli*. As for the Communists, they transferred the cultural battlefield into the very heart of the cinema, and in the 1960s they were mostly concerned with denouncing the advancing ethos of commercial profit, favoured by the invasion of American capital, which was pushing Italian art films and social criticism to the margins.

The second condition rested not exactly on an upheaval, but certainly on a far-reaching rebalancing of forces between cinema and television in favour of the latter. Such a rebalancing was due not so much to an incipient crisis in Italian cinema – a crisis that was destined to assume unambiguous outlines and alarming dimensions in the 1970s – but to the influential and pre-eminent position that television, as a medium and as an institution, had built for itself and was firmly holding on to in the late 1960s within the Italian culture industry. It was in full awareness of television's conquest of the centre-stage that the Rai management made a complete *volte-face* in the policy of separateness that it had followed for over ten years, and decided that the time had come to ally itself with its erstwhile competitor.

The adoption of the new policy of close encounter with the cinema was unquestionably premised on the proud self-perception that television, both as medium and institution, had reached maturity, strength and power in the national context. And precisely this well-established national lead offered fertile ground for cultivating ambitions with a wider geographical range. Indeed the cinematic turn in the television drama sector was closely connected with the Rai's wish to emerge from the domestic market by creating the conditions for international circulation of its products. Italian cinema had achieved a similar success, if only intermittently, in the course of its history, and in the 1960s especially 'it enjoyed an extended boom in markets throughout the world' (Brunetta, 2009: 168), thanks both to author films like *La dolce vita/The Sweet Life* (Federico Fellini, 1960) and to genre films like the 'spaghetti-western' created by the director Sergio Leone. Turning to the cinema was the equivalent of acknowledging that the film industry had at its disposal the resources of internationalization that television both lacked and needed. Thus to some extent the proud self-awareness with which the Rai resolved to embark upon the alliance was counter-balanced by the irreplaceable role of the cinema in enabling television to achieve its ambition.

The rise of the miniseries

L'Odissea/Odyssey (1968) was the first fruit of the collaboration between the two media. The seven-episode television drama, based on Homer's second epic, was made by producer Dino De Laurentiis, an outstanding figure in the Italian cinema industry.[15] One of the first to take the road to large co-productions (for instance *War and Peace*, King Vidor 1956), he could boast of a long collaborative experience with international partners. De Laurentiis had already produced an adaptation of Homer's epic poem – the film *Ulisse/Ulysses* (Mario Camerini, 1954), starring Kirk Douglas, which was one of the biggest box-office successes in the 1950s – and his interest in a remake was well known in cinema circles. He gladly welcomed the Rai's proposal and used the funds from Europe (France, Germany and Yugoslavia) that flowed into the project, to create a very spectacular work, commensurate with his style and his grandiose vision of the cinema. *Odissea* was shot on location in Homeric places, with a cast of international stars, under a cinema director (Franco Rossi, trained as a neo-realist) and it benefitted from the special effects created by Carlo Rambaldi, the future winner of three Oscars. It broke sensationally from the *sceneggiato* model, though the scripts still kept some trace of this, and only one year after *I promessi sposi* it inaugurated a new wave in Italian TV drama, marked by an unmistakable cinema imprinting.

The subsequent theatrical release of *Odissea*, in a shortened version, ensured its 'cinematic respectability' and paved the way for other 'amphibian' dramas; these too were made with the idea of being shown on both the small screen, in instalments, and the big screen as one-off films. The partnership among Italy, France and Germany was reconfirmed in the co-production of a second epic adaptation in seven parts, this time of Virgil's *Aeneid* (Franco Rossi, 1971); whereas *La vita di Leonardo da Vinci/The Life of Leonardo da Vinci* (Renato Castellani, 1971), was co-produced with British partners. The five-part biography of the great Renaissance genius pushed the process of cinematization and internationalization of Italian TV drama a step further. The director Castellani was an important name in Italian cinema; he had made significant contributions to the neo-realist movement (*Sotto il sole di Roma/Under the Roman Sun*, 1948) and created the very popular genre of *neorealismo rosa* (pink neo-realism: *Due soldi di speranza/Two Cents Worth of Hope*, 1952). His career was studded with prestigious awards from the main European film festivals (Cannes and Venice, where he won the Golden Lion in 1954 for the film *Giulietta e Romeo/Romeo and Juliet*). Furthermore *La vita di Leonardo da Vinci*, having been acquired by CBS, achieved for the first time the objective of introducing a

Rai product into the American market (the British partner may have acted as guarantor). It was a felicitous entry, as the work received two Emmy nominations and won a Golden Globe for the Best TV Special. Later the CBS also acquired the six-part Biblical drama *Mosé/Moses the Lawgiver* (Giancarlo De Bosio, 1974), once again an Italo-British co-production starring Burt Lancaster in the leading role, which he had already played in *The Ten Commandments* (Cecil De Mille, 1956). *Moses* was co-scripted by the English novelist Anthony Burgess and the Italian Vittorio Bonicelli; the music was composed by Ennio Morricone. It was however the NBC that guaranteed the six-part drama *Gesù di Nazareth/Jesus of Nazareth* (1977); this was directed by Franco Zeffirelli, a former pupil of Luchino Visconti internationally known for his adaptations of Shakespeare (*La bisbetica domata/The Taming of the Shrew*, 1967; *Giulietta e Romeo/Romeo and Juliet*, 1968) and his operatic films. It was recently said of *Gesù di Nazareth*: 'This particular production, with a stellar cast headed by British actor Robert Powell, remains the biblical drama in television against which all others are judged' (Marill, 2007: 106–107).

Obviously the titles I have mentioned represented the very best products of the new cinematic course taken by Italian TV drama; they were, so to speak, the Rai's 'jewels in the crown' in those years. Substantial budgets, high production values, renowned authors, a stellar cast – not to mention the complex creative and organizational machine of the co-productions – made these titles into something rare and out of the ordinary, events in the true sense. The bulk of TV drama continued to conform with the much more modest standards of the *sceneggiato*; but this itself was undergoing a metamorphosis and was being transformed once and for all into 'filmed *sceneggiato*'.

The cinematic turn was a seminal moment in the history of Italian TV drama. Indeed, it marked the dawn of and set the standards for the miniseries, or more precisely it shaped and legitimized the ideal–typical model of the form destined to become a true national hallmark: 'so embedded in and at the same time such an embodiment'[16] (Kerr, 1982: 6) of Italian TV drama.

In recent years there has been some growth of scholarship concerning the rise of the miniseries internationally, not all of it in agreement with respect to time and place. As Elke Weissmann (2009) underlines in her reconstruction of the debate, there are authors (Creeber, 2001b) who accredit the invention of the miniseries to American 1970s television (beginning with *The Law*, NBC 1974, and *Rich Man, Poor Man*, ABC 1976), whereas others (Edgerton, 1991) properly locate the premises of this form in the British TV drama serials of the 1960s (*The Forsyte Saga*, BBC 1967, is regarded by many as a prototype). It is plausible that the British programmes that were beginning to be imported into the United States in the late 1960s 'provided part of the stylistic roots' (Weissmann, 2009: 54) of the American miniseries. In addition some Italian drama serials were broadcast on US networks in the following decade, as I have recalled earlier.

In the Italian case, the indigenous components seemed to prevail: the miniseries was rooted in the national tradition of the *sceneggiato*, whereas the new tradition of cinematic drama that came into existence within and through the birth and rise of the miniseries could similarly be traced back to a set of circumstances that were peculiar to Italy. But this indigenous path to convergence between television and cinema ended up in reality leading Italian TV drama along the trail that had already been blazed by the 'alien' American television. The latter, since the 1950s, had been entering into symbiosis with Hollywood, and furthermore the US networks had begun, in the early 1960s, to finance the large-scale production of made-for-TV movies. It is in fact from these that the American miniseries (Edgerton, 1985), with their clear legacy 'of a tradition of more cinematic television dramas' (Weissmann, 2009: 52), can be said to have descended later, after assimilating the structural and stylistic lesson of British drama serials. Not by chance, when the great American miniseries, starting with *Roots* (ABC, 1977) and *Holocaust* (NBC, 1978) reached Italy, the acclaim that welcomed them – *Holocaust* was the first and only American drama to be included in the annual top ten – was favoured, if only in part, by the recognizability of the form that bore a strong resemblance to the Italian miniseries. But meanwhile American television drama had made a massive entry into the Italian television landscape.

The flood of American imports

As is widely known, the Italian television scene experienced a far-reaching and turbulent transformation from the mid-1970s onwards when commercial networks began to appear, first locally and then nationally (Baransky and Lumley, 1990; Buonanno, 2004a). The transformation, which took place in a regime of deregulation, put an end to the monopoly of public television and created the preconditions for the Rai–Mediaset duopoly.

The most immediate effect of this evolution was an enormous expansion of televisual offering. The rapid transition from scarcity to availability (Ellis, 2000) was brought about as much by the proliferation of broadcasting channels as by the extension of broadcasting hours: for the first time the flow of programming was extended to the whole day, never before covered in its entirety by public television. The viewing hours that had traditionally been neglected by the Rai, such as night-time, became strategic for private television channels, which were able to broadcast overnight without competition, creating new segments of viewers and attracting advertising with the offer of free night-time slots.

In consequence, an urgent need for content arose that could only to a very limited extent be supplied by domestic production capacity. Completely overturning the 20-year-old practice of sparing and cultured use of films by public television, the new private networks started to fill the schedule's empty spaces with a profusion of movies: mostly old films that could be acquired cheaply on the market, as well as more recent productions (not infrequently screened in breach of copyright). The advent of commercial television in Italy generated large-scale phenomena of Americanization in television drama supply, which I shall address shortly. But it is important to bear in mind that this was anticipated and accompanied by an unprecedented and unequalled cinematization of television supply, which grew exponentially in the 1970s until it reached the order of thousands of cinematic titles broadcast each year. 'The cinematic patrimony of the entire world, which seemed destined to be forgotten, became newly accessible and began to circulate in a chaotic and tumultuous manner at all hours of the day and night on all channels' (Brunetta, 2009: 248). The Rai itself did not opt out of the trend and gradually increased its film programming, which rose from 100 titles per year in 1976 to 400 at the beginning of 1980. With the inception of the three national networks of the private company Fininvest, owned by Silvio Berlusconi, the film became a strategic means of competition between public and commercial television; and the battle between competing networks, especially after Fininvest acquired a package of 350 cinematic titles never before shown on TV, was fought more and more often with fresh films that were a box office success. The screening of theatrical movies in prime time was intensified to the point that the standard length for this time slot ended up being rearranged according to the cinematic running time of 1½ hours. The domestic production of TV drama, mostly destined for prime time, had to accommodate this standard; and even today the preferred length of parts and episodes of Italian TV drama is 1½ hours – not only for the miniseries but also for the series.

In any case Italian TV drama was at that time the most scarce of the resources available, even more for the new private channels that had entered the television market without their own library or any production experience. Therefore the commercial networks, which were to start producing a modest quantity of TV drama only in the second half of the 1980s, went ahead with massive imports; and the stimulus of competition induced public television to do the same, thus breaking its own 20-year-old tradition of resolute self-sufficiency. At the beginning of the 1980s the Italian television market had the dubious honour of being the biggest European importer of foreign programmes: primarily from the United States, as well as from Brazil and Japan.

In terms of programming policies, a truly radical break with the past occurred, especially with regard to the now unrestricted opening up to American products. Up to the early 1970s, Italy still was 'one European market declared poor for U.S. product' (Seagrave, 1998: 145). The Rai did not spend much on American imports, also because of its 'annoying' (to the American exporters) practice of acquiring only a few episodes at a time for the same series. Of course we should not believe that American TV drama was entirely unknown to, or unpopular with, the Italian viewing public. The domestic comedy *I Love Lucy* (CBS, 1951–1957), broadcast in 1960 for only 13 episodes, may have been a complete failure; but the anthology *Alfred Hitchcock Presents* (CBS and NBC, 1955–1965) and the legal drama *Perry Mason* (CBS, 1957–1966), both screened from 1959, were well entrenched in the schedule of early television and in viewers' preferences. In the 1960s, it was the turn of *The Addams Family* (ABC, 1964–1966), *Twilight Zone* (CBS, 1959–1964), *Dr. Kildare* (NBC, 1961–1966), the westerns *Bonanza* (NBC, 1959–1973) and *The High Chaparral* (NBC, 1967–1971). However it was only in the second half of the 1970s, after the end of public television's monopoly, that American imports started to flow abundantly and continuously. The period saw the arrival in Italy of, among others, *Gunsmoke* (CBS, 1955–1975), *Columbo* (NBC, 1968–2003), *Mash* (CBS, 1972–1983), *Kojak* (CBS, 1973–

1978), *Happy Days* (ABC, 1974–1984), *Starsky and Hutch* (ABC, 1975–1979), *Charlie's Angels* (ABC, 1976–1981), as well as the big miniseries *Rich Man, Poor Man* (ABC, 1976), *Roots* (ABC, 1977) and *Holocaust* (NBC, 1978). *General Hospital* (ABC, 1963–) was the first soap opera ever to be broadcast in Italy. The flood of US drama series and serials continued with still greater intensity for almost all of the following decade: 'Italian television bought so much American product in 1980 that it moved into second place as an import market, trailing only Canada' (Seagrave, 1998: 204).

In fact, a high rate of Americanization of the audiovisual products on offer was nothing new for the Italian public; they had already experienced and enjoyed it on the big screen in more than one historical circumstance, as I have recalled in the preceding pages. In this case, furthermore, the undeniable predominance of American TV drama on the small screen occurred within a somewhat more cosmopolitan range of foreign contents, inclusive of Latin American serials and Japanese cartoons.

In any case, those were the years of an exhilarating televisual experience. In the framework of an impetuous and deregulated conversion of the Italian TV system into a duopoly, Italian viewers were faced, and became acquainted, with new genres such as the sitcom and the drama serial, and were exposed to an unceasing supply of American police drama series (see Chapter 5). Female viewers for the first time got to know, and became hooked on, soap operas and *telenovelas*; for their part, children and teenage viewers at that time developed an avid enthusiasm for Japanese cartoons, which came to fill a vacuum in the domestic programmes for children and adolescents. In fact, the great transformation in the televisual scene was becoming part of the daily experience of the Italian public and was turning into a unique opportunity for total immersion in a 'great narrative flow' (Curti, 1990: 323). Sitcom and cop shows, hospital dramas, serial dramas, soap operas, *telenovelas,* cartoons ... a simultaneous plurality of formulae and genres was pouring forth from the screens, creating new reading competencies and new consumption choices and preferences, and offering for the first time the pleasures of continuous serials in the two-fold North American variant (the open serial) and the South American variant (the closed serial). Imported programmes were, on the whole, well received by the Italian public, whose preference for cultural goods of a foreign provenance should be borne in mind. Obviously we must be careful not to assume that all foreign productions were irresistibly attractive (the appeal of cultural proximity, a prerogative of domestic television, has hardly any rivals in any circumstances). However it is true that in the mood of voracious and frenetic consumerism encouraged by televisual availability (which marked the end of 20 years of a relatively meagre diet) there were probably no titles or personalities of foreign and mainly American series and serial dramas that failed to enter the public awareness, if not the preferences, of the majority of Italian viewers at that time. And while the era of the *sceneggiato* was on the wane, this Italian word for it was also on the way out and it was beginning to be superseded by the English word 'fiction', which was more in tune with the new international trend in television.

The sudden introduction of a great narrative flow from abroad into Italian television was one of the most forceful indicators both of the transition between the Rai monopoly and the inception of the duopoly, and of the difference between public and private broadcasting. Although the Rai did not refrain from competing with Mediaset (in those years still called Fininvest) in the imports sector, the intensive filling of the programme schedules with foreign material was beyond doubt practised primarily by commercial television. In the mid-1980s, 48% of the broadcasting time of the three private national channels, as against 12% of the three Rai channels, was monopolized by TV drama, almost all of it imported (Silj, 1992: 14). Furthermore, commercial television had from the start built the schedules and organized the programming of its own channels in accordance with the American networks model – the one that had suggested the concept of 'flow' to Raymond Williams (1974) – just as it had imported philosophies and techniques of self-promotion and marketing from the United States (Freccero, 1986).

In hastening to assume and display close proximity with American television, Italian commercial broadcasting was operating a complete reversal of the cultural policies of public television. This was an integral part of an elaborate strategy of identity-building that made similarity to the American model a marker of the difference from the public broadcaster – at the same time putting the non-national at the service of a project of national establishment.

In fact for commercial television the prospect of well-established entrenchment in the national scene was largely related (especially in the pioneering phase) to its capacity to be, and to make itself overtly perceived by, viewers as a television option that was different from the Rai; and nothing could have turned out to be more convincing and effective for this purpose than the adoption of an 'American way of television'. 'Private TV must be American in order to build for itself a distinctive identity' (Freccero, 1986: 136); resembling American television served the key objective of making room for itself in the domestic market.

The transformation of the Italian television system, which came about through the genesis and development of commercial broadcasting, was thus accompanied by a process of internationalization, more specifically of Americanization, unequivocally characterized more than any other indicator by a true deluge of imports from the United States. This process was powerfully fostered by the programming and acquisition policies of private television, just as it was instrumental in favouring its consolidation.

The Italian response to *Dallas*

In this regard, it is worth recalling that the American prime-time serials, namely *Dallas* (CBS, 1978–1991), played an important role in restructuring the Italian television landscape. The *Dallas* phenomenon may well have impacted on the whole of Europe and beyond with its huge popular appeal (Katz and Liebes, 1991), provoking alarm and anger in intellectual and political circles about the dangers of the 'Dallasification' of culture; but in Italy the phenomenon was a crucial episode in the competition between public and private television, working entirely to the advantage of the latter. In the wake of its success in the US, *Dallas* was at first acquired by the Rai; but whether because of a certain disdain for American products, which they were nevertheless forced to import, or in particular because of the absence of a seriality culture in the professional milieu of public television, the programme was neither understood nor appreciated. In spring 1981, *Dallas* was scheduled outside prime time on the Rai's first channel as a series made up of independent and self-sufficient episodes; i.e. it was aired without respecting the chronological sequence of the instalments, which is an essential part of the serial's structure. Following its inevitable failure, the Rai surrendered its option on the rights and *Dallas* moved to commercial television. They made it the event of the season, turning it into an important weekly appointment in prime time on Channel 5 – the future flagship of the private sector – and promoting it with an unprecedented volume of publicity. *Dallas* thus became a means of establishing and consolidating commercial broadcasting, and served as a true Trojan horse in the dismantling of the Rai's monopoly (Schlesinger, 1990).

Italian 'fiction', as the home-grown product began to be called from that time on, did not remain immune from changes that could be traced back, directly or indirectly, to the new internationalized and Americanized television environment. There was hardly ever any attempt at open or hidden imitation but rather a quest for distinctiveness, in accordance with the style of public television, which was still the only producer of domestic drama. The changes may have reflected, if only in part, a physiological evolution in the indigenous storytelling system that was leaving the *sceneggiato* era behind; but the arrival in force of the American 'other' in Italian televisual space was not a factor that could be left out of consideration in domestic drama policies.

In response to internationalization from abroad, brought in by foreign imports, the Rai produced programmes that were 'internationalized from within' – though not in the same way as the *sceneggiati* adapted from foreign novels. This time the works of fiction were big-budget historical miniseries, mainly biographies of great Italians – *Marco Polo* (Giuliano Montaldo, 1982, Emmy award for Outstanding Miniseries); *Verdi/The Life of Verdi,* (Renato Castellani, 1982); *Cristoforo Colombo/Christopher Columbus* (Alberto Lattuada, 1985, two Emmy nominations); *Quo Vadis?* (Franco Rossi, 1985) – made in co-production with both European and non-European partners. Direct heirs of the first generation of the filmed dramas that arose from the cinematic turn of the late 1960s, these fine television products further enhanced the standards of the miniseries and established the image of the Rai as the maker of 'sumptuous' television epics.[17] The scenarios and the international cast, the cinematographic pedigree of the stars and the directors, the *éclat* of the programmes, which, despite their Hollywoodesque inspiration, were redeemed by the guarantees and testimonials of European quality, led to prestigious products, endowed with wide appeal, which were destined to engender much-publicized television events. And as the nature of the co-productions made them suitable for 'travel' across borders

(Selznick, 2008), Italian personages and stories entered into the awareness of foreign viewers, as a partial reversal of and compensation for Italy's condition as a net importer. The subjects were purposely chosen; portrayals of famous travellers and navigators such as Marco Polo and Christopher Columbus testified to the historical contribution made by Italians to the discovery and experience of foreign lands, well beyond Italy's borders.

The *sceneggiato* had given priority to stories of other times and other places. The new course of domestic drama did not suddenly stop drawing on the historical and literary past, but started a process of 'presentification' that moved ahead the chronological 'centre of gravity' from the nineteenth century to the twentieth, opening the door to a contemporary narrative stream. In the same vein, foreign stories began to give way to Italian ones, which focused on the social issues and the everyday life of the country. Pioneering this trend, the miniseries *Storia di Anna/The Story of Anna* (1981) brought to public attention for the first time, in an unusual crude realism style, the problem of teenage drug addicts. It is not easy to establish to what extent the 'national turn' of Italian drama in the 1980s represented a direct reaction to the challenge of Americanization – our own country against the foreign 'other' – or whether it was a tendency already inherent in the post-*sceneggiato* Zeitgeist that was furthered by the invasion of drama from the United States. In any case, 'the Italian response to *Dallas*' – that is, *La Piovra* (*The Octopus. Power of the Mafia*) – took shape in the context of the national turn.

The case of *La Piovra* (see Chapter 3) is without doubt the most remarkable in the whole history of Italian TV drama, owing to the unprecedented popularity and status as an authentic 'media event' gained by the fiction since its first appearance in 1984, when it was soon acclaimed as the 'Italian response to *Dallas*'. The huge success of the programme with both audience and critics prompted the Rai to carry on with a story that was originally conceived as a single stand-alone miniseries; in fact *La Piovra* turned into a saga, and unfolded over the years into a sequence of ten miniseries before coming to an end in early 2000.

The amazing and enduring popularity of *La Piovra* must be ascribed first and foremost to its quintessential 'Italianness', which made it into a 'text of identity' *par excellence* of domestic drama. This prerogative emanated from a set of elements endowed with large resonance, recognizability and credibility in collective Italian culture.

Being a Mafia story, *La Piovra* revolved around a dramatic issue deep rooted as much in social reality as in the Italian imagination. The reality of the early 1980s was a fierce power struggle within the Sicilian Mafia; this was the cause of unequalled carnage, which, in addition, claimed a great many lives among representatives of the State (police officers, magistrates and local politicians). However the definition of 'Mafia story' does not adequately capture the narrative's ambitious purpose of unmasking the treacherous relationships between crime and power, in their twofold embodiment: the deadly power of organized crime, and the criminal connections of political and financial power. Inherent in *La Piovra* was a sort of obsession with conspiracy theories (Sparks, 1992: 143), this being the main inspiration for its complex and visionary plots involving collusion between Mafia bosses and the powers that be, allies in pursuing their mega interests. Effectively symbolized by the tentacled metaphor of the octopus, the vision of a world infiltrated by crime right through to its innermost institutional mechanisms strongly resonated with the 'culture of suspicion' and mistrust of political power, which (for a number of historical reasons) is a permanent feature of the Italian collective mentality.

The protagonist Inspector Cattani, to this day an unforgettable icon of the popular hero, was for his part a primary success factor of *La Piovra*. Cattani was a typical Italian character in his captivating mixture of honesty and unscrupulousness, exhilaration and despondency, in his vacillation between a desire for justice and a thirst for vengeance, in a deep anarchism betrayed by his impatience with the restraints of legal formalities. Typically Italian, furthermore, was his tragic figure as hero–martyr doomed to sacrifice his life, fated to succumb in the fierce but unequal struggle against the overwhelming forces of evil.

Nevertheless, this quintessentially Italian TV drama was not totally without foreign influences; the 'school', so to speak, of American action movies and cop shows for example was evident in the scripts and the direction style. Besides, the narrative formula of *La Piovra*, which it is appropriate to regard as the first long-running Italian serial, refashioned the formulae of the continuous serial that had been introduced by imported products (I shall have more to say on this in the next chapter).

La piovra was 'the Italian response to *Dallas*': not only because it contrasted the image of oil-producing Texas with the landscape of Mafia-dominated Sicily, and emulated the international success of the American serial (*La Piovra* is today still the most widely sold Italian TV drama in the world), but also because it adopted the formula of *Dallas* and adapted it in consonance with Italian tradition. The result was a serial *sui generis*, influenced by the serialized narratives imported from America, yet unmistakably Italian in being a successful 're-territorialization' of the foreign models.

By the end of the decade, the escalating success of *La Piovra* was accompanied by a decline in the popularity of US imports.

Notes

1. In the words of the director Sandro Bolchi, regarded as one of the fathers and the greatest master of the *sceneggiato*: 'There was then a belief that the viewer could not perceive certain rhythms, and on the other hand the requirements of the TV studio entailed plenty of speech, without cuts ... in *Karamazov* the dialogue about the Grand Inquisitor between Ivan and Alesa lasted for 20 minutes' (quoted in Pinto et al., 1988: 52).
2. In this way the Rai managed to kill two birds with one stone: they strictly limited the offer of films in television programming, and at the same time demonstrated their wish to safeguard the traditional watching of films in the cinemas, following the agreements stipulated with the National Association of Cinema Operators. In order to restrain the feared competition from the new medium, many exhibitors came up with a fairly odd initiative: television sets were

installed in many theatres, and the film projection was deferred when the most popular TV programmes were being broadcast, so that the audience could watch them from their seats in the cinema. Of course this attempt to combine the watching of films and television was destined to come to an end, as television viewing lost its initial public and collective character and was transferred to the private spaces of the home.

3. At the start of the 1970s, Italy was still regarded by the American film industry as a poor market; 'since only two features were allowed telecast per week, it set a maximum on Hollywood features of no more than 52 a year' (Seagrave, 1998: 145).

4. To name just a few: *Roma città aperta/Rome, Open City* (Roberto Rossellini, 1945); *Paisà* (Roberto Rossellini, 1946); *La terra trema/The Earth Trembles* (Luchino Visconti, 1947); *Ladri di biciclette/Bicycle Thief* (Vittorio De Sica, 1948); *Riso amaro/Bitter Rice* (Giuseppe De Santis, 1948); *Stromboli* (Roberto Rossellini, 1949); *Cronaca di un amore/Story of a Love Affair* (Michelangelo Antonioni, 1950); *Achtung! Bandit!* (Carlo Lizzani, 1951); *Bellissima* (Luchino Visconti, 1951); *Umberto D* (Vittorio De Sica, 1952). For a complete filmography, see Wagstaff, 2007.

5. Mussolini seized power in 1922, but the Fascist government did not impose an embargo on foreign films until 1938.

6. The mobilization of thousands of Fascist militants (Blackshirts), coming from all parts of Italy and invading Rome in October 1922, has gone down in Italian history as 'the march on Rome'.

7. In the early 1950s more than one-third of Italian cinemas belonged to the Catholic chain of church halls (Forgacs, 1990: 121).

8. The *Centro Cattolico Cinematografico* (Catholic Film Centre) was a religious organization set up in 1935 to give pastoral guidance to the faithful on watching films. The CCC published periodic booklets containing analytical reviews of films released, in which consideration of the artistic merit of the products was invariably associated with moral judgements. The final assessment was based on the latter, expressed in a range of ratings (from Everyone to Excluded).

9. To the appeal of the film was added the twofold attraction of the cinema, as a public and private space: it was a place for displaying visibility and meeting the community, and at the same time a space protected by darkness, where one could surrender to amorous and erotic advances (before the spread of car ownership offered couples an even more intimate refuge).

10. Set in the seventeenth century, during the Spanish occupation of Lombardy, *I promessi sposi* is a historical novel and at the same time a very perceptive socio-anthropological 'treatise' on the Italian identity. The obligatory reading of this book in secondary schools has ended up by making it unpopular with many generations of schoolchildren; but there has never been any question as to the greatness of Manzoni's masterpiece and its deep roots in Italian culture. An entire repertoire of words and phrases borrowed from the work survive in the Italian language to this day.

11. In the course of the twentieth century three cinematographic adaptations of the novel were made, respectively by the directors Mario Bonnard (1923), Mario Camerini (1941) and Mario Maffei (1963), with somewhat erratic artistic results and success.

12. The expression was coined by the director of *I promessi sposi* himself, Sandro Bolchi (see note 1).

13. In fact some filmic infiltration could be identified even in the very theatrical *Promessi sposi*. Each instalment opened with the brief filmed scene of a small boat rocking in the waters of a

lake; furthermore the cast included – along with a rare team of the greatest performers from the Italian theatre – the actor Massimo Girotti, protagonist of *Ossessione* (Luchino Visconti, 1943) and of numerous other films, both art and commercial. He was known as the 'Italian Paul Newman'.
14. A literary adaptation of Giovanni Verga's novel, one of the masterpieces of nineteenth-century Italian *verismo*. For its part the *sceneggiato* was regarded as the masterpiece of Giacomo Vaccari, a television prodigy who died young. He made the adaptation into a highly expressive work with a very personal style, which received critical acclaim at the time.
15. He was later to become a mogul of the Hollywood film industry. A few years after directing *Odyssey*, Dino De Laurentiis left Italy for good and moved to Los Angeles, where he died in 2010.
16. In the early 1980s Paul Kerr wrote that 'the classic serial … seems so embedded in and at the same time such an embodiment of British television' (Kerr, 1982: 6). This observation could equally refer to the Italian miniseries.
17. Concerning *The Life of Verdi*, note this quotation from an article published on 24 October 1983 in the *New York Times*: 'As is usual with Italian epics, whether made for television or the movie screen, the production is sumptuous. … The usual extraordinary statistics are bandied about: 100 actors, 18,000 extras, 4,000 costumes, filming on locations ranging from Milan and Venice to Leningrad and London. Scenes at La Scala, as it was in the nineteenth century, are positively magnificent' (O'Connor, 1983).

Chapter 3

The Political Career of a Popular Fiction:
La Piovra (The Octopus: The Power of the Mafia)

A phenomenon of popularity

In the 1980s, when the programme schedules of both public and commercial Italian television channels became internationalized following massive waves of imports from abroad, and successes achieved by American series and serials, Latin American *telenovelas* and Japanese cartoons seemed to justify – and in any case were arousing – 'cultural panic' in many sectors of public opinion on account of the dreaded 'colonisation' of the tastes and consumption models of domestic audiences, a peculiarly Italian TV drama gave rise to a phenomenon of unheard popularity, destined to remain unequalled even in the future. I am referring to *La Piovra/The Octopus: The Power of Mafia* (hereafter *La Piovra*; Raiuno 1984–2001), which I have briefly introduced in the previous chapter.

Just as (Abbott: 2009) attaining blockbuster status, thanks to its very high ratings, would in itself be insufficient to make *Lost* one of the most thought-provoking and emblematical phenomena of contemporary television, so the importance of the case of *La Piovra* rests only partially on its huge and long-lasting success. However, it must be recognized that ratings of such magnitude (up to 17 million viewers and a 60% audience share) acquired at that time the exciting significance of a resounding victory of the local over the global – the Italian antidote to *Dallas* – while if we look back at them from the present-day scenario of fragmentation, those successes offer reasons for nostalgic pride in the great results that domestic drama was able to achieve in the past.

In fact, *La Piovra* constitutes a phenomenon that in many ways is unique in the whole history of Italian TV drama and in all probability unrepeatable. This is explained by its unprecedented narrative structure, the generic hybridization ahead of its time, the impressive mythopoetic impact of its imaginative and symbolic power, its astute timeliness in creating an ongoing epic narrative of the extremely harsh conflict between the Mafia and the State that was taking place at the time and, perhaps the most important of all, to its capacity of gaining a firm place in the agenda of national political debate.

I shall deal with these various aspects in the present chapter, which is dedicated to a case study of *La Piovra*. And as I agree with Jason Mittel (2009) that it is appropriate for television scholars to allow space for a personal appraisal in their (conventionally neutral and value-free) critical and interpretative work, I shall not refrain from defining *La Piovra* as a magnificent drama, a milestone in the history of Italian television fiction, worthy of special attention and in-depth analysis, independently of the large number of viewers and fans, by reason of its high concept, narrative form, textuality and production.

Nor is it by chance that *La Piovra* to this day holds the record as the Italian TV drama with the highest sales abroad: it has been exported to over 100 countries and in some of these (Russia, Germany and France) has gained real popular appeal. As far as I know, it is also the only Italian TV drama mentioned in international literature: Richard Sparks (1992) includes *La Piovra* – broadcast in 1985 on Channel 4, which co-produced it with the Rai– in his book on the drama of crime in television.

As I shall explain more clearly later in this chapter, *La Piovra* is a *sui generis* serial: its macrotext is made up of an ensemble of 10 (four-to-six-part) miniseries, produced and broadcast at annual or biennial intervals over a timespan of 17 years. The first edition goes back to 1984, the last to 2001. My analysis takes the perspective of the seventh edition, to cast a comprehensive look at the narrative of *La Piovra* throughout the decade (1984–1995) when it was in effect the unrivalled core story of Italian television. The three successive miniseries that were broadcast between the second half of the 1990s and the beginning of the twenty-first century merely ensured good ratings for a story swinging back and forth in time – the eighth and ninth editions were prequels set in the 1950s, the tenth returned to the present day – which was by now losing its magic, and the power of its mythology to arouse profound resonances in Italians' collective sentiments.

Bond and beyond

The title of this chapter 'The political career of a popular fiction' will be instantly recognized by anyone who is familiar with the field of cultural studies; it is in fact a quotation from the title *Bond and Beyond: The Political Career of a Popular Hero* (1983), a well-known and much acclaimed cultural analysis of the 'Bond phenomenon' carried out by Tony Bennett and Janet Woollacott at the beginning of the 1980s.

The quotation, far from being merely evocative, incorporates and proclaims a twofold enunciative intention. The first intention relates to the analytical approach adopted in the text of *Bond and Beyond* and indicates that numerous theoretical and methodological inputs from that work will be freely taken up and applied to the analysis of *La Piovra*, without this being tantamount to the mechanical reproduction of a given model. The second and more transparent enunciative intention, by contrast, refers to Bond as a cultural phenomenon and, in suggesting a possible analogy between the two cases, carries out the preliminary operation of endorsing *La Piovra* and placing it among the outstanding expressions of popular Italian culture at the end of the twentieth century.

Obviously, the analogy is partial, if only because of the disproportion between the 'global' popularity enjoyed by the figure of James Bond in his day and the mainly 'local' or national popularity of *La Piovra*. Among the few but significant anecdotes concerning its popularity in foreign countries, at least one is worth quoting: the proposal, sent to *Pravda* by some Russian viewers, that the persecuted Inspector Cattani should be offered political asylum in the (then) Soviet Union. Quite apart from the remarkable paradox of political asylum in a country with an illiberal regime, the episode – if true – is a perfect indicator of that transition of a fictitious character to real life that is so much a part of popularity phenomena. Nevertheless, the success of *La Piovra* outside Italy still remains a limited occurrence and is in no way comparable to the truly global or trans-national scale of Bond's popularity or, to take another example, that of *Dallas*. However the merely partial equivalence of the two cases does not prevent us from assigning *La Piovra* to the same category of profound and lasting phenomena of popular culture to which Bond belongs, or used to belong. -

The political career of a popular fiction ('a hero' in the original title): this quotation is not fully justified unless the concept of a 'political career' – a further feature of the affinity between the 'Bond phenomenon' and the '*piovra* phenomenon' – is brought into the picture. The fact of being political, in a sense not indicating party politics as such, and therefore leaving alignments, positions and affiliations out of consideration, is not an anomalous property of *La Piovra*. For some time scholars have acknowledged that 'entertainment is, or may be, political' (Blumler et al., 1985: 258); and every tale dealing with issues that are relevant to the public and social sphere – crime, corruption, war, the nation, class, race – is liable to take on a political significance in the broad sense. More recently 'the enduring encounters between entertainment and politics' (Van Zoonen, 2005: 2) have been thematized in their multifarious articulations in the light of the refreshing hypothesis that such an alliance – conventionally regarded as a deplorable and dangerous *mésalliance* – could even prove to be beneficial to citizenship.

What is peculiar to *La Piovra*, however, is the intensity of its politicization and the fact that it was the cause and focus of controversy and very heated political and ideological debate. This politicization directly participated in the process of producing and reproducing the '*piovra* phenomenon'.

An *intertextual* octopus

It has to be pointed out, to begin with, that the '*piovra* phenomenon' requires the adoption of an analytic intertextual approach. In being applied to an object that does not contain the reasons for its own success entirely within itself, this approach demands that we go beyond the primary texts of *La Piovra*, understood as individual and discrete narrative units, to place them in the context of the relationships that they maintain both with each other and with 'other texts' or secondary texts of discourses concerning *La Piovra*, which have been produced by different subjects and circulated by the news media. In other words, I should reconstruct the network of factors that have co-produced and reproduced, from one seasonal success to the next and in the intervals between one success and another, the popularity of *La Piovra* itself.

By adopting such a perspective, I intend to acknowledge a long-lasting reflection on televisual textuality and, more generally, on the texts of popular culture that featured in the media and cultural studies some decades ago – running the risk of seeming (mistakenly) outmoded, useless indeed in the changing trans-media multi-platform digitalized landscape of contemporary television. I do not wish here to revisit a debate – not lacking in excesses of abstractness or controversy – between schools of thought and intellectual streams, which I reconstructed when it was still 'alive' in the early 1990s (Buonanno, 1994); instead I will confine myself to extracting from it and acknowledging the compelling lesson that analyses and readings focused exclusively on this or that primary television material prove, to a greater or lesser extent, to be incomplete or biased (which obviously does not mean either useless or unworthy) in their capacity to fully illuminate phenomena that are always, or nearly always, constituted by and constituent of relationships between texts, media and – not least – subjects.

In this connection, the contributions of John Fiske, and especially of the already quoted scholars Bennett and Woollacott, are the most useful for my purposes: in each case, starting with an acknowledgement of a plurality of levels and textual typologies, the concept of intertextuality is crucial.

Fiske, within a category of intertextuality defined by him as 'vertical', proposed over twenty years ago an analytical distinction between primary texts, secondary texts and tertiary texts (Fiske, 1987: 117). Although it would be pleonastic to specify what is meant by the term 'primary text', there is some sense in bearing in mind that materials and promotional forms of every type, critical columns and journalistic coverage in its entirety, make up a set of secondary texts whose function is to put into circulation interpretative frameworks and selected meanings and commentaries, even if contradictory or conflicting, on the primary text. In turn, tertiary texts are the products of the initiative and relational activity of the viewers: letters sent to newspapers or to television networks and in particular exchanges of views, conversations and public and private discussions that may relate to the primary or secondary text or interact with other tertiary texts. The Internet, with its proliferation of blogs, forums, fan sites, chat rooms and social networks, has created the conditions for a huge expansion of secondary and tertiary textuality and has furthermore enabled tertiary textuality – which in the ephemeral forms of the once prevalent conversational style was, and remains, destined to vanish without trace, except perhaps in the memory of those who took part in it – to be traceable and to a greater or lesser extent durable as it materializes, as it were, in writings posted on the Internet. This kind of tertiary textuality, which did not exist in the 1980s and had only just begun in the first half of the 1990s, in any case remains inaccessible for my retrospective case study of *La Piovra*.

The advantage of the notion of vertical intertextuality is its articulation into analytical categories of textuality that are immediately empirical and reliably self-evident: the feasibility of the distinction between primary and secondary texts, to limit ourselves to two levels, is difficult not to agree upon. Furthermore, as Gripsrud has pointed out, 'this kind of categorization maintains the centrality of the text proper ("the primary text")' (Gripsrud, 1995: 130), while acknowledging the vital importance of other categories of texts.

Whereas Fiske tends to leave the relationship between the diverse categories of text implicit or to some extent taken for granted, the concept of *intertextuality* is cogently thematized by Bennett and Woollacott. This is not likely to be confused with a system of references or an interplay of quotations from one text to another – that is to say, with intertextuality in the acceptation originally introduced by Julia Kristeva: 'We intend the concept of *intertextuality* to refer to the social organization of the relations between texts within specific conditions of reading' (Bennett and Woollacott, 1983: 45). Cultural phenomena are peculiarly intertextual, not only because they are produced and diffused by a plurality or a whole set of texts, but also because their very conditions of existence and functioning reside in the system of constant or changeable inter-relationships that take root within this set of texts. The James Bond figure cannot be analysed without taking into consideration the heterogeneous ensemble of 'James Bond texts' – novels, films and related 'micro-narratives' such as biographies of the actors, newspapers, advertising – all of which helped to model and remodel over time the cultural and ideological significance of the hero. 'We would suggest', the authors state in the introduction, 'that it is impossible to analyse any particular text … without at the same time considering its relations to other texts of a similar nature' (Bennett and Woollacott, 1983: 6).

Bennett and Woollacott push this theoretical position to the point of sustaining the substantial equivalence of texts in relationship; there exist no privileged texts, or primary ones in Fiske's definition, in relation to which the other categories of texts can be situated; otherwise one retreats to the essentialist and individualizing concept of textuality, that instead rests solely on the relational dimension. Yet it is not necessary to accept such a radical corollary in order to adhere to a theory of cultural analysis that proves very convincing, in effect, in sustaining and demonstrating the importance of intertextuality, and the need to incorporate it into an approach that aims at accounting more completely for the objects and phenomena to which it applies.

The origins of *La Piovra*'s success

Originally, the story was to have been entitled 'Il romanzo di Loris' (Loris's Novel) and narrate the loneliness of a policeman who, having failed to come up with any proof in a case he was investigating, transformed the enquiry into a provocative novel. In an interview with the regional daily *Il giornale di Sicilia* on 21 March 1984, the scriptwriter Nicola Badalucco described the original subject of *La Piovra* in terms of an intimist and introspective story, in the style of Pirandello. As it never became the intimist and Pirandellian story envisaged by its authors in the first draft of the script, *La Piovra* proved from its inception to be a narrative destined for and inclined towards metamorphoses – just as its eclecticism, the fact of its being a combination of genres and diverse styles, was embedded from the start in the cooperation between Damiano Damiani, an author of social and political cinema who was well-known for having directed numerous movies about the Mafia (including *Il giorno della civetta/The Day of the Owl*, 1967) and Ennio De Concini (winner of an Oscar for *Divorzio all'italiana/Divorce Italian Style*, Pietro Germi 1961). De Concini was one of the most active and famous screenwriters in Italian cinema, his work ranging across a broad spectrum of popular genres from peplum to comedy. This group of authors with a cinematographic background, to whom must be added the famous musician Ennio Morricone (career Oscar in 2007, Oscar nominee several times in the 1980s for the soundtracks of *Once Upon a Time in America*, Sergio Leone 1984; *The Mission*, Roland Joffé 1987; *The Untouchables*, Brian De Palma 1987), gave a pedigree to the prototype of *La Piovra*, raising its profile above the status and reputation of an ordinary TV drama and injecting into the viewer's horizon of expectations a surplus of interest in a product that proved to be ennobled by its relationship with the cinema.

Despite taking a different form with respect to the original idea, the narrative of *La Piovra* interweaves so many elements of private affairs into the main plot, tied to the Mafia theme, that a definition on the lines of 'a story of sentiments' could also be justified. And it was the family and love story of a policeman, engaged in an investigation into the Mafia, that the promotional material tended to exploit in order to arouse and cultivate audience expectations. On the other hand, the actual presence of a director such as Damiano Damiani guaranteed a social component in the story; his name was always accompanied by selective and well-targeted filmographic citations ('the director of *Il giorno della civetta*'). Thus the twofold public and private register of *La Piovra* constituted a true resource, allowing promotional efforts aimed at attracting categories of viewers (for example women) who might not have been very interested in watching a straight Mafia story. The opening of *La Piovra* confirmed and at the same time re-ordered both the versions and expectations: establishing the primacy of the Mafia story, the first episode opened with a televised news report from the scene of a Mafia crime; then the protagonist Inspector Cattani was introduced in a guise that could not be more private: in his pyjamas, filmed in his bedroom in the morning while having a quarrel and then a passionate reconciliation with his wife.

Different titles were considered, and ruled out. In this regard, it can be said with reasonable certainty that a product that was already displaying pre-requisites for success in abundance, by virtue of its cinematographic pedigree and the attraction exercised by the mixture of Mafia violence and emotional turmoil, would have lacked a clearly decisive factor in its immediate and lasting popularity if it had been differently entitled.

In an interview published on 5 March 1995 in the Rome daily *Il messaggero*, the scriptwriter Ennio De Concini traced back the genesis of *La Piovra* to the 'inspired idea' of conjuring up the spectre of an obscure threat, playing on the assonance (in Italian) between the word 'piovra' and l'OVRA (Opera Vigilanza Repressione Antifascismo/ body for control and repression of antifascism), the secret police of the Fascist regime. For his part the producer Sergio Silva – known as 'the father' of *La Piovra*, and in fact the only continuing presence in a team of authors that saw many changes of directors and scriptwriters over time – instead confirmed a choice of title that was more directly prompted by the characteristics of the sea monster: a fierce and intelligent creature, able to survive if its tentacles were cut off. In any case De Concini was right in calling the idea 'inspired', but not because it was an original invention, which it was not; on the contrary it drew on (albeit entirely unconsciously) a symbology that already had wide and time-honoured currency in the collective imagination. Boats dragged down into the depths, or fortuitously rescued from the coils of huge tentacles, in much popular imagery; the 'giant octopus with fearsome eyes' that generations of adolescent readers have encountered in one of the most exciting chapters of Jules Verne's *Twenty Thousand Leagues under the Sea*; the portrayal of alien invaders in the first science fiction films in shapes similar to a stylized octopus; the evil Octopus, arch enemy of the superhero Spiderman; the Bond film *Octopussy* (Glen, 1983), where the octopus stands for the SPECTRE (and here, in the interweaving of criminality and politics, we are already very close to *La Piovra*): the danger, the exploitation, the criminal power and the obscure yet all-embracing threats that emanate from these things have often been represented, in literature and popular iconography and cinema, in the tentacular forms or under the name of the octopus.

Thus by having recourse to a powerful symbology of evil that was already lodged in the unconscious and in the collective imagination, the creators of *La Piovra* carried out a very effective operation in activating that *modus operandi* of popular genres that rests on the powerful appeal and the well-proven promotional capacity of the already known. Obviously the operation would not have been so effective had it not been intertwined with elements of innovation: that is to say, if the designation of evil and, in a sense, of the 'enemy' had not been accompanied by the identification of the same evil and the same enemy with the criminal organisation, the Mafia. Not that the Italian cinema and even TV drama had previously failed to confront the problem, but *La Piovra* was the first TV drama to proclaim from the title an identification between the Mafia and Evil, which had never been so programmatic and absolute, and which made its appearance in a climate of opinion already predisposed to welcome it, share it indeed.

Criminality, and even more the culture of the Mafia, is a long-established evil of Italian society. Nevertheless both the ability of the traditional Cosa Nostra leadership to cope with its internal conflicts without attracting too much attention, while at the same time ensuring the immunity of its own members – thanks to its network of alliances with institutions and State officials at local and national level – and the tendency of State authorities, for various reasons, to underestimate the problem, allowed the Mafia phenomenon to develop in relative invisibility for many years as far as public awareness and press attention was concerned. The situation changed suddenly and dramatically at the end of the 1970s when the criminal Corleone group, hitherto marginal in the geography of the Mafia, began its ascent to power and thus initiated a strategy of out-and-out carnage that left over 1000 dead among the Cosa Nostra affiliates in just a few years. For the first time in the history of the Mafia, the very institutions of the State came under attack: politicians, magistrates and police officers became the targets of deadly assaults. The Mafia thus arose as a sociopolitical 'emergency' that could no longer be underestimated. In the early 1980s the Italian Parliament approved a law against the specific crime of Mafia membership, while an anti-Mafia team consisting of an elite of magistrates and functionaries of the security apparatuses set up wide-ranging investigations in Sicily that were to lead to the charging and trial of over 400 Mafiosi. The connections and instances of collusion between the Mafia, politics and business emerged (at least in part) from the thick cloud of suspicion that had always enveloped them, and began to assume the clearer contours of provable facts (Arlacchi, 2009).

Consequently the Mafia phenomenon in its multi-dimensional and truly tentacular configuration became a prominent and burning issue in public discourse in the 1980s, raising media attention and collective concern about organized crime to levels never previously reached in Italy. All this very probably helped both to fertilize the inspirational terrain of *La Piovra*'s narrative with ideas and echoes of recognizable 'real-life' reportage, and to create a reception context that made viewers favourably disposed to welcome and follow a drama that had resonances with the top issue of the moment.

A further factor engendering a generally propitious atmosphere for, or any rate a sustained interest in, *La Piovra*, was the debate (very heated at that time) about television's system and culture. This was in the early 1980s; and in the still new scenario of the 'mixed system' there was an acknowledged risk that public television, under the pressure of aggressive competition from private television networks, might yield to the temptation of fighting them on their own ground and thus renouncing 'culture'. Commercial television channels were accused in particular – this was during the years of the success of *Dallas* – of serving as transmission belts of cultural colonization by means of 'low-quality' American products that were alien to domestic customs, problems and values.

Therefore, expectations and reception of *La Piovra* were affected by the symbolic overload of meanings it came to embody in relation to issues of major political and cultural relevance: the identity and functions of public as opposed to private television, Italian identity versus the risk of Americanization, and not least television versus the cinema. Not by chance, the complete success of the operation aroused satisfaction from all sides, as is proved by the following quotations from the main daily papers of that time.[1]

'*La Piovra* ... is a demonstration of how TV can be made, by concentrating upon quality as in the cinema, representing our own themes and problems' (s. gar., *L'Unità*, 19 March 1984)

'*La Piovra*: perhaps one of the possible models of cultural commitment on the part of public service, as compared to the competition from commercial TV' (Surchi, *Il Popolo*, 18 March 1984)

'*La Piovra* ... demonstrates that the Rai has in fact not lost the ability to positively perform its function not only as a public service, but also as a major producer of culture and information' (C.S., *L'Avanti*, 23 March 1984)

'... bringing Italian stories of today to the small screen serves to rescue us, if only for a few hours, from the cultural colonisation of *Dallas* and the like' (Gavioli, *La Repubblica,* 21 March 1984).

The first edition of *La Piovra* was not the one that reached the highest average or peak ratings: both these records were held by *La Piovra* 4, with an average of 14 million viewers and a peak of 17 million for the final episode, when Cattani dies. But the first edition was the one that achieved the biggest increase: almost a doubling of viewers between the first episode (8 million) and the last one (15 million). This increase in viewers was matched by a great deal of public and private discourse, which quickly spread from everyday conversations to newspapers and to television itself – the last episode was followed by a debate in the studios of Rome, Naples and Palermo, with connections and interviews on location – thus making *La Piovra* a true 'television event'.

If I have so far emphasized the extra-textual and contextual elements – the cinematic aura, the evocative appeal of the title, the promotion of the personal, private aspects of the story and at the same time its concern with a dramatic public emergency, the circumstances of an interpretation in terms of the cultural policies of Italian television – this is because I wanted to give prominence to the unexpected or neglected role that these factors play: not, for sure, in determining a success or an event, but in helping to bring it into existence and to make it function in the presence of, and in relation to, other textual factors that cannot be left out of account. In the case of *La Piovra* the paramount textual factor – and, it could be said, the victorious one – was the true theme of the story: the Mafia.

Mafia plots

Nothing but the Mafia, the great national obsession – as present in real life as it is dominant in the collective imagination – could have given *La Piovra*'s powerful stories such an abundance of gripping narrative material, ready for and predisposed towards every type of fictional metamorphosis.

Within the range of popular genres, the Mafia can in fact be regarded as an unsurpassed resource for the conception and development of stories in which the entire panoply of archetypes, motives and ingredients of popular narration based on crime is unfolded: positive and negative heroes, one group armed against others, betrayal and revenge, savagery, blood and tears, blackmail, conspiracies, lust for and conflicts of power, greed for money, corruption, punishment, justice. All this, and more besides, is the basis for the powerful attraction that crime, especially violent crime, and stories about crime have always exercised on the collective imagination in an inextricable mixture of fascination and repulsion. It is not by chance that crime is the main substance of newspaper reports, as it was in the past for the tales of storytellers. One could not fully comprehend the popularity of *La Piovra* without recognizing that the Mafia, as well as arousing repulsion and moral condemnation, does undeniably exercise a fascination – though perversely, that of evil.

Nor can one entirely comprehend why *La Piovra*'s stories should have been so successful and regularly provoked a debate on their degree of realism without grasping the deep affinity of the narrative with Italian culture's penchant for secret conspiracies and power plots. Mafiosi, managers, entrepreneurs, politicians, big wheeler-dealers, evil geniuses, united in a shady alliance to the detriment of society: it is on this conspiring backstage that *La Piovra* has turned the spotlight, giving substance to and acknowledging the myriad suspicions of a collective mentality that is inclined, indeed hypersensitive to, the evocation of 'plots'.

From one edition to the next, *La Piovra*'s narrative was increasingly in tune with that sort of irresistible national penchant for speculation on the hidden agenda, that identifies the cause and the explanation of many events in society in the secret plans worked out behind closed doors in powerful circles. This certainly does not mean ignoring or denying that poisons, cloaks and daggers, plots and mysteries, are actually a part of Italy's past history and even more recent events; but all this served to create and nourish the forceful, larger-than-life conspiratorial image that *La Piovra*'s fictional stories have simultaneously shared and enhanced.

La Piovra did not confine itself to exploiting the Mafia in full as a narrative resource – and thus was soon to be accused of making too many concessions to the fictitious – but thematized it as the problem, or rather the *social evil*, of present-day Italy, adding to the treatment of the story not only a cipher of engagement and civic passion but also those references and allusions to real life, or rather to Italian news reports, that in giving space to a 'recognition game' that spread and grew from one edition to the next, ended up by entering into a sort of implicit pact between the narrative and the viewers and became a constant factor in structuring the expectations of the public. For many reasons it would be out of place to associate with *La Piovra* the same type of compulsive 'forensic fandom' (Mittel, 2009: 128) we find in certain contemporary cult series; nevertheless, one of the ways in which the narrative cleverly inspired the commitment and aroused the pleasure of viewers consisted without doubt in subtle and astute instigation to speculate on the clues, mysteries and suspicions scattered or hidden on purpose along the trail.

Quite surprisingly, this helped to confer on *La Piovra* the credentials of a 'television drama that helps one to know' (Gavioli, 1984: 15).

> Anyone who knows about the Mafia knows that the serial *La Piovra* is a good show, but it is above all good education. Using the communicative power of television, it explained to Italians that the Mafia was not merely that Sicilian gang of criminals, murderers and kidnappers that was already being talked about during the Fascist era, ... but that its web of responsibility and complicity spread out just like the tentacles of an octopus to a large section of society and the economy in the South, had contacts in government and justice offices in Rome, did business with a number of respectable banks in Milan and Rome and had their lobby in Parliament (Bocca, 1994: 1).

> With *La Piovra* Italians *came to know* (my italics) that the Mafia was ferocious, that it handled huge sums of money and that there were many cowards who colluded with them and some, just a few, brave idealists. (Deaglio, 1995:8)

Such a good reputation can in all probability be numbered among the factors of a long-lasting success, since a Mafia story that combines entertainment and information, fact and fiction, is likely – if it is well made, as *La Piovra* generally was – to attract and satisfy a more heterogeneous, and therefore larger, audience than would be drawn by a story of either pure entertainment or authentic, well-documented realism.

On the other hand *La Piovra* has, precisely because of its two-faceted nature, been exposed to criticisms and heated debate taking the opposite view: it has in fact been accused either of turning a much more threatening and complicated reality into a simplified piece of fiction or of purporting a degree of adherence to real life such as to allow viewers to presume that the serial sought to unveil, if only by allusion, dark underhand dealings and hidden, uncomfortable and disquieting truths. Whereas the first line of argument soon made its appearance, the second took shape and was gradually and progressively strengthened as the narrative, in one edition after another, seemed to raise the stakes in portraying the infiltrations and connections of the Mafia within high places of political and financial power. A further contentious argument, or rather the most constantly reiterated, maintained that a story with realist pretensions like *La Piovra* was running the risk of circulating images of reality that were not true yet were credible and trusted despite, or rather by virtue of, the force of conviction inherent in their nature of fictional make-believe.

Hence a politicization of *La Piovra*, that is to say an emphasis and a symbolic overload placed on its meanings, aims, implications and political effects, which was without equal in the history of Italian television drama. In this connection, for example, the episode reported on the jacket flap of a book taken from the screenplay of *La Piovra 5* is symptomatic.

> On 7.10.1989 the troupe of *La Piovra* were being transferred to Palermo on an Alitalia plane departing from Rome. ... A distinguished gentleman of about 50 with an authoritative air struck up a friendship with a likeable girl in the cast ... and confided to her with a touch of benevolent reproof that in the days immediately before the final instalment of *La Piovra 4* ... there had been a meeting in Rome at high ministerial level, during which the possibility of forbidding it to be broadcast had been aired.' (Petraglia et al., 1990)

It was feared, the mysterious person was said to have explained, that the death of Inspector Cattani might cause public unrest. But in the end, it was decided to defer such an unusual measure.

It was precisely in the 'political career' of the narrative that the popularity of *La Piovra* found one of its conditions of existence and survival. Not merely did this strong politicization help to sow the seeds of even more intriguing and exciting interpretations in the reception context; it also acted as an incessant stimulus to discourse and newspaper coverage, that is to say to the production of secondary texts that were able to keep the interest and attention alive and awake even between one edition of *La Piovra* and the next, thus making it an authentic and unusual inter-medial continuing story.

La Piovra, for its part, fed and revived interest in and attention to the Mafia phenomenon. The VHS versions of several editions sold in newspaper kiosks, together with booklets of a Mafia story in instalments (Bentivegna, 1995). Non-fiction itself and the reading of non-fiction on the Mafia drew inspiration from the televisual octopus:

> In the second half of the 1980s, the success of a television serial like *La Piovra* has enormously increased the number of people who are interested in reading journalistic reportage or memoirs on the activities of Cosa Nostra and its allies. (Tranfaglia, 1994: 19)

Newspapers and non-fiction, on the other hand, were soon won over by the small but significant linguistic revolution created by *La Piovra*: the words 'Mafia' and 'Cosa Nostra' practically vanished from ordinary language, book titles and newspaper headlines, to be replaced by the tentacular metaphor of the sea monster, while Italian language dictionaries updated the entry for 'piovra', adding the new meaning of 'criminal association with a tentacular organisation, Mafia' (Gabrielli, 1989: 2642). In fact the televisual octopus not only effectively helped to make the wider public aware of the Mafia phenomenon; it also successfully carried out an operation of re-denomination through which, in putting its own stamp on the Mafia, the octopus construct to some extent freed itself from the televisual matrix to become an autonomous linguistic hallmark that incorporated a certain conception of the Mafia itself in a way that was (in the Italian context) universally recognizable.

When events of this kind occur – that is, when a character or, as in the case of *La Piovra*, a name or a make-believe symbol emerges from the original text itself to assume something similar to an autonomous life or existence, becoming part of the repertoire of cultural reference points that are significant for an entire community – we are faced with a popularity phenomenon in the fullest sense of the word. The autonomy from the textual conditions of existence, state Bennett and Woollacott, is witnessed by the fact that these reference points work and assume a sense that is inter-subjectively shared also by and between 'those who are not directly familiar with the original texts in which they first made their appearance' (Bennett and Woollacott, 1983: 14).

The various televisual editions of *La Piovra* have been watched by millions, but the number of those in Italy who have never seen an episode of *La Piovra* is certainly very high; and yet there is no doubt that for many, even if not all those who are not 'directly familiar' with the texts of *La Piovra*, the octopus metaphor still acts as an evocation and an activator of meanings that, albeit only vaguely, can be traced back to the nexus of Mafia and politics.

Social melodrama

When the process of détente between East and West started, the openly anti-Soviet attitudes hitherto demonstrated by James Bond became embarrassing and had to be toned down in the context of a more general de-politicization of the hero's adventures. The Bond films, the producers repeated, 'are not political but good old-fashioned entertainment' (Bennett and Woollacott, 1983: 191).

The anecdote is significant because it demonstrates how a controversial narrative, or one that is made controversial by particular circumstances, raises the question of a continuous definition and redefinition of its nature or the genre to which it belongs, with the purpose of containing the disagreement and orienting the expectations and interpretation of viewers in a direction that is appropriate or fitting for the circumstances.

Not by chance, one of the peculiarities of the 'Piovra phenomenon' is in the fact that its authors were constantly urged to supply the 'proper definition' of *La Piovra* as regards the perennial question concerning the relationship between invention and reality, fact and fiction, entertainment and engagement. Some declarations made in the autumn of 1992, at the time of the broadcasting of *La Piovra 6*, and in March 1995, before *La Piovra 7* was screened, may serve as examples; moreover, they will provide the starting point for discussion on the genre and formula of *La Piovra*.

La Piovra 6 was presented to Mipcom of Cannes in October 1992; on that occasion, recalling the heated political debates that had obstructed the making of the new sequel, the newspapers reported some statements by the director Luigi Perelli:

> The close relationship between fact and fiction has always distinguished this serial … This film has a special force, it is almost a civil struggle. It is pegged to Italian and international reality like few other serials. … (Fumarola, 1992: 41)

A few days later, during an interview with the daily paper *L'Unità*, Sergio Silva inscribed *La Piovra* ('my great professional and civil passion') in a relationship between invention and reality where indeed

> the facts seem to have drawn inspiration from the fiction. Even if *La Piovra* was and is a novel, everything that has appeared in the various episodes of *La Piovra* appeared subsequently in the newspapers … The great merit of this series was, in politico-social terms, that of portraying the connections … it made viewers understand how a low-level crime is linked with high-level interest … it taught people to look at reality. (Silva, 1992:19)

La Piovra 6 was broadcast from 20 November 1992 and obtained lower than expected ratings; it was judged to be too abstract and metaphysical and, in the opinion of many, not in keeping with the close, even anticipatory, relationship between an imagined story and Italian sociopolitical current affairs. In that circumstance, the screenwriters Rulli and Petraglia intervened to reformulate, indeed almost to reverse, the dosage of *La Piovra*'s ingredients, stating that '90% is invention' and re-establishing the anchorage of the story not to the news report in the strict sense but more generally 'to certain striking elements of our social life' (Conti, 1992). When the broadcast of *La Piovra 6* was concluded, they were to write:

> If there is one thing that we sought to reflect … it was not the *news reports* of the political misconducts of these years. What we tried to convey every time was an *atmosphere*, even if in the simplified narrative form of the popular novel. (Petraglia e Rulli, 1992)

During the presentation of *La Piovra 7*, recalling the heated debate and criticisms that this edition had provoked even before it was broadcast, Sergio Silva eventually declared: '*La Piovra* is not a political film, at most it is a historical account that contains political but also strongly melodramatic elements' (Piccinini, 1995).

If we refrain from seeing in these declarations a mere expression of communicative tactics in keeping with changing circumstances, or of divergences or disagreements within the group of authors, we can more usefully discern the relative malleability of popular texts and their capacity (within limits) to be inflected or interpreted in different directions and to different ends, incorporating into their own popularity a degree of slippage, wavering and ambivalence of sense and genre. Film reportage, real-life novel, historical account: *La Piovra* has managed to be defined in terms that established it as a text-to-be-read against a changing background without losing its recognizability or ceasing to function as a principle of unifying classification.

All this was made possible by the peculiar heterogeneity of the *La Piovra* formula itself, among other things. It has rightly been observed on a number of occasions that *La Piovra* resists being confined within a specific genre, in the sense that we so define, for example, the action-adventure, thriller or science fiction. In fact *La Piovra* was an eclectic and metamorphic mixture of various trends and genres: cinéma-vérité or social engagement, a vein that was more explicit or more covert according to the situation, but always decipherable between the lines in the constant allusions to facts and personalities of an Italy beset by scandals, corruption, mysteries; the police drama, naturally, the *film noir*, the Gothic and even the western – in some sequences of ambushes and clashes between criminals and the police – not to mention the love story, as well as sophisticated elements of art films or echoes of the theatre and the radio (consider the frequent monologues).

It would not be mistaken to define *La Piovra* as a post-modern narrative *pastiche*, an implacable and haphazard hybrid that may perhaps be regarded as an original and anomalous genre apart: the 'piovra' genre, capable of displaying its own trademark, arousing its own expectations and constituting and supplying its own referential horizon.

It is however difficult (though not impossible) for very popular phenomena to happen and to be perpetuated simply within the referential horizon that they themselves have created, and *La Piovra* is no exception to this; like saying that if the 'piovra genre' works, or has worked, this is also because it is enshrined in a well-tested narrative formula. Here I am using the notion of formula in the sense, proposed by Cawelti, of archetypal or universal narrative; archetypal narratives are those that we find at the root of stories that manage to achieve widespread popularity in various epochs and societies, from time to time recombining within the same formulaic model the different themes and cultural materials that have interest and significance for every specific epoch and society. The formula for the heroic adventure story, for example, governs chivalric literature as well as the western genre or the spy story.

So the basic formula of *La Piovra* is the social melodrama (to convey the idea immediately, one might say that social melodrama finds its most grandiose and famous expression in Victor Hugo's *Les Misérables*). Cawelti describes this formula's structural characteristic as 'the combination of melodramatic structure and character with something that passes for a "realistic" social or historical setting' (Cawelti, 1976: 261). The plot unfolds according to the conventions of melodrama in such a way as to ensure maximum emotional satisfaction, while 'the social setting is often treated rather critically with a good deal of anatomizing of the hidden motives, secret corruption and human folly underlying certain events or institutions' (Cawelti, 1976: 261).

The synthesis between melodramatic structure 'and something that passes for realistic' exercises a particular attraction, because it allows us to yield to the pleasure of the narrative while at the same time having the comforting sensation that we are learning something important about real life. Social melodrama, Cawelti continues, benefits from whatever may give the story the appearance of profound social significance, and strives to make us feel that it is offering us the opportunity of penetrating beyond the surface of events and institutions to discover 'the dirt beneath the rug, the secret power behind the scenes' (Cawelti, 1976: 262).

This tendency or ambition to reveal unsuspected or unspoken truths links social melodrama to the tradition of 'muck-raking'; the progressive 'muck-raking' movement, as is known, generated a huge amount of social criticism in the United States between the end of the nineteenth and the first two decades of the twentieth century. This social criticism was also voiced in literature – Upton Sinclair and Theodore Dreiser were part of this trend – and in aggressive investigative journalism, dedicated in particular to the unmasking and denunciation of political scandals.

But social melodrama came into existence first in Europe at exactly the same time as the *feuilleton*, with which it coincided in some respects. Eugène Sue's *Les mystères de Paris/The Mysteries of Paris*, with the intense drive of its crusade against the many social evils of the nineteenth-century metropolis, may be considered a true social melodrama. The fate of *Les mystères de Paris*, amongst other things, immediately throws light on the conflicting effects of a formula that can arouse opposing reactions: tremendous popularity and heated controversy at the same time. Sue was to be accused of political propaganda and scandal mongering and, in the course of a parliamentary session, a deputy was to accuse the *Débats* – the newspaper in which *Les mystères* was being published – 'of having made its readers walk through the Parisian sewers for a year' (Bianchini, 1968: 96).

When we consider the immense popularity of works such as Harriet Beecher Stowe's *Uncle Tom's Cabin*, Victor Hugo's *Les Misérables* and Margaret Mitchell's *Gone with the Wind*, and of authors such as Eugène Sue, Charles Dickens, Wilkie Collins and Irving Wallace who created sure-fire best-sellers out of social melodrama, we can fully understand that we are faced with a formula, an authentic 'basic' narrative archetype, that is capable of having a very wide and profound impact on the collective imagination. And it is precisely in this blend of melodrama and social criticism, of emotional appeal and intention to inform, of spectacular treatment and scandalous material, that we recognize the ambivalent formula of *La Piovra*. When the authors in the passages cited earlier speak of a story that has taught its readers how to look at real life yet is 90% invention, a story that was almost a civil struggle but also a popular novel, they are in effect speaking – consciously or otherwise – of a social melodrama.

It may be useful to cite some examples, to show how *La Piovra* fully meets the requirements of the formula. Social melodrama uses various techniques to intensify emotions. One of the most important and effective of these is weaving important historic or social events into the tale, preferably ones that are dramatic and large scale: wars, trials, assassinations, ceremonies. In addition to heightening excitement, the melodramatic use of an event or a public spectacle serves to reinforce the impression of the story's truthfulness, thanks to 'something that passes for realistic' and thus plays a part in influencing and modifying the fate of this or that character. The bomb at Palermo railway station in *La Piovra 5*, with all its power to evoke real-life tragic events etched on the memories of viewers, is one possible example.[2]

Another more interesting instance of the melodramatic use of a public event can be found in *La Piovra 7*, in the long funeral scene leading to the story's dénouement. The scene is constructed in such a way as to evoke recognizably the funeral ceremony for Judge Giovanni Falcone,[3] his wife and his bodyguards, assassinated by the Mafia in 1992 ('the massacre of Capaci', from the name of the place in Sicily near which the assassination took place). What served to jog people's memories was in particular the inspired prayer of a young woman, bearing close resemblance to the wife of one of the murdered bodyguards who gave a heart-rending and moving address from the altar at Falcone's funeral.

The scene does not completely succeed in creating the intense climax for which it was intended and designed; but it undoubtedly 'works', in the triple sense in which a public spectacle in a social melodrama must work:

(1) it provokes a rush of emotion, both because it recalls memories – still recent and vivid when *La Piovra 7* was screened – of sad moments in the collective life that were shared by everyone, and because viewers are aware that the entire ceremony takes place, in the fictitious story, under threat of an assassination;

(2) it deploys something that can easily pass for realistic, in that it recalls a real life public event and gives the story a flavour of truthfulness, which social melodrama needs in order to confirm that access to the truth is being offered;

(3) finally, through the impact that it exercises on certain characters, the public spectacle of the funeral leads the story to a conclusion that is consistent with the conventions of melodrama: being a moral tale, this is in principle incompatible with the ultimate triumph of evil.

In speaking of a conclusion that is consistent with the moral vision of the melodrama, we touch on a point that could be potentially controversial. *La Piovra* has often been accused of pessimism and of adhering to the vision of a world dominated by the triumphant forces of evil; this makes it difficult to reach, convincingly, the consoling conclusions that are regarded as typical of melodrama. Here there is probably a misunderstanding to be dispelled, concerning not so much *La Piovra* as melodrama.

It is entirely true that *La Piovra* was never intended to be a 'consoling narrative'. The authors have always admitted this: 'The Piovra will not become comforting', said the director Luigi Perelli, referring to *La Piovra 6*, 'we are participant witnesses of dramatic phenomena and it would be immoral, at a time like this, to tell a story in which good triumphs' (Caprara, 1992: 22).

In truth, no edition of *La Piovra* has been able entirely to avoid some sort of final triumph of good, even if at the price of the death of the heroes; at the end of *La Piovra 7*, for example, the guilty people either die or collaborate or are dragged before a court of law. The convention of an at least partially happy ending is respected. In fact it is no more than a convention, which – in *La Piovra* as in melodrama, or rather in *La Piovra* because it is a melodrama – can coexist perfectly well with the gloomy vision of the maybe not truly, or no longer triumphant and unassailable, but nevertheless still huge and tentacular, force of social evil.

The fact is that not even melodrama lends itself to being entirely traced back to the orthodoxy of a consoling formula. Remove the 'last five minutes' or so of the melodrama, and the rest is all wickedness and crime, spectacularly victorious: 'it is beyond all doubt', states Peter Brooks, that 'despite the ultimate triumph of virtue, it was the moment of evil triumphant that fascinated' (Brooks, 1996: 34). It is accordingly no surprise that the authors of *La Piovra* should have always seemed to be happily inspired in their construction of superb figures of wickedness: the powerful and 'respectable' Mafia lawyer Terrasini; the enigmatic and Machiavellian Espinosa, collector of Italy's secrets; and above all Tano

Cariddi, a character of potentially legendary stature on account of the captivating charm of his malign geniality and the almost metaphysical grandeur of his criminal plans.

Again according to Brooks, the final moment, in which by convention rewards and punishments are dispensed and justice is meted out to the evildoers, is of secondary importance in relation to the authentic core of the melodrama, which is turning the spotlight on the signs of good and evil: 'What counts is clarification and recognition of the signs of conflict, and this may be true even when expulsion cannot be achieved and virtue succumbs' (Brooks, 1996: 203).

The virtuous outcomes of the moral conflict that is always portrayed are, in other words, less important than the true function of the melodrama, which resides in the identification of the antagonistic forces and, in particular, the recognition and disclosure of evil, and the assertion that it must be fought without any surrender to its perennial threat and power. For this reason the melodrama may turn out to be valuable 'in the recognition of what we have to deal with, and what – in all its limitations – we most often have at hand for dealing with it' (Brooks, 1996: 206).

If *La Piovra* was not, and did not aim to be, a consoling narrative, this happened without any fundamental contradiction of the principles of melodrama and the formula of social melodrama; no other formula, indeed, would have allowed *La Piovra* to better express the profound affinity of the story with a culture, or widespread areas of a culture such as in the Italian case, that tends to be sceptical rather than trusting in the possible triumphs of things such as honesty, lawfulness and justice. This affinity is undeniably among the primary factors of the wide and lasting popularity of *La Piovra*.

The fascination of the loser

On 20 March 1989, watched by over 17 million viewers who had been kept on tenterhooks by an exceptional press campaign concerning the fate of the character, Inspector Corrado Cattani died at the hands of Mafia killers. He was the protagonist of the first four editions of *La Piovra*. (In the preceding weeks rumours had circulated that two different versions of the final instalment had been shot; it would be decided at the last minute which of the two would be broadcast, according to the mood of the public and the actor Michele Placido's decision as to whether or not he wished to continue playing the part of Cattani. A popular magazine had announced a competition among its readers on 'What fate awaits our hero?')

The next day the national daily *La Repubblica* had a headline on its front page 'Assassinated like Cassarà'[4] (Bolzoni, 1989: 1).

The Mafia attack on Cattani was carried out in the final episode of *La Piovra 4* with a stunning, indeed excessive, number of bullets. Some sceptical critics, who would have preferred a plainly realistic depiction of the execution, attributed this to the poor aim of the killers, whereas all evidence showed that the exaggerated firepower deployed by them was intended to enhance the resistance and the legendary powers of endurance of the hero.

In fact, Cattani is much more than just the protagonist of the first four editions of *La Piovra*: he is the only and all-time hero. The character Davide Licata was his successor in the narrative (editions 5 and 6), but not in the collective imagination and popular mythology, where Cattani remains a loved and unforgotten icon. *La Piovra* itself acknowledged the irreplaceable primacy of Cattani when in the seventh edition it went back to the thread of the story of the inspector's death as though Licata had never existed, forestalling the conditions for the emergence of a new individual hero.

The character of Inspector Corrado Cattani, portrayed by the actor Michele Placido with a frowning, melancholy face and dark good looks, an idol for female viewers, made a major contribution to building and consolidating the fortunes and success of *La Piovra* in the 1980s: fortunes and success which, although they did not decline much after the

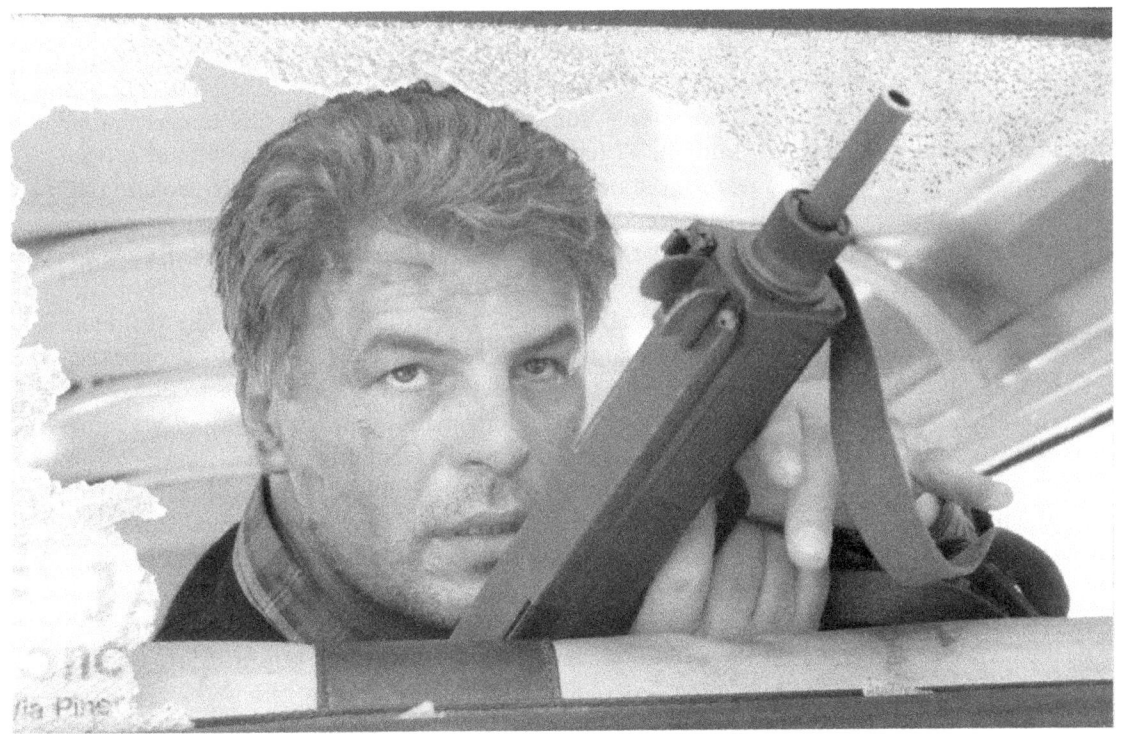

Figure 3.1. Michele Placido as Inspector Cattani in *La Piovra* 4 (Raiuno, 1989). Courtesy of RAI.

death of the inspector, were never as great as they had been during the 'Cattani cycle' years and editions.

And it is easy to understand why. One of the basic functions of popular narratives is responding, through exemplary stories of lives and endeavours, to the need for symbolic characters, sometimes superhuman, sometimes merely human, on whom readers or viewers can project their expectations, hopes, dreams and ideals: heroic characters, in short, who express and embody what we would perhaps wish to be and in whom we can confide, even if we do not identify with them. The heroic figures that from time to time arouse enthusiasm and win approval speak, in a certain sense, about us; they bring out into the open the areas of daily and social life where we are most acutely aware of doubts, dilemmas and conflicts; they deploy the strategies and actions needed – or so we like to imagine – to tackle problems; they drive their actions towards the outcomes that we dream of in our hopes and fears. Cattani is one such figure, a recognizable expression of part of ourselves and of our identity.

In some ways, Cattani was a classic and universal model of the popular hero: an honest and upright man, a loner, struggling against the forces of evil. But beyond that, he was also and above all a typical Italian hero, one who shows moods and embodies peculiar traits of an Italian identity that is perhaps not widespread, but deeply rooted in the tradition of Italian history and culture.

An undeniably complex character – sometimes superhuman in his temerity and invulnerability, sometimes 'human, all too human' – Cattani could be defined as the 'imperfect positive hero', a fearless but not blameless knight (if you take into account the failures and irregularities in his career). In the first edition we see him giving in to Mafia blackmail and publicly disavowing the results of an inquiry that had brought him close to discovering the members of the organisation: a yielding that even in its intense dramatic force sanctioned the primacy of personalistic family affections – his adolescent daughter had been kidnapped by the Mafia and came to a tragic end after being raped – as opposed to the universalism of professional ethics. Wounded several times in his affections, the character will assume a vengeful air: a degree of arrogance and irascibility in his fight against crime, a fight that was often conducted as a private affair.

Subsequently (*La Piovra* 2) we see the protagonist double dealing with a criminal organisation and the secret services: an apparent collusion, that seems to have little – to put it mildly – to do with normal, legal and legitimate investigative methods of inquiry into, or monitoring of, crime.

In the third edition, the character reveals a deep loss of ethical co-ordinates, mistrust of the justice system and a cynical and bitter view of a world where the powerful and wicked are the winners: a *Weltanschauung*, so to speak, that will accompany him to the end.

In the fourth (and, for him, the final) edition Cattani, now a man who has nothing more to lose, abandons himself to vehement and passionate reactions of moral indignation – he gets to the point of almost strangling the evil Tano Cariddi with his own hands – and gives full rein to his contempt for legal procedures: like the time when, to the cry of 'we'll do it our way', he drags his devoted collaborators into investigative exploits that are far from conforming with the rules

Then at each step, the inspector engages in amorous relationships or intense friendships with women who are directly or indirectly linked with criminal circles: witnesses, accomplices, daughters and wives of persons under investigation, in an inextricable tangle of the public and the private.

This is enough to outline the ambivalent traits of an imperfect hero, and perhaps more appealing precisely because of this, a blend of honesty and unscrupulousness, of self-abnegation and despair: oscillating between a yearning for justice and a thirst for vengeance, an enemy of crime at all costs, including the costs of illegality. 'A maverick police chief', inclined to 'rash actions', is how he is defined several times in *La Piovra* 4, where the protagonist's maverick character is the subject of an explicit thematization.

Passionate, sentimental, perhaps a bit of an anarchist, one who perceives the law and formal justice as strange and remote ('you keep on talking to me about the law and justice, all written in capital letters; I think of the dead', he says to judge Silvia Conti, his partner in the investigation and in his private life), he is a personage in whom it is not inappropriate to recognize at a glance features that are specific to the Italian temperament and culture, for better or for worse. *La Piovra* 4, which marked the definitive exit of Cattani from the narrative, but not from the pantheon of popular heroes, tends to emphasize the contradictory aspects of his character. He had never been seen simultaneously so determined and aggressive and so ready to surrender, unarmed, to homicidal gunfire; so threatening and furious and yet so inclined to be moved to pity; detached from the world yet tenaciously attached to his enemies. He shouts to Cariddi that he will follow him all the way to Hell, he swears to Espinosa (the enigmatic character in whom is incarnated more than one protagonist of murky events in Italian politics, thus triggering the game and pleasure of recognition) that he will follow on his heels wherever he goes; he is brusque on surface, and good in his heart.

The prologue of *La Piovra* 4 effectively summarizes this contradictory nature of the hero. Cattani is showed in the course of action against drug traffickers who make use of hired or bought child drug pushers; grasping his weapon, a hard and concentrated expression on his face, the inspector bursts in with his men into their hideout, throws himself on one of the traffickers and, having brutally shaken him and manhandled him, pushes him against the sharp edge of a broken glass door threatening 'Speak or I'll kill you'; meanwhile the thin and frightened children emerge from a trap door, and suddenly Cattani's inner good side also emerges: dismayed and moved, overcome with suppressed emotion, he caresses them, asks their names and gives one of his rare smiles.

But the hero of *La Piovra* is also, indeed above all, something other than this; in his most authentic persona, one could say in his mythical persona – as a realistic assessment, always inappropriate and reductive in cases of this kind, shows him to be imprudent, hot-headed and adventurist – his charm is the tragic charm of the loser hero.

Figure 3.2. Inspector Cattani (played by Michele Placido) helps Judge Silvia Conti (played by Patricia Millardet) after she has been assaulted by Mafia criminals, in *La Piovra* 4 (Raiuno, 1986). Courtesy of RAI.

In truth the story leaves us little doubt on this point: Cattani does not cease to fight strenuously against evil, against the 'monsters and murderers who are devouring our country' (those are his words), but he does it with the gloomy and embittered spirit of one who has no trust or hope in the ultimate victory of the forces of good. Cattani is a brave and stoical character, who, forced on a number of occasions to acknowledge that 'they have beaten us', never fails to do his duty, though he is increasingly angrier about it; yet he is under no illusion that he can change the rules of the game and the relationships of power. He is a pessimistic and disenchanted hero, rather than a fervent and trusting champion of good (and still less of the law), and at the same time a problematic and sorrowful character, to the point that he sometimes seems 'a soul in torment', in whom a deep layer of Italian identity can without hesitation be recognized.

Gun-toting, ever more indignant and furious, Cattani fights the powers of organized crime, which reveal themselves hand in glove with an Italy known for its corruption, scandals and mysteries. Cattani may embody the revolt of the just and the honest against the overwhelming amount of inequity; but he also expresses something of our more covert and more undeniable 'Italianness': a barely contained impatience with the restraints of formal legality, a vengeful impulse that feeds on personal feelings of revenge and – last but not least – a vision of the unlimited power of evil, that in actual fact makes him a loser. Cattani is the hero of our loved – and hated – legacy of pessimism.

The metaphysical vision of a world dominated by the forces of evil, the scepticism concerning the effectiveness of law and justice, the fascination exercised by the figure of the loser who yet affirms his victory on the moral plane: in short all the things that Inspector Cattani incarnates and expresses belong undeniably to an ancient tradition of Italian intellectual and political culture. As has been convincingly discussed (Montanari, 1995), both the lasting inheritance of medievalist religiosity with its universe of bleeding martyrs and, above all, the long experience of invasions and foreign domination – from which is derived a conception of power as an eminently overbearing, cruel and tainted force – have created and ensconced in collective Italian culture the conditions for a true conflation between heroism and martyrdom. From history (the martyrs of the Risorgimento or the Resistance) to contemporary crime news (Falcone, Borsellino and the numberless victims of the Mafia) to the imaginary – Inspector Cattani, in fact – the Italian hero *par excellence* is a person who is called upon and doomed to sacrifice his life, which he loses in the unsparing but unequal fight against an entity that is excessively powerful because it has a dual nature. In fact the Italian hero – and *La Piovra* could not have staged this twofold evil better – finds himself fighting against the deadly alliance between the power of evil (the criminal organisation) and the evil of power (the corrupt or infiltrated institutions that are colluding with organized crime). Only an invulnerable superhero, like the imaginary ones in graphic novels, could emerge unscathed and victorious from such a battle; a human hero is inexorably destined to succumb, earning the martyr's halo and achieving an everlasting victory on the moral plane.

For this reason – because from the very start a foreboding of sacrifice hovers over the hero's head – Cattani's death in the fourth edition of *La Piovra* is a foreseen or foreseeable death, an essential part of the character's profile. The decision of the actor, by now tired, weary of the role as was widely known, can do no more than anticipate an outcome that had been inscribed in 'the way things are'. In the end, unarmed and unprotected, Cattani will go towards his expected and heralded death, that seals his identity and the sad and intense allure he has of a loser hero.[5]

Italian-style serial

Critics of the later editions of *La Piovra* claimed that it had now turned into a soap or *telenovela* (Peirce, 1995: 7). Accusing a TV drama of being a soap or a *telenovela* is a labelling game that is often found on the pages of Italian newspapers; as it is used in a more or less indiscriminate way to define anything that is to be critically evaluated, or rather disparaged, the label would have no special significance were it not for the fact that in the case of *La Piovra*, it is to some extent appropriate. *La Piovra* can in truth be regarded as an open serial, a kind of soap opera (the first serialized drama, even if *sui generis*, produced in Italy); and, one should also add, a soap opera in spite of itself and in spite of its authors who invariably rejected such a comparison as being inadmissible and thoroughly contemptible.

Apart from any evaluation, it is possible to argue that on the formal level (that is, in some of its structures and narrative procedures) *La Piovra* is related to the serial family of soaps and *telenovelas*. In some ways, it may seem paradoxical that a product that hailed on its appearance as 'a response to *Dallas*' should have ended up by assuming some of the key characteristics of the serial form. In actual fact, what is seen to be at work in the serialization of *La Piovra* is the interpenetration between the 'global' and the 'local' in terms of narrative formulae.

This reminds us that the process of media globalization affects not merely cultural content, values and lifestyles conveyed by televisual products but also, and no less importantly, formulae and formats, genres and narrative models. Furthermore and above all, it provides a vivid and eloquent testimony to the true dynamics that are set in motion by a culture and a local tradition in the presence of, and as a result of, media encounters with other cultures. The anxiety-inducing 'master narrative' that has long been in circulation and has achieved credit in this regard, speaks of the 'local' – understood as a 'given' of long-lasting and pure authenticity and specificity – that is constantly threatened with cultural colonization and loss of identity by the 'global' (that is to say America). Instead, what is most often observed in real life is the re-appropriation and reworking, within and in accordance with local or national contexts and traditions, of foreign elements introduced by the import of trans-national products. The consequence of this reworking is normally a hybrid: it is also understandable that supporters of an intact cultural purity should see in this – as is always seen in the hybrid – a regrettable contamination. Yet it is through hybridization with the global that local identities are ceaselessly reconstructed: reconstructed, furthermore, in *new and original forms*. 'Authenticity has increasingly to be judged *a posteriori* not *a priori*, according to local consequences not local origins' (Miller, 1992: 181). To return to *La Piovra*, it is therefore not by defending its unshakeable diversity from and opposition to the soap opera that we ascribe value to its 'Italianness', but by acknowledging the originality and the entirely Italian specificity of the formula that *La Piovra* has created by contaminating itself with the serial.

To make this acknowledgement possible, it is essential first to adopt an *intertextual* approach and consider *La Piovra* not so much as a mere ensemble of distinct and separate primary texts, but rather as a set of texts-in-relationship. If we look at each edition as a self-standing unit, we inevitably risk adhering to a definition of *La Piovra*'s narrative formula, which is the same as its production formula: and this is what institutional and journalistic sources have always done, presenting each new edition as a miniseries or, equally erroneously, as a TV movie.

Instead, an intertextual approach, whose subject is the interrelated ensemble of the primary texts of *La Piovra*, allows us to observe how the reiteration and the inter-linkage of the same production formula could give rise to a different narrative formula: or to a serialization which, in this specific case, bases its originality on a peculiarly syncretistic and negotiating device such as the 'stop-and-go', where both narrative traditions, national and international, are acknowledged. -

La Piovra was not originally created as a long-running story; it became this subsequently, on a wave of success with the press and public, which encouraged its authors to extend – 'success prolongs things', as they said at the time of the *feuilletons* – a story that was originally planned to be confined to a single miniseries. Damiano Damiani, director of the first edition, always declared that *La Piovra* was created as the precise opposite of a serial narrative and consistently refused to direct the sequels. In the beginning, therefore, it was a miniseries, a cinematographically revised version of the old *sceneggiato*. The miniseries is the typical formula for domestic TV drama: it epitomises and conveys Italian TV drama's tradition of 'weak' or 'short' seriality.

The miniseries is a self-sufficient narrative formula and, above all, a closed narrative: the story starts, unfolds and ends within the span of the (two to six) canonical instalments. But these constituent features clearly turn out to be modified when – as in the case of *La Piovra* – the thread of the story is taken up anew and freshly unravelled in a sequel and still again in other sequels. Although each new sequel or new edition is presented in the production format of the miniseries, the collapse of self-sufficiency – in that each miniseries relates to the preceding and the subsequent ones and has a past and a future – and the revocability of the narrative closure, in that the story brought to a conclusion in each miniseries is liable to be continued in the next one, create the conditions for a fresh and eclectic narrative formula that is closed and open at the same time, made up of short stories that are completed yet linked together, inscribed on the horizon of an interrupted (by the lengthy intervals between one edition and another) and yet equally continuing story. In this way, *La Piovra* has built its own serial formula, on the well-achieved hybridization between the weak seriality of Italian narrative tradition (the miniseries) and the strong seriality of the international tradition (the genuine serial). And in this hybridization, unlike the surrender to the hegemony of imported narrative models, what really emerges is the interactive and changing character of tradition and identity, as the formula of *La Piovra* traced and followed an authentic and original 'Italian road to seriality'.

I shall shortly turn more analytically to the open-ended narrative structure of *La Piovra*, but I now revert to the initial statement concerning the affinities of *La Piovra* with the soap opera: affinities and similarities that, although they are not at all surprising, have gone unnoticed both by the defenders of *La Piovra*'s different nature and by those who accused it, though in generic terms, of having become nothing other than a soap.

We can start with the destiny of the protagonists. As I have pointed out (see also note 5), *La Piovra* 'killed off' its protagonists – in keeping with the sacrificial concept of heroism that was discussed in the previous section – and survived their death and replacement. Such a survival testified to a popularity strong enough to resist the shocking and repeated removal of a basic and familiar device as the continuity of protagonism. But this was not an unprecedented phenomenon, in that it belongs to the tradition and conventions of soap opera. 'Soap operas regularly kill off even the most central of characters' (Allen, 1985: 77), yet the formula is made distinctive by a radical and structural discontinuity of protagonism. As loyal and expert viewers know well, the protagonist (male or female) of one season can disappear forever, or remain in hiding for a long time, or change role or identity. Indeed protagonism is cyclical and changeable in soap opera; the story seems always to be able to manage without indispensable or irreplaceable characters and goes ahead just the same, not despite but even thanks to its interchangeability and alternating protagonists. The same goes for *La Piovra*. In this regard, the surprisingly self-reflecting nature of the title should be noted: by evoking an animal that can survive the cutting off of its tentacles, the metaphor of the octopus comes to symbolize not only the Mafia but also a story that can survive the cutting off of its protagonists.

A further affinity concerns the memory of the narrative. *La Piovra 7* opens with the words of Silvia Conti, as she takes a bitter and painful stock of her life: 'These years have been full of anger and grief, but also of happiness … with Corrado and Davide we have won so many battles … but now I am alone'. Although they are joined in mourning and remembrance by the woman who loved them both, Corrado and Davide – that is, Cattani and Licata – occupy very different positions not only in the collective imagination, but also, what is especially interesting in this context, in the memory of the narrative. Indeed *La Piovra 7*, although it retained close links with the 'Cattani cycle', allowed the shorter 'Licata cycle' to fall into complete oblivion; this was regretted by some observers at the time, but here again it is a conventional device that belongs to the soap opera repertoire. Soap opera is characterized by a huge textual extension generated by the long duration and by an equally extensive accumulation of history and memory of the characters and the plots. This being so, it not infrequently resorts to 'oblivion' or other devices of partial or total reversal of narrative developments, in order to re-establish interrupted or lost continuities, remove segments of the story that could restrict or contradict new dynamics or steer the plot in the direction dictated by unforeseen circumstances. The oblivion of Licata's short cycle was intended to lighten and simplify the textual richness of *La Piovra*, which by entrusting the removed parts and characters to the memories of long-standing viewers was able to reshape the past of the narrative in a more linear and unitary way: the

The Political Career of a Popular Fiction

unifying principle being clearly Cattani – 'investigation into the death of Inspector Cattani', read the subtitle – whose icon was repeatedly reintroduced into the visuality of *La Piovra 7*, as was the scene of his murder. The fact is that the name and character of Cattani belong to the repertoire of cultural references that are significant and resonant even for those who have no direct familiarity with the texts of *La Piovra*: particularly the new and younger segments of the viewing public at whom the seventh edition was aimed, as testified by a cast of characters that was untypically crowded with young, even adolescent, figures.

The rejuvenation of the community of characters, sometimes accompanied by a brutal elimination of those members who are bit ancient and *passé*, is a classic way of 'revitalising' a soap opera. Thus by freeing itself of part of its own past and at the same time introducing young people, *La Piovra* carried out a rejuvenation that could not have been done better in a genuine soap. The press had announced well in advance, nearly two years before the broadcast, that *La Piovra 7* would be 'more youthful' and would include adolescents. This sort of anticipatory information, which is part of the promotional initiatives run by press offices, is routine for a wide range of products and programmes and is therefore not exclusive to *La Piovra*; but it was one of *La Piovra*'s constant prerogatives, in which one recognizes, beyond the signs of exceptional popularity, functions that are closely related to the specific narrative formula.

Revelations, speculations, exercises in prediction and whatever else may be deployed in journalistic secondary texts, play a crucial role in relation to soap opera, of which they constitute not a mere additional or ancillary element but an essential means of relating to viewers. A narrative that long-lasting accumulation makes virtually and factually unstable, discontinuous and reversible needs more than anything else to create and maintain a reception context that is open to and ready for any amount of mutability. Soap opera audiences are accustomed to expecting anything, as 'the only narrative certainty is that things change' (White, 1994: 337), and they derive pleasure from uncertainty; but this uncertainty must be rationed and controlled to some extent, so as to remain within the limits of tolerability and still be acceptable and enjoyable. Advance announcements and clues about changes in plot or characters, disseminated and put into circulation via news media, are more than just curiosity or material for gossip columns; they perform the twofold and interrelated function of confirming the image of a changing and unpredictable narrative and at the same time confining the changes (by making them well known or capable of being guessed at or at least suspected) within a horizon of relative predictability, if not of absolute certainty. And it is precisely at the intersection of unlimited openness and partial enclosure of expectations that narratives like soap opera and *La Piovra* – in the intertextual and inter-medial cooperation between press and television – create and cultivate the relationship with their own viewing public.

This same combination of unlimited openness and partial enclosure is characteristic of the anomalous, ambivalent and open-ended narrative structure of the soap opera. Yet we can say that the formula inclines decisively towards the first of these two poles, that is to say towards openness, the moments of resolution and temporary closure being episodic and secondary in the narrative organisation. As is widely known, in fact, the most singular property of the soap opera formula is to be seen in the absence of the *telos*, or ultimate end of the story, or narrative closure of the text: a true infringement of the canonical rules of storytelling, which demand a story that is structured with a beginning, a development and an end (Buonanno, 2002). The soap has no ending, it is not slanted towards a point of resolution or a true conclusive moment, and this characteristic – very much a constitutive component of its formula – turns it into a never-ending story, inscribed in a dimension of potentially inexhaustible continuity, capable of unfolding for years without *an* eventual final episode (productive closure) becoming in a true sense *the* final episode (narrative closure).

The absence of narrative closure draws a clear divide within the serial family, between the soap opera and the *telenovela*: these formulae are too often confused and conflated in common language and journalistic discourse, but are in reality separate from the opposite 'teleological' orientation. Whereas the soap opera is open, the *telenovela* is closed: that is to say, it concludes with a definitive ending towards which the narrative trajectory is heading (Buonanno, 2002). Narrative closure, for its part, is not a mere requisite but a principle of textual organisation that in turn shapes public expectations; for example in the case of the *telenovela*, which in this respect is not unlike the miniseries except in the number of instalments, the narrative trajectory tends to privilege the final part of the text and above all the last instalment, where the whole story reaches its conclusion. Viewers also await the final dénouement with increased interest and expect satisfaction from it.

Let us see, going back to *La Piovra*, how each of the seven editions that followed one another (first annually and then every two years) achieved the highest ratings in coincidence with the last instalment (Tab. 1). That means that viewers appreciated and shared the teleological tension of the single and successive 'octopuses', and harboured particular expectations towards the ending (they knew, in particular, that they could expect an ending each time): narrative closure, which is one of the two components of *La Piovra*'s open-ended formula, here finds full expression and recognition in both the textual organization and the dynamics of viewing.

Table 1 *La Piovra* (1-7). Audience of each miniseries' finale episode.

Edition	Season	Episodes	Most-watched last ep. (in millions)
La Piovra	84–85	6	15.2
La Piovra 2	85–86	5	16.5
La Piovra 3	86–87	4	13.8
La Piovra 4	88–89	6	17.2
La Piovra 5	90–91	5	14.4
La Piovra 6	92–93	6	9.2
La Piovra 7	94–95	6	10.6

But although the moments of resolution have – from the institutional, textual and audience perspective – much greater importance in *La Piovra*'s narrative formula than in soap opera, *La Piovra* succeeded over its entire televisual lifespan in being perceived and enjoyed as a story that could have an inexhaustible future. According to Christine Geraghty a permanent 'sense of the future', correlated with the systematic postponement of a true ending, is one of the distinctive hallmarks of the soap opera. A narrative formula among other things is characterized by and is inseparable from the horizon of expectations that it itself contributes to structuring: 'Soap operas do not encourage such expectations [of resolution] and the longer they run the more impossible it seems to imagine them ending' (Geraghty, 1991: 11).

The same thing could be stated concerning *La Piovra*: its narrative encouraged and sustained in viewers the expectation of a 'never-ending story' over a period of more than ten years, when it systematically alternated interruptions and resumptions, conclusions and fresh starts, and survived the deaths of its two heroes. In the case of *La Piovra* it is highly improbable that a miniseries finale was enjoyed by the Italian viewers as the definitive end of the whole story, regardless of the degree of their involvement in the tense atmosphere of the last instalment.

All this has important implications for meaning making. As narrative theories remind us, the ending is the perspective from which a story, finally considered in its entirety, acquires order and sense and reveals its moral by dispensing rewards and punishments and declaring victories and defeats. But if one knows in advance that an ending is only partial and likely to be revoked, and (as is often the case) is already projected into the future, then that ending does not have the same significance or the same function in providing a stable and definitive moral perspective. See for instance the ending of *La Piovra 7*: Tano Cariddi, having appropriated the floppy disks that contain the proof of murky crimes and Mafia and politics misdeeds, buries them like the seeds of the 'flowers of evil', which (as all this hints) he will go back to harvest in a nebulous future.

La Piovra's stories always ended with some sort of defeat of criminal plots – massacres thwarted, the guilty unmasked and hauled before a court – even at the cost of the life of the hero. However those defeats and corresponding victories were rendered provisional by the provisional nature of the finale, as the outcome of a conflict that was always on the verge of flaring up again was in fact left open and constantly postponed. Perhaps it is not entirely true, or rather not entirely convincing, that the absence of total narrative closure in the serial 'means that the open serial '... can raise any number of potentially controversial and contentious social issues without having to make any ideological commitment to them' (Allen, 1985: 21). In reality, an open-ended narrative like *La Piovra* incorporates a position in its own formula, even without needing to involve the intentionality of the authors.

In proceeding by means of partial closures along a horizon of almost unlimited openness, *La Piovra*'s narrative affirms the instability and uncertainty of any outcome of the struggle between crime and justice; and gives us the one and only certainty that this struggle (just like a soap opera) is a true never-ending story.

Television event

It was a Sunday in March, just after eight o'clock in the evening, and half of Italy was asking the same question. Would Inspector Corrado Cattani, the hero of *La Piovra* number four, be killed at the end of the last instalment? The newspapers were suggesting that this would be so, but were not ruling out a sensational *coup de théâtre*. Rocca di Loto, an unknown village in the furthest and least-visited corner of Sicily, was no exception: people had gone home and sat down in front of the television. (Deaglio, 1992: 11)

Il figlio della professoressa Colomba/The Son of the Teacher Colomba, a short novel by Enrico Deaglio (a journalist and Mafia expert), opens with a group of people watching television in a domestic setting on the evening of 20 March 1989, when 'half of Italy' is getting ready to watch the most famous and memorable episode of *La Piovra*. The domestic setting, in the small Sicilian village with deserted streets – 'Ooh, there's not a single car going past, Mother Rai has beaten all the records this evening' says one character (Deaglio, 1992: 18) – is the home of the teacher Colomba, who on this occasion has invited two important friends to supper; then two other guests, unexpected and perhaps unwelcome but begged to stay just the same, arrive 'to watch *La Piovra*, with all the naturalness of next-door neighbours' (Deaglio, 1992: 13).

'Please forgive me if I ask you to explain things', warns one of the guests. '*I have to admit that I'm not a good Italian* (my italics), some of the episodes were wasted on me' (Deaglio, 1992: 14). Then the small and closely knit group concentrates on watching *La Piovra*, sometimes silent, sometimes making comments, and finally bewailing the fate of the murdered inspector: 'So he's really dead, poor guy', said the marine biologist, '*Sorrisi e canzoni*[6] was right' (Deaglio, 1992: 21).

This scene, which takes up nearly the whole of the novel's first chapter, offers a twofold and convergent interest in the frame of a cultural analysis of the *Piovra* phenomenon. In the first place, it incorporates in the diegetic reality of a fictional story (*Il figlio della professoressa Colomba*) a piece of the diegetic reality of another fictional story, namely *La Piovra*; in so doing, it revives and reinforces the memory of a powerful moment in national televisual storytelling and again confirms *La Piovra*'s mythical status. But at the same time the scene in the novel recalls a very real moment: the death of Inspector Cattani may belong to TV drama, but the appeal of the last episode of *La Piovra* 4 to viewers who had never been so anxious or so numerous (the audience share reached 60%) belongs to real life and is numbered among the biggest television events of the last 20 years (and more).

The empty village streets; the festive and ceremonial nature of the domestic scene, underlined by the presence of distinguished guests; the reunion, partly organized and partly unforeseen, of a group of neighbours and acquaintances; the engagement in the viewing, which brings about both face-to-face interaction between the viewers, and a form of para-social interaction with the fictional characters: 'He stared at the screen and kept repeating: It's a trap, don't go there' (Deaglio, 1992: 17); the perception and awareness of dealing with something that strikes at the roots of Italian national identity: 'I'm not a good Italian, some of the episodes were wasted on me'. The novel does not offer us all this with the credibility of ethnographers' observations and research protocols; nevertheless the scenario seems broadly recognizable and convincing to us, and chimes in with our experience of viewers and/or our knowledge of scholars, as it belongs to the phenomenology of television events (Dayan and Katz, 1992). It is precisely in this frame that I intend, in conclusion, to analyse the *Piovra* phenomenon.

Figure 3.3. The dead body of Inspector Cattani (played by Michele Placido) riddled with bullets fired by mafia killers, in *La Piovra* 4 (Raiuno, 1989). Courtesy of RAI.

Even though the death of Cattani powerfully evokes the idea and condenses the image of an 'event', we must not isolate individual segments of the narrative and moments of viewing, but understand the more general factors and connections that created and preserved for *La Piovra* the conditions of an uninterrupted, so to speak, eventful regime. Indeed if we review the main elements of the definition of a media event, we find a good many that are without any doubt pertinent to *La Piovra*. First and foremost, *La Piovra* cannot be regarded as a 'routine' programme just like any other content that is part of the regular flow and regular habits of television viewing. There were gaps of years between one edition and another; and the broadcast has always entailed an interruption in or a modification of the routines of the schedule, so as to guarantee the best and most strategic placing for the programme's 'big comeback'.

Furthermore, each new edition of *La Piovra* was announced and advertised so far in advance, and with such continuous and intense promotional activity that there was no contest with the marketing of other television programmes, even popular ones; viewers' memories were reawakened by celebrating the national and international success 'of Italy's best-loved *sceneggiato*'; the topical moments of the story were recalled, the deeds of the heroes revived, authors and actors were repeatedly interviewed, political controversies were raked up. 'Here is a preview of the situations, characters and actors in the most popular *sceneggiato*', promised a long article in the weekly *L'Espresso* of October 1994, five months before *La Piovra 7* was broadcast (Mammì, 1994).

All this came together to create a climate of great expectation on the part of the large and heterogeneous public that the different media involved in the promotional campaign – newspapers, magazines and television – had been able to reach; and this expectation was interwoven with a sense of duty, indeed of obligation of viewing, as if *La Piovra* were something that one could not or should not miss. Regarding this point, which according to Dayan and Katz is a constitutive element of media events, the case of *La Piovra* is exemplary of the peculiar way in which the image of an unmissable event, or in other words the construction of *La Piovra* as a must see, was systematically propounded by the press – drawing, among other things, on the testimony of 'special viewers'. Judges, politicians, prominent intellectuals, and personalities from show business – and finally even Tommaso Buscetta, the Mafia boss turned State's witness, presented by newspapers as 'the man who had struck Cosa Nostra a mortal blow' (D'Avanzo, 1995: 6), – were solicited at each edition of *La Piovra* to give their comments, opinions and criticisms: favourable or unfavourable, these reactions served in each case as a confirmation and example of a proper and indeed unescapable norm of viewing.

The comments of the 'special viewers' were generally obtained and recorded in interviews, mostly by telephone, on the following day; but quite often, a different procedure was used, namely a screening of *La Piovra* being watched by selected witnesses, together with journalists. When this happens, two further components of media events can be seen emerging into public visibility, which would otherwise pass unnoticed because they normally manifest themselves within the domestic sphere: the gathering power, and the capacity to reconfigure the spaces where the events are consumed and discussed into spaces where a public opinion is formed and expressed.

By offering people an opportunity to be together, media events temporarily suspend the tendency to 'individualize' television viewing: 'People invite others – families, friends and neighbours – to share the experience' (Dayan and Katz, 1992: 206). And it is precisely this shared experience that the newspapers' presentations insisted upon: '*La Piovra*. We saw it with Ayala',[7] (Amurri, 1992); 'The last instalment of the serial arouses new controversy. "Panorama" saw it with four special viewers' (Berbenni, 1995).

As these discussions took place between public figures and were destined to be disclosed in the press, they did not have the freedom and informality of an ordinary conversation between family members, friends and neighbours in a private living room; rather they expressed the influential opinions of the opinion makers, who helped to expand the volume and diffusion of public discussion on *La Piovra*. In fact the gathering of 'special viewers' seemed to do nothing but isolate and condense the capacity of media events to generate interactions and discussions, which, even when they take place in normal conditions away from the media's eyes and ears, play some part in the processes of public opinion formation and expression.

The Mafia and politics

The attention of the news media is a fundamental component, and at the same time a condition of possibility and a factor of production, of events such as *La Piovra*: events that would not exist as such, even if they were popularity phenomena, if they did not impose themselves forcefully on the newsworthiness and journalistic thematization. This kind of event not only electrifies the audience, but also magnetizes the media, generating coverage and stimulating an intense and focused debate 'on a given issue or set of issues ... Media events seek to enrol support but they also attract opposition. Their agenda-setting powering acts like a magnet, gathering protests and demonstrations' (Dayan and Katz, 1992: 199).

This is exactly how it was with *La Piovra*, in particular the seventh edition. In the course of the 1994–1995 television season, at least 400 articles about *La Piovra* were published in the daily press and magazines. This huge coverage was related only in part to the stars or the narrative content or artistic quality or the reception of the programme and other such features; it coincided primarily with a heated debate that focused on the political aspects of *La Piovra* and was constantly rekindled by fresh controversy. The intentionality and warnings of the authors, who saw in the politicization of *La Piovra* a risk factor for the programme's survival and who exerted themselves as never before to insist that '*La Piovra* is not a political film', are entirely irrelevant in this respect; the primary texts of *La Piovra* may not be political, but nevertheless they offered a pretext and a subject for a political debate, which, particularly in the Italian context, was likely to have an intensely magnetizing effect on the attention of the news media.

La Piovra's career could supply innumerable examples in this regard, but it will suffice to confine ourselves to the seventh edition and to the 'incidents' that preceded and accompanied it. The first of these happened well before the broadcast, which went out in March 1995. In October 1994, the prime minister Silvio Berlusconi, on an official visit to the Russian Federation, held an impromptu press conference at the Italian Embassy. At the end of the meeting, as if to soften a dialogue with journalists that had dealt with rather serious matters, someone observed that a Russian network was at that time broadcasting the serial drama *Passioni*, imported from Italy and produced by the commercial television company owned by the prime minister. Berlusconi said that he was pleased about this, adding straightaway that he hoped that 'no more shows would be made about the Mafia. It was a worldwide disaster. Thanks to *La Piovra*, a negative image of our country has been propagated almost everywhere...' (Palombelli, 1994: 2). It should be noted marginally (but not too marginally) that the concern expressed by Berlusconi, and by others before and after him, about the image of Italy propagated abroad by *La Piovra* is intrinsic to a perception of *La Piovra* itself as an event; media events, in fact, shape the international image of the society to which they belong, 'offering the opportunity of a solemn "presentation of self" to other societies' (Dayan and Katz, 1992: 201). Whether the programme was a self-presentation of a Mafia-ridden society, as the critics would have it, or of a society that was energetically fighting the Mafia, as supporters of *La Piovra* proclaimed, cannot be established and is in any case of little importance; but it is worth pointing out how one and the same interpretative frame, namely that of an influential media event, could unwittingly unite opposing perceptions of the international effects of *La Piovra*.

Anyway, the statements of the prime minister were destined to arouse great excitement in the journalistic media. Opinion makers, politicians, representatives of the anti-Mafia commission, *La Piovra*'s authors and actors and television executives all intervened in the 'new anti-piovra crusade' (Corbi, 1994: 3), which in laying itself open to the re-evocation of a long series of precedents went back – or rather was led back – to the same political humus as the criticisms levelled at neo-realist films. 'It's the usual accusation already uttered by Andreotti at the time of *Ladri di biciclette/Bicycle Thief* (De Sica, 1948). You shouldn't wash your dirty linen in public' (Placido, 1994: 25).

Very similar scenarios took shape on other occasions. Less than a week before the broadcast of *La Piovra 7* in March 1995, the film director and senator Franco Zeffirelli expressed his regret about a promotional campaign, which in his view was spreading 'messages and concepts that are very damaging for Sicily and therefore for the whole Italian nation' (Fumarola, 1995: 31; Garambois, 1995). Some time afterwards, taking their cue from the then current broadcast of *La Piovra 7*, it was the turn of a group of senior Sicilian prelates to complain about the exploitation of spectacular aspects of the Mafia and the perilous reductionism of the Sicilian Mafia cliché (Garbesi, 1995: 19).

In defence of *La Piovra* the voice was heard (among many others) of the authoritative opinion maker Giorgio Bocca, who had already intervened on Berlusconi's declarations: 'Please don't touch our Piovra' entreated the title of a long article in the magazine section of the daily paper *La Repubblica* (Bocca, 1995: 7).

'Please don't touch our Piovra' is a title that proves particularly effective in epitomising the true cipher of the discursive production generated as a reaction to the controversy and the attacks levelled against *La Piovra*. Taking the cue from the critical or hostile statements, in actual fact the news media (with a few mild exceptions) were deploying a corpus or a chorus of opinions argued in various ways, in support of *La Piovra* and in open controversy with its detractors. In other words the media, though giving space to opposing views and dissent, unequivocally adopted the point of view of approval and consensus.

The consequence, only apparently paradoxical, is that the assaults each time provided an opportunity for a great public tribute to *La Piovra* and brought about 'status conferral' and valourization of the programme in the face of those assaults. We need only recall how the artistic status of *La Piovra* was raised by the analogy with the accusations levelled at the masterpieces of neo-realism or the almost heroic aura that being the object of political crusades or persecutions confers.

It would be exceedingly reductive to perceive this specific 'treatment' of *La Piovra* by the news media as being nothing more, for example, than a question of taking sides, of expressing political and ideological views that were in disagreement with the political and ideological positions of the opponents (Berlusconi, Zeffirelli, the Church hierarchy). In truth, what could be observed here is a further prerogative of media events: they may not be in a position to arouse unanimous consensus and therefore they remain exposed to criticism and accusations, but they are characterized also by the fact that manifestations of hostility towards them tend to be inhibited, repressed, rejected, even ostracized. In short, hostility towards media events is very *unpopular*.

La Piovra's political career, inseparable from its status as an event, is closely connected – as I said in a previous section – to a symbolic structure endowed with powerful resonance, recognizability and credibility in Italian collective culture: collusion between criminal power and political power. Thus nothing could have been more effective in raising the status of *La Piovra* as a great event than the extraordinary coincidence of the broadcast of the seventh edition with the announcement that Senator Giulio Andreotti[8] had been committed for trial for association with the Mafia.

The story was on the front pages of the newspapers on Friday 3 March 1995, flanked by reports on the inside pages of the deadly ambush of a cousin of the Mafia informer Totuccio Contorno. On the front page of the far-left daily paper *Il Manifesto* was a prominent headline: 'The Piovra is back (perhaps not only on TV)'. On the same day there was a press conference presenting *La Piovra 7*, where people were asking 'whether the Andreotti trial will harm the Piovra on TV or promote it' (Piccinini, 1995), or 'what impact the new series will have on the viewer, after the committal for trial for Mafia association of the politician who for decades has been identified with power?' (Cappelli, 1995: 33).

But this is not the point. The triangle formed by the televisual *La Piovra*, Mafia crimes and the Andreotti trial sketched the extended outlines of an unprecedented public scene, where a true drama of Italian sociopolitical life was lived out, represented and in turn staged; and all this, as the front page of *Il Manifesto* amply demonstrated, lent itself to encapsulation in one resounding symbolic reference: the octopus, or *La Piovra*. Asking whether the Andreotti trial could harm the televisual piovra or promote it is the wrong question, or irrelevant in those terms, as there had never been such a close conflation between news reports and TV drama, between real legal proceedings and imaginary ones, between facts and fiction: it is worth recalling that *La Piovra 7* concludes with the trial of a powerful and evil politician. So rather than exercising or undergoing reciprocal influences, true life and fiction lent themselves as never before to an interpretation against the background of one and the other, within one and the same horizon of meanings, within the framework of one and the same event to which both equally contributed.

The opening of *La Piovra 7* was characterized by what newspapers defined as a 'striking coincidence' with news reports; but it is the way in which the coincidence was staged by the journalistic media that made it into something different. When the nephew of Tommaso Buscetta (whose long article about the first episode of *La Piovra 7* was published by *La Repubblica*) became the victim of indirect revenge, the news reports and comments on this latest Mafia crime were placed on the same pages and close to the articles about the televisual piovra; thus the photograph of Buscetta flanked the photograph of the actor Ennio Fantastichini, who played the part of Saverio Bronta, first the murderer of Cattani and then state witness in *La Piovra 7* ('a hybrid of Tommaso Buscetta and Tano Badalmenti', the papers speculated: Caprara, 1995: 11). And the photo of Judge Gian Carlo Caselli, prosecuting magistrate at the court of Palermo, was placed next to that of Inspector Cattani.

In the simultaneous presence of fact and fiction within the same spaces of informative reality, therefore, one could see a new type of media event coming into being, whose 'liminal' character did not reside – as happens with ceremonies, including televisual ones – in the suspension or transition between the secular and the sacred, between what is and what could or should be, but in the suspension of and transition between sociopolitical reality and television fiction, under the insignia of the same unifying principle.

In supplying this unifying principle with its own symbol and its own underlying structure of meanings, in constituting – thanks to the coincidence of unforeseeable and maybe unrepeatable circumstances – the laboratory of a new typology of television events, *La Piovra* set the seal on its political career as a popular fiction, protagonist of a lengthy season of the Italian imagination.

Notes

1. I would like to thank Sergio Silva for his generosity in giving me access to his personal archive of promotional and journalistic texts concerning *La Piovra*, of which he was the primary creator and producer. Naturally, as this documentation was not collected and preserved for the main purpose of serving as research material and as a source of quotations, and is made up for the most part of press cuttings and photocopies, it was not always possible for me to find all the information (author, date, title, page number) which should normally be included in a complete bibliographical reference.
2. The real-life event referred to is the terrorist attack known in Italy as 'the Bologna massacre'; on 2 August 1980 the explosion of a device hidden in a suitcase that was left in Bologna station caused 85 deaths and left 200 wounded. The perpetrators of the attack were never identified with certainty. The final episode of *La Piovra 5* staged a similar threat at Palermo station, but avoided extending it to this tragic end. Although the Mafia was not involved with the Bologna massacre, it is nevertheless true that in the framework of their strategy of intimidation against the State they simulated a terrorist attack on Christmas Eve 1984, exploding a remote-controlled device on a train that caused the deaths of 17 passengers and wounded 200 others.
3. Judge Giovanni Falcone, who had a deep understanding of the Mafia's true nature, was one of the most enlightened and perspicacious investigators and prosecutors of Mafia crime. In May 1992 he was the victim of a powerful bomb attack just outside Palermo, ordered by the bloodthirsty Corleone boss Totò Riina. Together with his colleague and friend Paolo Borsellino, who was himself assassinated only three months later, Giovanni Falcone was listed in *Time Europe Magazine* (13 November 2006) as one of the heroes of our time.
4. Antonino Cassarà, deputy police superintendent of Palermo, was assassinated by the Mafia in 1985.
5. Inspector Cattani left no heirs in *La Piovra*; nor did other heroes of comparable popularity take his place in the collective imagination. The fifth and sixth editions of *La Piovra* did, however, introduce a new protagonist (Davide Licata) who despite being very different from Cattani and, perhaps for this reason, destined to be removed from the memories of the narrative, should be recalled because he equally belongs to a rank of sacrificial characters and hero–martyrs. In turn, Captain Antonio Arcuti, protagonist of *La Piovra 8* and *9*, the two prequels set in the 1950s, ends up by being assassinated by the Mafia.
6. *Sorrisi e canzoni* (Smiles and songs) was, at that time, the most popular television listing magazine.
7. Judge Giuseppe Ayala was the public prosecutor in the so-called maxi-trial of Palermo (1986–1987), when more than 400 people accused of Mafia crimes stood trial.
8. Andreotti, a Christian Democrat and seven times prime minister, was one of post-war Italy's most powerful politicians and was continuously at the centre of the Italian political scene for over 50 years. He was the inspiration for the character of the Italian politician Licio Lucchesi in *The Godfather* 3 (Coppola, 1990). An enigmatic and charismatic figure for whom the nickname 'Giulio the Star' was well suited (hence the title of the grotesque biography by Paolo Sorrentino, *Il divo*, 2008), Andreotti was interrogated several times by the Italian magistrates about his supposed connection with the Mafia; he always managed to emerge unscathed from these accusations, but has not been able to dispel the serious suspicions about his collusion with Cosa Nostra.

Chapter 4

A Place in the Sun: The First Italian Soap Opera

Escape from fiction

It may be true that *La Piovra* can be considered as a *sui generis* open serial, a soap opera in spite of itself. The fact remains, however, that until the mid-1990s there was no homegrown production of truly serialized television narratives in Italy, be it open or closed continuous serials. The first domestic daily soap, *Un posto al sole/A Place in the Sun*, was screened in 1996, when Italian television was already more than 40 years old. A latecomer to the national TV drama scene on which it was destined to make a profound impact, *A Place in the Sun* has been the fruit of 'well tempered' cooperation between local and global. In this chapter I shall present the case study of the first Italian soap opera, pointing out how players and formats from abroad proved to be an instrumental resource in laying the grounds for a much awaited re-launch of domestic TV drama.

In order to understand the nature of the cultural and industrial revolution brought about by the daily soap, we need to recall that since the inception of Italian television (see Chapter 1), creative talents and professional circles (authors, directors, actors, producers, networks executives) had regarded seriality as a US-dominated cultural form, to be unconditionally resisted and rejected. This stance embodied both the elitist cultural background of public television and the shunning of foreign commercial models that was a prevalent feature in the identity-building process of early Italian television. As a result, the Italian drama industry, which was designed to deliver only short-running formats, had never set up the production system or matured the know-how that was required to produce long-running series and serials.

At no time more than the 1980s, at the height of the major transformation of the Italian television system, did the deeply rooted and widespread rejection of seriality make its presence felt, in the face of the great narrative flow coming from the United States.

However one may wish to regard it – a window of opportunity open to the horizons, both wide and unexplored, of transatlantic televisual imaginary, or a threatening invasion by an alien culture liable to contaminate the purity of the homegrown product, or even some other viewpoint – the wave of American imports that followed the advent of commercial television was characterized by an incontrovertible factual element, in that it was made up of serial products (comedy and drama series, serial drama, soap opera, *telenovelas*) and represented the first large-scale arrival of seriality, the narrative modality typical of 'popular', in Italian televisual space.

Faced with the popularity of foreign drama series and serials at the beginning of the 1980s, the Rai decided to consider for the first time the idea of producing domestic serials and long-lasting series, in competition with American imports. A minority group of Rai executives, led by the innovative manager Massimo Fichera (at that time the vice-director for new technologies), were mindful of the need to establish a production-based system of domestic drama and accordingly developed a strategic project along these lines (Brancato, 2007; Silj, 1988). The proposal sparked off intense discussion within and outside television milieux. Issues of identity and otherness, national and international ways of television, tradition and change informed the debate both intellectually and emotionally. There was much opposition to what was perceived as a surrender to 'alien' modes of production and narration and an unacceptable way of becoming willingly 'Americanized'. Influential cinematographic circles were hostile to a project that might threaten or weaken the financial engagement of public television in the national film industry. Television writers and producers were deeply concerned about the prospect of undergoing a dramatic change of professional routines (and mentalities). Consequently, the project was dropped. Public and commercial television would continue to compete with each other in subsequent years alongside a massive acquisition of American products, a truly paradoxical consequence of a rejection of seriality that was expressed in the name of autonomy from America.

The Rai's refusal to adopt a system of serial production, and thus to convert the cottage industry of Italian TV drama into a true 'factory-based' televisual industry, put a substantial block on the development of domestic TV drama until the mid-1990s (the production of comedy series initiated by private television in the late 1980s was too small scale, and indeed too 'homespun', to serve as a driving force in the industrial take-off of seriality).

As a consequence of the situation outlined earlier – the exploitation of foreign 'canned shows', which offered better value for money in comparison to the more expensive domestic TV drama, and the refusal to put in place an industrial production system, seen as a betrayal of national tradition – Italian TV drama entered a decade of increasing decline. In fact, the early 1990s were characterized by an authentic 'escape from fiction' by Italian broadcasters. Economic factors seriously influenced this state of affairs, as public and private television had crossed the threshold of the decade weighed down by huge debts, to the extent of thousands of billions of lire. Moreover, private channels had to take on the costs of setting up news editorial offices, under obligation of a new broadcasting law (the Mammi law, 1990); it seemed almost inevitable that fiction production should undergo more or less radical cuts, being the most expensive of television genres.

Furthermore, the escape from fiction took place in the early 1990s in the midst of political turbulence,[1] in which both public and private television were involved, though each in different ways. This turbulent environment helped to spread a climate of anxiety and instability within the broadcasting companies, dissuading them from investing in medium- and long-term production projects and processes. Thus resources and funds were diverted from drama, and channelled to cheaper and fast-producing programmes: news, current affairs, variety shows, talk shows and mostly reality shows, the new rapidly growing genre in the early 1990s that promised to guarantee, more than TV drama, a positive balance between financial costs and good ratings. In Italy, domestic drama was cleared from the schedules to make room for the reality shows, whose invasive presence in public and private schedules served to some extent as a 'surrogate fiction', able to satisfy almost for free the demand of the audiences for stories 'coming from our own backyard'.

In this connection, suffice to say that, in the 1995–1996 season the supply of Italian TV drama reached a historical low of just 130 hours.

Turning point

Over the 2005–2006 television season, first-run domestic fiction aired on the broadcasting channels amounted to more than 700 hours; scarcity had turned into plenty, through a process of increase that had lasted for ten years.

In fact, TV drama had developed into the 'central storytelling system' (Newcomb, 1988: 88) of Italian society in the decade at the turn of the century. In a country where reading books and newspapers is hardly a widespread habit, and where the national cinema ceased in the 1970s to be a medium of popular entertainment, television had taken on and fulfilled the role of the contemporary super narrator. The late 1990s and early 2000s witnessed a true rebirth of both the production capacity and the popularity of local drama, along with the inception of the Italian television industry.

The re-launch of domestic TV drama was set in motion in 1996, a year now considered to be the threshold of the 'second golden age' (to borrow the definition from Thompson, 1997) of national TV drama. It coincided with the industrial production, run by the global player Grundy International, of the first ever Italian continuous serial, the daily soap *Un posto al sole/A Place in the Sun* (hereafter *A Place in the Sun*), which is still on air today on Rai 3, the third channel of public television.

The cooperation and deal between the Rai and Grundy was a sort of paradigm or epitome of the nexus between the local and the global, which in diverse combinations is at the origin of a wide range of contemporary television formats and contents. It did not merely lay the foundation for mass production, where only a cottage industry had previously existed, or enhance a poor fictionscape by adding a certain amount of 'volume television'; it also precipitated a small 'cultural revolution', in that it opened the way for the legitimization of the most popular forms of televisual storytelling, namely the continuous serials that had long been banned from the production culture and practice of Italian TV drama. In actual fact, the introduction of a daily soap in the domestic TV drama scene has entailed a true reversal in Italian broadcasters' strategies.

The rebirth of domestic TV drama owes much to the turning point marked by the first daily soap. In subsequent years, the serial formulae proved crucial, as serials boosted the productive capacity of the infant Italian industry. They soon became popular with the viewing public, thus extending the range of domestic shows that enjoyed success, cult status and critical acclaim. In this respect, Italy represents a case of a national system of drama production and consumption that has been imbued with new life and strengthened by the processes of change set in motion by the import and adoption of foreign elements (whether they are production companies, know-how, formats or formulae).

The road that eventually led Italian television to experiment with the continuous serial formula was long, difficult and obstructed by entrenched production practices and cultural elitism. Far from being an unexpected conversion on the road to Damascus, the change matured in the 'compelling environment' that was taking shape in the mid-1990s. Broadcasters at that time were put under heavy pressure to produce more original drama, as a result of a number of different but converging conditions:

– In the wake of the European directive 'Television without frontiers', Italian broadcasters were required by law to reinvest fixed shares of their net revenues from licence fees (public television) and advertising (commercial television) in national and European production of TV drama and film; the Parliamentary debate on the law, definitively approved in 1998, started in 1995.

– Although pay-TV penetration in the mid-1990s remained at a preliminary stage, the thematic channels carried by the digital platforms (Telepiù, Stream) were already drawing sizable quantities of movies and sporting events, taking them away from terrestrial networks; in consequence, the latter needed to have a larger amount of valuable content available in order to fill the void.

– The popularity of foreign, that is to say US, TV drama was on the wane, owing at least in part to audience saturation. As the biggest European importer of readymade programmes from the United States and Latin American countries during the 1980s, Italy had been almost addicted to international television; but the foreign imports' run of luck was coming to an end, and national drama had to take its place.

– Finally, and perhaps most importantly, in the midst of the processes of globalization – and possibly as a counterpoint to them – the viewing patterns of mass audiences in Italy (and elsewhere) were being reshaped by a deeper desire for storytelling infused with cultural proximity (Straubhaar, 1991): demands and choices of television viewers were driven by an intensified predilection for national homegrown drama. This was not at all a new phenomenon – even in the *Dallas* years domestic TV drama, if available, proved more attractive than US imports (Silj, 1988) – but it gained more weight and visibility at a time when imports were losing ground in viewers' preferences.

This set of circumstances was able to convince Italian broadcasters to put an end to what in the early 1990s had become in truth an escape from domestic drama. Public television initiated the trend by taking the controversial decision to produce a daily soap. For a television industry and culture that had for decades tenaciously opposed the idea of long seriality, the decision represented a complete volte-face.

The close encounter of local and global

For the sake of precision, it has to be pointed out that a number of attempts to create homegrown long-running drama (but not a daily soap) had been previously made by private television. Continuous serials, in the closed variant of the *telenovela*, were produced at the beginning of the 1990s to be aired in prime time on the Mediaset channels. These included both the Italo-Argentine co-productions (Mazziotti, 1996), and the homegrown closed serials such as *Edera/Ivy*, *Passioni/Passions* and *Camilla* (O'Donnell, 1999). Despite a few good results, the project of opening up prime time slots to serialized domestic drama failed and was therefore abandoned. The idea was probably premature, at a time when the presence of a domestically produced serial would have seemed unorthodox even in daytime. However, the disappointing outcome of the experiment was first and foremost due to other factors, in particular the misalliance between the foreign and the domestic, in that neither of the two was endowed with the right credentials to make such a break with tradition palatable.

The 'alien' Latin American *telenovela* adopted as a model was the least suitable narrative formula for this purpose. In Italy – indeed probably in Italy more than elsewhere – it is difficult, if not impossible, to find a genre as undervalued and discredited as the *telenovela*, which has become the epitome of the lowest aesthetic and cultural level of televisual seriality. The word has come into common parlance and into journalists' vocabulary, with the derisory meaning of a thing or topic that drags along inconclusively through ostensible *coups de théâtre* and a lot of standing about. What is more, the early 1990s saw a massive fall in the popularity enjoyed by Latin American serials in the previous decade. This was brought about by intensive programming that made the schedules of Rete 4 (Mediaset's 'female' channel) practically mono-generic. Nor for its part was Italian commercial television, almost an absolute beginner in drama production, in a position to deploy and impose the cultural hegemony that would have been necessary to support a similar innovation.

In order for long seriality to be turned into a constituent part of the domestic television landscape, it was imperative for the initiative to be assumed by a player that enjoyed acknowledged authority on the national television scene. A daily soap was dangerous territory to cross, threatened by the apparently immeasurable gap between something seen as frivolous and culturally insignificant ('only a soap opera') and the relevant issues that it was likely to raise and inject into public debate: cultural identity and tradition, televisual quality and the role and destiny of the Italian television industry.

The project called for a player that could reliably offer guarantees concerning the risky operation and be robust enough to withstand the criticism and controversies that would be aroused. Public television had a sufficient patrimony of authority, credibility and strength and – given the pressing and inescapable necessity to expand production capacity – decided to invest this patrimony in the project of the first Italian soap opera, just the opposite of what had happened in the 1980s. This was destined to introduce into the domestic television landscape, and above all to legitimize the continuous serial as a narrative formula and production mode.

As the continuous serial's narrative formula and production mode were completely alien to Italian television culture, the expertise and know-how had to be sought outside national boundaries. Like other European broadcasters, the Rai turned to the global player Grundy, who had initially built up remarkable experience as a producer of television entertainment in Australia. The company had been the first to export soap formats to European markets, and had the required human resources and skills for adapting the original templates in accordance with the different national contexts of the importing countries (Moran, 1998; O'Donnell, 1999).

The deal between the Rai and Grundy stipulated the adaptation of the hugely popular – at home and abroad: Croft, 1995; Hobson 2003 – Australian soap opera *Neighbours*, a major asset of the Grundy library. A communication strategy was agreed and put jointly into practice by the two players, with the aim of preventing or softening the criticism and disapproval towards an undertaking that could be perceived in Italy as a cultural imposition. This communication strategy entailed, for instance, recalling the 'Australianness' of Grundy as the ambivalent but perhaps positive feature of a foreign partner who, if nothing else, was not American. And, more important, it was centred on the claim of the 'Italianity' of the soap from the very moment of its conception; the entire promotional campaign that preceded and accompanied the launch of *A Place in the Sun* made this claim its leitmotif, insisting that 'all the stories, all the actors and all the settings' were Italian.

On the one hand, it was imperative to minimize the part played by Grundy and the contribution given by the 'foreigners' (which generated unceasing controversy among Italian television producers); on the other hand, it was precisely the foreigners who offered a fundamental element of guarantee. As a matter of fact, they guaranteed production standards that local personnel at that time would not have been able to meet, because of their complete lack of experience. This matter understandably had to be handled with care, so as not to offend the sensibilities of creative talents and local producers, but it helped to forestall or tone down public scepticism. The expectations or curiosity regarding a 'completely Italian' soap opera in fact coexisted in many viewers – those who had learnt to appreciate the pleasures of the continuous serial through American soaps such as *Guiding Light, Loving, The Bold and the Beautiful* – with a degree of suspicion, if not prejudice, about a homegrown serial consigned to inexpert Italian hands. But the proven experience of Grundy allowed them, if nothing else, to concede the benefit of the doubt.

In fact, Grundy played an irreplaceable role. Obviously, the company was capable of fully mastering the dramaturgical model, the organization of scriptwriting and the 'factory-based' system of production of a daily soap. They put to work their own skilled human resources, but at the same time a process of 'learning by doing' was fruitfully activated and there was a gradual transfer of know-how from the global partner to the local personnel who were asked to cooperate in the bilateral endeavour of the first Italian soap opera.

But no extenuating circumstances were conceded by the critics when *A Place in the Sun* went on air in the access prime time of the Rai's third channel, at the beginning of the 1996–1997 television season. After the encouraging results of the first broadcast episodes, the ratings of the serial dropped dramatically, and an unprecedented barrage of merciless reviews was unleashed on the 'autarkic telenovela', sarcastically re-christened a 'flop-opera'. This gave the Italian producers a pretext to campaign against the low quality of a costly operation that placed too much trust in the 'foreigners'. Surprisingly, a few intellectuals – the semiotics scholar Paolo Fabbri, the anthropologist Marino Niola and the novelist Angela Bianchini – intervened in the controversy, arguing that the soap was original and enjoyable. Criticism and controversy, attacks and self-defence proved that the first Italian soap opera was a contested terrain where questions of national identity and cultural autonomy were debated and where the interests of those involved were set against the interests of those who felt excluded, and people vied with each other to state their opinion, or rather 'the legitimate opinion', concerning the worth of the operation and the quality of the product.

A Place in the Sun took more than one season to attract regular viewers and retain their loyalty. The Rai chose a line of perseverance, exercising the privilege of a public service television that could allow itself to keep a show on the air that was unprofitable in terms of ratings, but instrumental in the growth of Italian TV drama. This staying power paid off. Already during the second season the criticism was giving way to congratulations on an 'excellent programme' of Italian television; and the feared Trojan horse of Americanization was widely acclaimed as constituting the 'first true bastion' against the American invasion. To a large extent, the volte-face of opinion on the first homegrown soap was attributable to the eloquent evidence of its Italianity.

An Italian sense of place

'If you are familiar with *Neighbours* (another Fremantle/Grundy soap) then this is like "Ramsay Street-by-the-sea" with a bit more spice and drama thrown in for good measure' (http://bestuff.com/stuff/un-posto-al-sole, accessed June 2008). These lines, posted on a fans' forum, aptly introduce the (now forgotten) issue that long pervaded the initial debate on *A Place in the Sun*: whether or not, and to what extent, the first Italian soap opera was an adaptation of the *Neighbours* format.

As mentioned before, the two partners have insisted from the start on the 'programmatic originality' of *A Place in the Sun*, which was conceived and written in professional dialogue and cultural negotiation within a creative teamwork made up of Australian and Italian authors. Among these were Wayne Doyle, head writer of *Neighbours,* and the Naples-born story editor Gino Ventriglia. Standing midway between the agreements of a formal deal and an astute communication strategy, the truth is that resemblances, echoes and resonances from *Neighbours* or other Grundy-branded soaps such as the German *Unter uns* (see O'Donnell, 1999: 115) to be found in the concept and early development of *A Place in the Sun*, seem to corroborate the assumption that the latter was, loosely at least, modelled on pre-existing formats. Nevertheless, *A Place in the Sun* adapted and re-contextualized the Australian model to a considerable extent, introducing features and contents that were specifically and unmistakably Italian into the world of the serial, starting from the multi-layered articulation of the 'place'. 'Place' is a crucial component of a soap's identity and an acknowledged strategic resource both as a narrative device and a cornerstone of viewer's sense of familiarity. It is therefore important for us to see how *A Place in the Sun*, by comparison with *Neighbours*, outlined the geography and brought about the localization of its own social world.

Displaying a title that immediately conjures up the sunny Italian weather celebrated in many popular Neapolitan songs – such as *O sole mio*, made internationally famous by Elvis Presley as *It's Now or Never,* and *Chist'è o paese do sole* (*That's a Sunny Country*) – *A Place in the Sun* is set in the southern city of Naples, where it is also produced and shot. Naples is a highly recognizable and familiar setting for Italians, owing to its traditional presence in popular films, music and theatre. Furthermore, in the mid-1990s the city was at the height of a phase of splendour and rebirth, known as the 'New Neapolitan Renaissance'. *A Place in the Sun* exploits Naples as a sumptuous scenographic resource for the numerous scenes shot on location, giving this soap a brightness that is unusual in the genre, and as a linguistic and stylistic resource – the Neapolitan accents, the humorous tone of some of the characters and situations – which reinforces the overall effect of cultural proximity and recognizability. With the precise aim of awakening an immediate sense of familiarity, the opening scenes of the first episode deployed the whole repertoire of conventional Neapolitan iconography: alleyways, street urchins, peddlers, washing hung out to dry, against the backdrop of a cacophony of voices and music.

Within the larger context of the big city, the more localized scenario of the narrative is an area in the historic centre of Naples. American, Australian and English soaps are set for preference in working-class areas or suburban residential districts. The change of location made in *A Place in the Sun* is significant in its cultural specificity. In Italy in general, and Naples in particular, suburban areas summon up a menacing picture of run-down districts on the edge of cities or dreary dormitory towns. City centres with a concentration of fine historic architecture, however much they may be perceived as uninhabitable because of insecurity and disorder, still convey the core identity of the

A Place in the Sun: The First Italian Soap Opera

Italian city (one of the enduring differences between European and American lifestyles) in addition to being the object of dreams and aspirations about luxurious living.

The unexpected inheritance of a large apartment in the historic centre of Naples is, not by chance, the starting point of the story that unfolds in *A Place in the Sun*. This leads to the most inward and significant of the spatial reference points, the true social setting of the soap: the *palazzo* (this Italian word means both a block of flats and a palace) looking on to the Bay of Naples. Here we no longer have the 'horizontal' or 'egalitarian' structure of a street-level setting, as in *Neighbours* (or *Coronation Street*, or in the German soap *Lindenstrasse*). Instead, the 'vertical' and hierarchical structure of the building stands for the peculiar 'social geometry' of *A Place in the Sun*. Here, in owner-occupied apartments located on various floors, resides the inter-generational and socially stratified community of the characters of the soap, from the aristocratic elites to the middle and working class: not so much a community as a microcosm of Italian society.

Figure 4.1. The Palladini Palace, home of the community of characters of the daily soap *A Place in the Sun* (Raitre, 1996–present). Courtesy of RAI.

The first domestic soap, by situating its own microcosm in a setting that would be familiar to most Italians – that is to say a heterogeneous condominium or block of individually owned flats – thus installed itself literally and unmistakably 'at home'. It should be added that the condominium is often referred to in Italy as a metaphor of national social life.

Obviously, *A Place in the Sun's* credentials of cultural belonging would need to be more analytically discussed and demonstrated with reference to its characters, plot lines, situations and problems (Buonanno, 1999). I have confined myself to highlighting just a few significant examples, which will suffice to identify the prerequisite of Italianity as the main factor that has contributed to the reappraisal of the prejudices and opposition regarding the first domestic soap opera.

Without any doubt, the continuous serial and its industrial modes of production made their way into the originally hostile Italian television landscape because, over and above other things, they gave tangible proof from the start that they were not the agents or conveyors of an unconditional cultural surrender to narrative and production models of 'alien provenance'. All the evidence confirmed that the specific features of Italian culture and society were perfectly capable of re-emerging from, and even taking advantage of, the serialization process; this was destined in a relatively short time to overcome the resistance of the creative talents and local producers, as well as the ill-concealed sense of shame of the cast members (the actors of *A Place in the Sun,* many of them making their debut but others coming from the traditions of theatre and radio drama, were assured from the start that they were lending their talents not to a soap opera but to a 'real drama', this definition having doubtlessly more dignified resonances). As the offspring of a loose format adaptation and a self-evident import and transfer of know-how from abroad, the soap opera *A Place in the Sun* – 'a delicious slice of daily Italian drama' according to 'The Wall Street Journal' (April 1998, day not available) – eventually succeeded in being acknowledged and enjoyed by viewers as an authentic expression of native culture (Capecchi, 2000). The visit paid to the production team and cast members of the soap by the prime minister, Romano Prodi, during an official trip to Naples in spring 2008 was intended to put the seal on the undisputed integration of *A Place in the Sun* into Italy's television industry and culture.

A seminal story

The interest of this case does not rest in – or rather is not confined to – the testing of the local element's strength, its capacity to put in place practices of adaptation, appropriation and reworking, and perhaps above all its resilience in the face of the foreign element. Although I in no way underrate the theoretical and empirical relevance of everything that can be included under the heading of 'indigenization' (which I have discussed at greater length elsewhere: Buonanno, 2008), I maintain that a more comprehensive account of the issues at stake needs to go beyond, or shift, the interpretative perspective.

A Place in the Sun: The First Italian Soap Opera

Figure 4.2. Patrizio Rispo and Claudia Ruffo as uncle Raffaele and niece Angela talking on the te;rrace of the Palladini Palace in the daily soap *A Place in the Sun* (Raiuno, 1996–present). Courtesy of RAI.

A Place in the Sun is not a 'success story' in the conventional sense. Over the years, even after overcoming the difficult initial phase, the soap has never achieved particularly high ratings: its loyal audience numbers an average of 2.5 million viewers, in line with the market share of the Rai's third channel in access prime time. Launched a few years after *A Place in the Sun*, and broadcast on the flagship channel Canale 5, the two daily soaps produced by commercial television have proved more successful. But no domestic daytime serial has so far managed to prevail over *The Bold and Beautiful*, (CBS, 1987–)

Figure 4.3. Wedding celebration in the alleys of Naples in the daily soap *A Place in the Sun* (Raiuno, 1996–present). Courtesy of RAI.

which is still the most popular soap in Italy – a challenging exception to the rule of the primacy of domestic drama. And not even the storylines and the issues raised in the domestic soaps achieve the wide resonance and provoke the intense debate that so often surround the British soaps and the Brasilian telenovelas, making them part and parcel of the discursive network of a 'popular public sphere'.

This is rather a 'seminal story': the case of a daily soap that marked a decisive watershed in the history of television drama and had far-reaching influence on the subsequent evolution of the Italian fictionscape. In a short span of time, other long-running serials have followed in the pioneering footsteps of the first domestic soap opera. The daily soaps *Vivere/Living* (1999–2008) and *Centovetrine/The Shopping Centre* (2001–) have appeared in the schedules of Mediaset's flagship Canale 5; the same public television later launched *Cuori rubati/Stolen Hearts* (Rai 2, 2002–2003), *Sottocasa/Downhome* (Rai 1, 2006–2007) and *Agrodolce/Bittersweet* (Rai 3, 2008–). Some of them were failures from early on; others have seen their initial success fade away with the years. Whatever the fortune of any single serial, it is worth emphasizing that the daily soap has been naturalized within the Italian television landscape. The radical change of the status of the soap is demonstrated by the fact that fiascos and cancellations now arouse open discontent and regret, even protests from the creative and professional circles; and loyal viewers 'left as orphans' have to work through their mourning.

An undeniable standardization effect arises from this – if Italy was for a long time different in not having homegrown soap opera, that difference has definitely disappeared – but the gains outweigh the losses. The serialization introduced by *A Place in the Sun* opened the way for a true television industry, gave stimulus to employment levels in both the creative and the technical sectors and brought into existence a star system and a nursery of talents. Daytime schedules, filled in the past only by imported series and serials, were enriched and diversified by the introduction of local drama; and the way was also paved for serialization in prime time, which happened only a few years later.

Long seriality entered prime time in the late 1990s. In June 1998, to give female viewers an alternative to the World Cup, the evening soap was tried out with *Incantesimo/Enchantment*, a hospital serial that was first broadcast twice a week on Rai 2 and then, once it had proved to be a success, transferred to the first public channel. The cancellation of the serial, which had run its course and been unsuccessfully turned into a daily soap in its last season (2007–2008), generated controversy and even a debate in Parliament.

The access to the prestigious evening slots has obviously reinforced the standing of serial drama, even though some deplore the 'soapization' of prime time fiction, which in truth is a phenomenon extending well beyond Italy (Henderson, 2007: 15). However, the fact remains that the miniseries preserves its historical position as the 'queen' of prime time and the trademark of quality Italian drama. Without removing or undermining the miniseries, prime time serials have joined it, bringing to domestic television the unquestionable benefit of a broader range and diversification of narrative formulae.

In conclusion, the turn to seriality that occurred in the mid-1990s in the context of specific and compelling conditions set in motion the re-launch of the Italian TV drama. This process had to be activated and managed by agreement between national and international players, as Italian television needed to import and learn from abroad production modes and formulae of serial storytelling that were alien to local traditions – and, what is more, were opposed and feared on account of their (supposedly) threatening foreignness. The result of such cooperation was the soap opera *A Place in the Sun*: 'a delicious slice of daily Italian drama'.

A Place in the Sun is by no means unique or exceptional in this respect. It joins the many cases that, in different parts of the world, testify to the capacity of indigenous television to convert contacts with and contamination by foreign or global cultures (not only televisual ones) into configurations that are broadly consonant with native culture (Buonanno, 2008). It is worth pointing out that this capacity seems in some way to be exercised *against* the varying degrees of threat or risk (or *in spite of* them) that foreignness still represents or evokes. All this testifies convincingly to the flexible resilience and dynamic vitality of indigenous television.

Not only just 'against' or 'in spite of', but *thanks to*: the Italian example suggests to me the plausibility of a different interpretative hypothesis about the relationship between the indigenous and the foreign, the local and the global, where the latter does not necessarily or exclusively represent a threat to be neutralized, or an obstacle to be overcome, but – switching the perspective – a resource to be capitalized.

The introduction of long seriality from abroad has opened up new opportunities for domestic TV drama. For the first time Italian creative talents have had the chance to conceive and tell long-lasting and never-ending stories, and a 'popular historiography' (White, 1994) of everyday national life has found stimulus and development, as never before, in the dramaturgical models that are inherent in the continuous serials. The specific contingencies in which these processes of change and growth have happened must not be overlooked. But they suggest that, given the right conditions, global players and foreign televisual cultures are likely to represent a vital resource for national players and local television cultures.

The same can be said of format adaptations, the other side of the seminal story of *A Place in the Sun*. From then on, the adaptation of foreign formats has become a regular practice within the Italian TV drama industry. The formats are acquired for preference from other countries of Mediterranean Europe, especially Spain, or from Spanish-speaking countries (in more recent times the networks have bought some formats from Argentina); and although the path of adaptations has been strewn with failures and unsuccessful hybrids, in specific cases the task of cultural translation is carried out so masterfully that the foreign provenance of the original concepts is barely noticed, or easily forgotten. One need only bear in mind that in a country like Italy, where the importance of family life is such an established and widespread tradition, the most popular prime-time family shows in recent years did not originate from the indigenous creativity of Italian scriptwriters, but were adopted and adapted from the format of Spanish family comedies (*Médico de familia/A Doctor in the Family, Los Serranos/The Serranos, Cuéntame como pasó/Tell Me What Happened*).

Un medico de famiglia/A Doctor in the Family, a long-running serialized series, was launched in December 1998 on the first public channel.[2] Like *A Place in the Sun*, *A Doctor in the Family* blended both otherness and our-own-ness, to quote Miller (2000: 156). In fact, it was a true format adaptation, indeed a well-adapted indigenization of the successful Spanish comedy *Médico de Familia* (Telecinco, 1995–1999). Portraying the daily life of a large household of three generations, the series managed to capture a multi-generational audience including children. The portrayal of an extended family, harmonious and united – an image endowed with a deep resonance in the family-centred culture still dominant in Italy – played a key role in establishing the programme in the viewing habits of a huge audience. Despite a degree of cultural affinity between Spain and Italy, the adaptation of the format entailed considerable work of 'cultural localization'. Greater emphasis was deliberately placed on the family group, a shift that can be perceived straight away from the title. This was changed from the original professional qualification of the protagonist – *Médico de familia*, equivalent to family doctor or GP – to 'a doctor *in* the family', thus emphasizing his role in the family community.

There is no doubt that since the 1990s the Italian television fictionscape has become internationalized as never before, by reason of the multiple and now coexistent practices of importing products and production models, acquiring and adapting formats and imitating or recycling formulae, genres and successful or trendy foreign concepts. The case of *A Place in the Sun*, and the others that I have cursorily mentioned, obviously do not recall the whole gamut of the modes and outcomes of this relationship. Nevertheless they help us to throw light on an area that has been left in shadow by the theorization and indeed the very thematization of native drama, its genesis and evolution: the area where, in and through the interaction (and even the opposition) between identity and otherness, between domestic and foreign, the conditions of possibility emerge for the elaboration and expression of true indigenousness in cultural production.

Notes

1. The turbulence was triggered by a whole set of factors: the controversy over the new broadcasting law, the judicial enquiries on political and financial corruption (an affair known in Italy as Tangentopoli, i.e. Bribesville, 'tangente' being a word for 'bribe'), which affected circles very close to Mediaset, the political ventures of Berlusconi, coupled with an anti-TV campaign of unprecedented proportions, a popular referendum on the privatization of public television, the high turnover of the Rai management.

2. It can be seen that public television was the first mover, both in daytime and in prime time. Commercial channels awaited the actions and results of their competitor before joining the trend themselves, despite the risk of losing opportunities: the format of *Médico de familia* was turned down by Mediaset before being acquired by Rai – precisely the reverse of what had happened in the case of *Dallas*.

Chapter 5

Mimetic Heroes and Ironic Leaders:
The Genesis and Evolution of the Italian Police Drama

The season of the detective story

Within the Italian dramatic landscape the genre that most epitomizes the process of indigenousness building through the multifarious interaction between domestic and foreign, local and transnational, is unquestionably the police drama. This chapter reconstructs the genesis and evolution of the television detective story as a national cultural form that has taken shape in constant tension with non-native and imported elements and influences.

From the 1990s onwards, the Italian detective novel or *giallo*[1] entered into what was defined by analysts of the publishing market as 'an explosive phase of growth' (Pischedda, 2007: 17). In fact, this literary genre, having long been confined to the peripheral territory of the bookstall before being admitted, belatedly and cautiously, to the shelves of the bookshop, is now enjoying a run of unusual good fortune that benefits national production in particular. Titles by Italian writers are well represented in publishing series and on the shelves of bookshops; and although the best-seller editions are still limited to a few cases, the average levels of circulation testify to a growth in the circles of readers who are interested in, if not passionate about, stories on crime and investigation.

An analogous occurrence is to be observed in TV drama. Here again we witness an exuberant flourishing of the genre, or at any rate stories about crimes and misdemeanours investigated and unveiled by professionals (police officers, *carabinieri*, lawyers, forensic experts) or by amateurs (priests, teachers), men and women, individuals and teams. Taken as a whole, this explosion of detective stories on television proves a good capacity to attract viewers, even when it does not generate phenomena of widespread popularity.

If, looking at the panorama of the first decade of the twenty-first century, I am induced to speak of an explosion of detective stories, this is because of the discontinuous trajectory of the genre in Italian television. Over the years, the police drama has gone through moments of great popularity and has left a certain number of 'classics' to the collective memory, as well as to television studies and archives. But it had never reached the point of establishing a solid and lasting productive tradition or building up a strong consumer preference on the part of Italian audiences, unlike other European countries such as Germany, the United Kingdom and France. The relaunch of Italy's television industry created the conditions for this to happen.

It is not implausible that the widespread perception of a rising crime rate in the country helps to maintain a high level of production and consumption of television police drama – even if what really frightens common citizens and threatens their sense of security, are the diffused forms of micro-criminality and 'predatory' aggression against persons and belongings, which rarely feature in a detective story's plot. Charlotte Brundson may well be right in counselling the greatest caution about 'too simple a correspondence between crime and unrest on the streets and crime on television' (Brundson, 1998: 223); however an observer and acute analyst of present times like the sociologist Zygmunt Bauman has not hesitated in relating the popularity of crime stories in films and television to the 'ambient experience of generalized insecurity' (Bauman 2002: 55) that characterizes the present human condition. Suffice it to say that the possible and no doubt complex connection between real and fictitious criminality in today's uncertain society remains to be explored in depth.

I shall reconstruct the historical evolution of Italian television police drama following the process of 'nationalization' or 'localization' of the genre: in other words, the transition from an original corpus of stories, which were largely and variedly 'foreign', to a corpus of stories that are recognizably 'domestic', that is to say Italian. We could also define this shift as the transition from 'stories from the sea' to ' stories from the soil', referring to the two archaic tribes of storytellers that Walter Benjamin evoked using metaphors that are as suggestive as they are insightful. In the opening pages of his magnificent essay *The Storyteller*, Benjamin writes of the pleasure that humans have always felt on hearing both stories of distant lands, told by the 'trading seaman' who has travelled all over the world, and stories filled with a sense of place and replete with local tradition, told by the 'resident tiller of the soil' (Benjamin, 1999: 84). These metaphorical figures of the sailor and the peasant illuminate the development of the Italian police drama, not so much in terms of binary opposition or schematic succession or alternation of types of storytellers and storytelling, as by casting light on the diverse forms of intersection and hybridization between them over time. Benjamin himself insists emphatically on the fact that 'the actual extension of the realm of storytelling in its full historical breadth is inconceivable without the most intimate interpenetration of these two archaic types' (Benjamin, 1999: 85): as used to happen in the workshops of medieval artisans, spaces where experiences of travelling afar and staying at home met, thus serving as a sort of 'high school' of the art of oral storytelling. A similar interpenetration can likewise be seen at work in the history of detective stories on Italian television.

Stories from the sea

The process of formation and transformation of the Italian police drama from the 'sea' genre (tales of distant lands) to the 'soil' genre (tales from the homeland) – without excluding various modalities of convergence and blending – can be reconstructed following three stages. The first stage runs between the end of the 1950s and the end of the 1960s; the second embraces the two successive decades; and the third starts with the 1990s and is still running. Like nearly all periodizations, this one is to some extent arbitrary, as neither the states of things nor, still less, the processes, can be segmented and enclosed into precise timespans (there are always anticipations, drifts and overlappings); but it nevertheless performs a useful function in applying a marked-out 'sequential structure' (Zerubavel, 1981: 2) to a half-century continuum. The three television eras identified by John Ellis (2000) – scarcity, availability and plenty – are also appropriate labels for each stage.

The first phase, at the origins of Italian television, coincided with the predominance and huge popularity of the genre of the *sceneggiato*, adapted for television from a literary source (see Chapter 1). In addition to the *sceneggiato*, Italian television originally cultivated detective drama, though as a genre of lesser importance. Police drama followed the same pattern as the *sceneggiato* by adapting 'classic' detective novels from Europe and the United States. During the 1960s, television adaptations from the novels of George Simenon, Arthur Conan Doyle and Rex Stout made characters like Maigret, Sherlock Holmes and Nero Wolfe household names for the Italian television public. These dramas were produced in Italy, but the stories had been created and were set in foreign geo-cultural contexts such as France, the United Kingdom and the United States. In retrospect, the international flavour of these first national police dramas can appear as a kind of anticipatory socialization process for Italian viewers, preparing them for the surge of foreign (especially American) imported cop shows, which proliferated in the programme schedules of public and private TV channels over subsequent decades.

Broadcasters' preference for the adaptation of international detective novels arose from the unquestioned assumption that the Italian public would not find domestic crime stories credible, given the absence (real or presumed) of a national collective imagination of crime in a relatively peaceful and crime-free country like Italy. Thus, the inception of Italian police drama was marked by a prevalence of 'stories from the sea', tales by storytellers from distant and foreign lands, rather than Italy.

Nevertheless, a certain Italian flavour (emanating from the soil) did manage to infiltrate these dramas. The crime stories that Italian television chose to adapt from the detective fiction of other countries were hardly faithful to their original source. To a certain extent, the stories underwent a process of adaptation and 'domestification' by the insertion or highlighting of elements that resonated with Italian culture. For example, in the case of Maigret, the background of the inspector's family life was given more prominence and visibility than in Simenon's novels, with Madame Maigret – a hazy and discreet personality – transformed into the figure of a maternal, nurturing Italian wife.

It is perhaps not by chance that it was precisely Simenon's novels that opened the series of adaptations of detective fiction in 1964, as Inspector Maigret bears little resemblance to the typical protagonists of the classic police drama; he does not have the gifts of strict deductive logic, but 'his intuitive immersion in a social atmosphere of a crime' (Cawelti, 1976: 130) and in the mysteries of the psychology of the individual, his moral scruples and his reflectiveness make him a police officer who is well endowed with the human insight, which Italians appreciate above all in their police heroes, and which Italian authors have always managed to confer on characters – starting with Lieutenant Sheridan, the forerunner of the policemen of Italian television.

The police drama series centred on the leading character of Lieutenant Sheridan – broadcast between the late 1950s and the early 1970s – combined tales of the sea and tales of the soil in various ways. In a sense, it was as if the peasant–narrator were pretending to be a sailor.

The investigations of Lieutenant Ezechiele Sheridan of the San Francisco police force were in fact based on original scripts by two Italian authors, Mario Casacci and Alberto Ciambricco (Ciambricco, 1975); but the protagonist and the stories were deliberately 'de-localized' and, as it were, made foreign by their American setting. This sort of camouflage was part of the tradition of the Italian police novel. During the entire Fascist period, Italian crime writers – with very few exceptions – had preferred to adopt foreign pseudonyms and set their novels outside Italy. This choice was in part dictated by prudence, as the Fascist regime did not approve of stories about crimes committed in Italy; it was therefore forbidden for a murderer in fiction to have Italian nationality. Furthermore this camouflage was also a way of getting round Italian readers' widespread love of all things foreign, which notoriously led them to prefer foreign novels, especially in the case of a genre like the crime story that was regarded as being alien to the national imagination.

The debut of the character Lieutenant Sheridan took place in the framework of an innovative formula that created a hybrid of the genres of police drama and quiz show. The programme was entitled *Giallo Club/Detection Club* and envisaged the participation of a few contestants who would be formally welcomed and entertained by a host/compère in the setting of a private club. Immediately afterwards the police drama would be broadcast and then interrupted just before the end, to give the contestants time to respond in secret to the 'who-dun-it' question. Then the end of the episode would follow with the unmasking of the guilty party by Lieutenant Sheridan; and the programme would conclude with prizes for the contestants who correctly guessed the culprit and the motive of the crime.

This new and intriguing formula ensured the immediate success of the programme; but *Giallo Club*'s true strength laid in the personage of Lieutenant Sheridan (played by the actor Ubaldo Lay), in whom the public recognized and appreciated an unmistakably Italian character, despite his American name. Shrouded in a white raincoat, with a serious expression and chiselled features in the style of Humphrey Bogart, Sheridan was a courteous and sensitive investigator, far removed from both the aggressiveness of American policemen and detectives and the coarseness of the stereotypical image (at that time) of the Italian *poliziotto*. He combined honesty and professional scrupulousness with the passions and shortcomings of the ordinary man, which made him a credible fellow human and, in a short time, a very popular figure and a true national icon. The character emerged from the texts that had created him and, taking on its own existence, became an advertising testimonial; the protagonist–actor had in turn to defend himself against constant requests to solve small real-life mysteries as if he were a real policeman, and remained definitively identified with Lieutenant Sheridan. Once the *Giallo Club* formula had run its course, Sheridan reappeared in autonomous series and miniseries, where his human vulnerability was revealed as never before by amorous intrigues, betrayed friendships and finally a serious injury that left viewers for ever in the dark regarding his fate.

In conclusion, Italian police drama seemingly wished to take on an eminently international characterization in the first phase of its history. It adopted authors and characters, told stories and portrayed settings that were not Italian; and even when dealing with original characters it preferred to use foreign names and settings. Nevertheless this strategy adopted by a genre held to be extraneous to national narrative tradition left some margins or interstices, in which elements began to take form that were destined in time to converge into the complete model of an Italian police drama: in particular the portrait of the protagonist as the common man, the mimetic hero.

In truth, there was something more than margins and interstices. Almost at the end of the 1960s, a police series of literary origin yet totally Italian (author, characters, settings) began to prepare the ground for what would become a pre-eminent trend in later decades. This was the series *I racconti del maresciallo/The Marshal's Tales* (Raidue, 1968), taken from a book that had just been published by the author and film director Mario Soldati. Through the character of Marshal Arnaudi, a scrupulous policeman who at the same time was capable of human compassion for the guilty themselves, the series introduced the typical Italian social figure of the *carabiniere*; and anticipated, by putting him in the setting of a small provincial locality, the elaboration of a further component that made up the future model of Italian police series.

Stories from the soil

The second phase of Italian police drama, from the 1970s to the end of the 1980s, coincided with the emergence of the domestic voice of the peasant storyteller, which had first resounded in *The Marshal's Tales*. The wave of stories by non-Italian authors had not entirely vanished; it was still nourished in the first half of the 1970s by *I racconti di Padre Brown/The Father Brown Stories* (Raiuno, 1970) from G. K. Chesterton's novels, *Giallo di sera/Evening Mystery* (Raiuno, 1971) from the detective stories of Louis C. Thomas, *Philo Vance* (Raiuno, 1974), the sophisticated creature of S. S. Van Dine. But the decade was marked by a sequence of homegrown police stories, either adaptations of works by well-known detective novelists (such as Augusto De Angelis, Loriano Macchiavelli) or original creations by television authors. In the frame of uniquely Italian stories, the police series *FBI Francesco Bertolazzi Investigatore/FBI, Francesco Bertolazzi Private Eye* (Raiuno 1970), *Qui Squadra Mobile/Here, the Mobile Squad* (Raiuno 1973–1976), *Il*

Commissario De Vincenzi/Inspector De Vincenzi (Raiuno 1974–1977) portrayed heroes who were typically non-violent, intuitive, discerning and endowed with human warmth rather than rationalist and methodical.

On the one hand, the Italianization of the television police drama helped to shape and cultivate the national collective imagination of crime, which had hitherto been considered too insubstantial a source of narrative inspiration for television scriptwriters. On the other, this change was made both possible and more credible by the increase in individual and organized crime rates in Italy during the same period. The Italian cinema industry of that era likewise seized on and exacerbated the 'sharp rise in quality' of local crime, giving life to the plentiful and popular sub-genre of the *poliziottesco* or Italian crime film; they were films about metropolitan violence (*Milana violenta/Violent Milan, Roma violenta/Violent Rome, Napoli violenta/Violent Naples, Napoli spara/Naples shoots*), fought equally fiercely by furious and implacable policemen like Inspector Callaghan and violent arms of the law in the homegrown version (Brunetta, 1991).

Alongside the cinema, TV drama consciously contributed to a representation of the new face of urban crime and the new *modus operandi* of the police. In particular, the ensemble series *Qui, squadra mobile/Here, the Mobile Squad*, a procedural drama set in a Rome police station and realistically inspired by true-life cases and enquiries, precisely because it explicitly referred to true facts from news reports, put the seal on the transformation of Italy into an environment that was by now rich in homegrown criminal activity, a credible source of crime imagination. The series, especially the second edition broadcast in 1976, was enormously successful.

And yet, especially in the 1970s (and still more in the 1980s) the landscape of television police drama seemed to be internationalized, crowded with tales of far-off lands as never before. But this phenomenon was no longer, or to a limited extent, generated in the field of national production which, as we have seen, had begun to tell stories set in Italy. This time the narrative voice of the seafarer truly came from overseas, indeed from beyond the oceans, and resounded in imported American TV drama.

Whereas before and during the 1960s, Italian public television had little recourse to American crime fiction (*Perry Mason* and *Alfred Hitchcock Presents* were among the exceptions), the 1970s and particularly the latter half of that decade witnessed a substantial expansion in the flow of imports from the United States – a trend that was to be accelerated later by the private networks. Keeping to the marine metaphor, there was a 'disembarkation' in Italy of such series as *Ironside* (1970), *Cannon* (1974), *McCloud* (1975), *Kojak* (1976), *Colombo* and *Police Woman* (1977), *Ellery Quinn* and *Barney Miller* (1978) and *Starsky and Hutch* (1979). In the next decade, with commercial television now well established, the flow of police drama imports included *The Streets of San Francisco* (1980), *Hart to Hart* (1981), *Magnum PI* and *Hill Street Blues* (1982), *CHIPS* (1984), *The Equalizer* (1985), *Miami Vice* (1986), *Murder She Wrote* (1988), *Hunter* (1989) and many more.

During the years when Italian television was moving towards and completing its transformation into a dual system and, more generally, shifting from the phase of 'scarcity' to that of 'availability', Italian audiences were exposed to an overwhelming supply of American police series. Some gained broad popularity, others enjoyed cult status among niche audiences; but there were few American police shows that did not reach Italian shores and enter the encyclopaedia of titles, texts and characters that directly or indirectly, to a greater or lesser extent, became familiar to Italian viewers.

So Italian television featured dozens of American series as against a handful of Italian titles. This imbalance inevitably prompted questions about the consequences. A wave of American police shows – attractive by virtue of their novelty and skilled craftsmanship, their dazzlingly high standards of production and their deployment of a wide range of sub-genres to satisfy various tastes – began to flow copiously from the screens as soon as Italian detective drama steeped in national realities began to be created and to prove its worth; certainly, this was not without an impact. But it would be going too far to assert that the foreign narrative voice had entirely overpowered the Italian one, as the field of homegrown police drama was not completely deserted in the 1980s. A new edition of *I racconti del maresciallo/Tales of the Marshal* (Raidue, 1984), *Cinque inchieste per un commissario/Five Investigations for an Inspector* (Raidue, 1982), a further attempt at renewing the 'giallo-quiz' formula with the investigations of the private detective Gianluca Spada as the protagonist in *Giallosera* (Raiuno, 1983), the series *Caccia al ladro d'autore/Hunt for the Author's Thief* (Raiuno, 1985) about thefts of works of art, testified to the intention to withstand. However there is no doubt that the 'peasant' voice that expressed itself through homegrown stories was faint, and left no significant traces in the collective memory or the creative fabric of the Italian police drama. Narrators of tales from far-off lands and peasant storytellers coexisted in that period; but the former, being more numerous and skilled, prevailed to some extent over the latter, who were hardly more than beginners and had no substantial tradition behind them.

Nevertheless, it is plausible to suppose that the large and prolonged availability of American police shows on offer ended up by structuring consumption patterns, and generating an extensive demand for the police drama as a genre in itself. When, again at the end of the 1980s, the American series' cycle of popularity began to wane as a result of a (perhaps inevitable) saturation effect, this extensive demand helped both to stimulate national production and to cultivate expectations and ensure a favourable reception context for the locally produced police series, which were now clearly preferred over anything foreign. Thus the somewhat paradoxical consequence of the surge of American cop shows on Italian television in the 1970s and 1980s was that of fostering, some time later and in conjunction with other circumstances, the revival of the domestic police drama.

At the end of the 1980s, the process of domestification of the television police series (which had been initiated a decade before but had lain dormant in the face of intense competition from imported programmes) was on the verge of being revitalized. With the dawn of the third phase, the new formula of the police series *all'taliana/Italian style* managed to achieve the task.

The funny detective

In the early 1990s, three successive series played a part in setting the standards of the nascent tradition, which was soon to establish a distinctive *Italian style* formula. *L'ispettore Sarti/Inspector Sarti* (Raidue 1991–1994) came first, a literary adaptation from the novels of the renowned crime writer Loriano Macchiavelli. The series was not exactly a popular success but soon became a cult, backed by the press and enjoying critical acclaim. The main character, a tragicomic detective whose actions bordered on the inept, received an award as 'television personage of the year' in 1991 (Buonanno, 1994). This was followed by *Commissario Corso/Inspector Corso* (Raidue 1992), whose central character was an affable detective from the south fighting micro-criminality in Milan, and *Un Commissario a Roma/An Inspector in Rome* (Raiuno 1993), in which a protagonist on the verge of retirement manages to reconcile his lengthy experience with the somewhat odd requirements of the new 'police code'.

Despite being heterogeneous in many respects, these three police series shared a double feature. First, they were amusing – by virtue of either the grotesqueness of their central character or the actors, popular film stars who had specialized in comedy roles. *Inspector Sarti*, with its clumsy and unlucky eponymous hero, performed a pioneering function in that it paved the way for police dramas aimed at making the viewers laugh. The two successive series followed in the same footsteps, as they relied on actors (Diego Abatantuono and Nino Manfredi) whose very names evoked the relaxing pleasures of the comedy.

It should be emphasized that the hybridization of comedy and police drama was not a complete novelty, but was rather a 'return of the already known' and a further borrowing from the cinema, in addition to bringing in film actors. The cinematographic genre of the afore-mentioned 'poliziottesco' that flourished in the 1970s had in fact developed a streak of humour alongside a vein of harsh violence (we need only recall the film series focused on the figure of a sloppy, coarse and unruly Roman policeman, nicknamed 'the garbage').

In addition, these series brought to the fore the family and personal lives of their main characters. The regular presence of mothers, wives, children, grandchildren and girlfriends inserted an enticing slice of private life into the public space of the police story. In fact, the personal and family lives of the protagonists were much more than mere background; they became a dense narrative strand, often interwoven with the issues and developments of the police plot. This specific feature played a major part in shaping the lead characters as 'mimetic' heroes: that is, individuals who epitomize the common human condition, as – apart from their special job – they are just 'like us'.

The police story *all'italiana* assumed an accomplished form and gained full approval from viewers and critics alike when the first edition of *Il Maresciallo Rocca/Marshal Rocca*

Figure 5.1. Gigi Proietti as the protagonist of the police series *Marshal Rocca* (Raiuno, 1996–2005). Courtesy of RAI.

(Raidue e Raiuno 1996–2005) was screened; it was the most successful Italian TV drama since *La Piovra*. A mature marshal of the *carabinieri* and, in his private life, a widower with three children, the main character was introduced by the promotional campaigns as 'a common everyday hero', an expert and wise investigator, full of humour, a paternal figure, natural and symbolic, a moral focus for his provincial community of Viterbo (Buonanno, 2000).

Embodied almost paradigmatically in *Marshal Rocca*, the new formula of the *Italian style* police series based its peculiarity and familiarity on a set of four essential components. The first of these was the blending of drama and comedy. Pre-announced and guaranteed by actors coming from film and stage comedy, humour permeated the police drama genre, in accordance with the deliberately hybrid style of the 'dramedy'. Aimed at revitalizing and lending a recognizable shape to the Italian police series, this hybridization with comedy was probably inescapable, given that comedy remained the only national cinema genre that still had popular appeal for large audiences in Italy (Brunetta, 1991). Moreover by introducing the relaxing presence of humour at a time when the American police series was becoming more bitter and sombre, domestic police drama managed to achieve a competitive advantage over its imported (American) counterpart. Maybe there was more than just a relaxing component. The Italian police dramedy seemed in this way to reflect a peculiar tendency of Italians to distance themselves from representatives of authority, institutional power and law and order by making jokes about them. Not taking them too seriously is a kind of taming device, a better way of coming to terms with the powers that be.

The second ingredient of the new formula was an 'estrangement' from the metropolitan milieu. This happened either by setting police stories in an ostensibly provincial location (either real or imaginary) or using the alternative approach of a 'provincialization' of the city. In the latter case, the series was seemingly set in a large city, usually Rome, but the metropolitan context was remodelled so as to evoke in many respects – urban spaces, relationship patterns, types of crime and other things – a provincial location and society. Rich in art and history, scattered among dozens of small and medium-sized towns that often have a magnificent urban structure, the provinces are effectively the prerogative and pride of Italy – which has never, or at any rate not yet, become a country of metropolises.

The third component of the formula was the intrusion of private and family life, the domestic sphere, into the narrative core of the police series. In more recent years, there has been no shortage of foreign police dramas in which a character's profile is enriched by fragments representing of his or her personal life. To cite just one example, viewers of *Without a Trace* (CBS, 2002–2009) could follow the devastating saga of the FBI special agent Jack Malone's divorce in the second season of the series.

But the formula of the police series *all'italiana* introduced more than just fragments of the private sphere, or an occasional intrusion into the home and personal feelings of the characters. It allowed an entire dimension of domesticity to unfold in detailed fashion, ranging from the preparation and consumption of meals to more intimate scenes (including glimpses at the bedroom) and the appearance of half-clothed characters at the breakfast table; it made ample room in the narrative diegesis, in parallel and interwoven with issues of crime and punishment, for issues of love and friendship, marital and intergenerational relationships, indeed any kind of situation in everyday family life. This was hardly surprising, given the practical and symbolic centrality of the family and the home in Italian cultural tradition and social life. What could be seen at work, in actual fact, was the influence of a specifically local cultural factor on both the thematic contents and the narrative structure of the domestic police series. Blending family stories into crime drama also proved an efficient marketing strategy, as it was instrumental in creating the conditions, if not the guarantees, for the police genre to appeal to diverse and therefore more extended categories of national audiences.

The hero is 'one of us'

A fourth and fundamental component of the formula was the characterization of the protagonists as anti-heroes, meant as representatives of average human beings with ordinary vices and virtues. Presiding over the construction of this figure of hero was a discursive strategy that, following Northrop Frye, we could call 'mimetic'. The reference here is to the well-known 'theory of modes' – a classification of literary works according to the hero's stature and power of action – elaborated by Frye (1957), taking his cue from a passage in Aristotle's *Poetics*. Following Frye's outline, James W. Chesebro (1987) has identified five discursive strategies or ways of constructing the figure of the hero, applying them to television texts: the mythic, the romantic, the leader, the mimetic and the ironic. Suffice it to say – without reviewing them all – that 'mimetic' (in Chesebro's terms, or 'low-mimetic' in Frye's) defines the hero, whose stature – including ability, intelligence and capacity to control his circumstances – is perceived as essentially equal to ours. 'If superior neither to other men nor to his environment, the hero is one of us: we respond to a sense of his common humanity, and demand from the poet [or author] the same canons of probability that we find in our own experience' (Frye, 1957: 34).

The Italian police drama that was being fashioned in the 1990s chose as its main character a mimetic hero: a 'common man' figure endowed with intellectual and temperamental resources and a capacity for controlling his circumstances, more or less equal to 'one of us'. The mimetic hero had been the object of constant tension in the Italian TV police series, with few exceptions during its history. But although he was by no means an original invention of the 1990s, it was only in this decade that he assumed accomplished and elaborate contours, organically related to the other components of the formula. We should not forget the discursive context in which the mimetic hero was taking shape, in explicit contrast to the so-called superheroes of the American police series: for example the authors of *Marshal Rocca*, when introducing the first edition, made it clear that they had not wanted to 'ape' American heroes.

In contrast, no superior gift or resource, placing him[2] above the common human condition, was expected to distinguish the mimetic hero of the Italian police series. The way in which he acted did not require or presuppose the soul or the physique of a fighter; rather, it was that of a simple, daily commitment to the honest and expert fulfilment of his work, to which he added a certain compassionate spirit, a non-violent attitude and an ill-concealed impatience with bureaucratic rules. He exhibited those qualities that Italians tend to approvingly attribute to themselves – refinement, wisdom, intelligence, tenacity, intuition, experience, sympathy – but he was not a man without defects, being inclined to impulsiveness, sometimes improvisation and a changeable temperament likely to emerge, first and foremost, in the occurrences of private life.

This increasing shift towards a mimetic-like heroism is not confined to 1990s Italian police drama. Chesebro (1987) observed the same tendency in the American series many years earlier. But it would not be implausible to maintain the hypothesis that, in the Italian context, the construction of a mimetic police hero has a more intense cultural specificity. Aside from cases of private eye or amateur investigators, the hero of the police series is an institutional figure, the representative of a State body charged with guaranteeing law and order. The conventions associated with the genre also require that he should be a winner – one who, at the end of the story, figures out the riddle, finds the culprit and brings him to justice.

This is (or was) somewhat in contradiction to collective belief in Italy. Although in more recent years the trust of Italians in the police force seems to have enjoyed a comeback, the national civic culture has traditionally been characterized by a basic suspicion of State institutions and agents. At most, Italians are inclined to nourish certain scepticism towards the capacity of the institutions responsible for law, order and justice to perform their tasks (Putnam, 1994). In building a character who, as much as possible, resembled 'one of us', the police story *all'italiana* aimed at making acceptable a social figure who was not so easy to metabolize in the national collective culture. Although formally representing the institutions, the television police hero came to represent the common man, thus making credible his victory over crime because, to a certain extent, the victory was achieved on our behalf.

It would however be a mistake to take too seriously the game of 'imposition of meanings' through which the narrative strategies of the police drama tried to corroborate the mimetic image of the heroes. In reality the construction of these characters was sometimes more complex; to understand them fully one would need to evoke other heroic figures and a discursive meta-strategy.

The heroic typology outlined by Chesebro places the 'leader' figure (or the high-level mimetic hero, in Frye's terminology) one rung higher than the 'mimetic' hero: the hero-leader is the one who possesses acknowledged moral authority, a firm sense of values, a clear vision of ends and of the means to achieve them; he is in a position to act in person and to mobilize and co-ordinate the actions of others to achieve such ends effectively. In other words, in Frye's words, 'the hero is a leader' (1957, p. 33).

Now the new police drama *all'italiana* was not devoid of hero–leaders (starting from the 'everyday hero' *par excellence*, the hugely popular *Marshal Rocca*). But we do have to look carefully to discern the prerequisites of the leader and the acknowledged authority of the chief behind the consummate play of appearances: the façade or mask, in the style of the mimetic hero, of this or that protagonist. Chesebro rightly warns that 'the mimetic form can be used to disarm us ... to create the impression' (1987: 30) of normality and typicality of characters and to portray them as models of human action and values that in fact do not – or not entirely – belong to the average profile of the common man. Mimicry readily shifts from simple imitation towards disguise, in order to hide oneself or hide something from sight.

Precisely this shift has at times been a feature of the construction of mimetic heroes in the Italian police series: they are shown as substantive yet unobtrusive chiefs, leaders but covert and appearing instead as 'one of us'. As their mimetic profile as common men is the result of an ironic strategy in the Socratic sense – pretending not to be what one really is – they could be defined as *ironic leaders*.

In the Italian character (for convenience I wish to invoke that most controversial category, the national character) there lurks unquestionably an ostentatious inclination, the cult of the art of appearances: a delight, not necessarily vacuous or presumptuous, in displaying status and power. But there also lurks the opposite inclination to play down, with understatement, privileges and resources of a personal and social nature. One can perceive precisely this strategy of minimization at work in the characters of ironic leaders in the police dramas of the 1990s: in creating the impression that the heroes are just like us, the strategy is aimed at raising the level of average man, and at the same time disabusing us of our perennial mistrust towards figures of authority.

A 'heritage' trilogy

More recently, from the late 1990s onwards, the television police series appears to have become an experimental laboratory for new forms, new narrative formulae and new cultural representations. The formula described in the previous section was not abandoned; indeed some of its components, notably humour, infiltrated the structure of the genre in all its manifestations; but it was no longer in the lead or exclusive in a landscape that was characterized by a wider and more diverse supply.

The catalogue of regular heroes was enriched by new 'ironic leaders'. Among the most lasting and popular of these is a provincial priest (*Don Matteo*, Raiuno 2000–) who infuses life into the character of a 'detective by chance', a champion of justice and above all of innocence. This protagonist pays strict attention both to material evidence and – thanks to his calling as a priest – to the recesses of the human soul to solve crimes, thus scoring regular victories over the more conventional and superficial investigations of official detectives. The *carabinieri* officer of the provincial town, who is decent and

Figure 5.2. Terence Hill as the protagonist parish priest in the investigative series *Don Matteo* (Raiuno, 2000–present). Courtesy of RAI.

willing but unable, to the point of being a laughing stock, tags along behind Don Matteo with amazed admiration for the firm effectiveness of his subtle intelligence and humane understanding, inspired by the religious faith. A priest and, one step behind him, a *carabiniere*: the cooperation and the unequal expertise in pursuit of truth shown by these two traditional emblems of social and moral authority depicts a curious portrait of the relationship between Church and State.

But the most famous regular hero of present-day televisual police drama is unquestionably *Il commissario Montalbano/Inspector Montalbano* (Raidue and Raiuno, 1999–), a character transferred to the small screen from the best-sellers of the Sicilian novelist Andrea Camilleri. The protagonist's self-introduction 'Montalbano here' (shades of 'The name's Bond. James Bond') has entered into everyday language and into that mode of endorsing genres and characters, which is parody.

Montalbano is a multi-faceted personage, dynamic and pensive, in the small agile body of the actor Luca Zingaretti; a bald yet fascinating police inspector, a lover of food and sensitive to female charm. He does not allow himself to be forced into the mould or style of other regular heroes, just as he shuns the conventional rhetoric of the 'ordinary everyday hero'; instead, he deploys the all too rare virtues of a man who is intellectually free, an acute and thoughtful observer and an understated natural leader.

Inspector Montalbano is the jewel in the crown of the new run of Italian police dramas, also because its 'Italianness' or rather its 'insularity' – all the action takes place in a small Sicilian town with the imaginary name of Vigata – has not prevented the series from being exported to a fair number of other countries. The television adaptation makes good use of and heightens the recognizability of a sophisticated yet popular literary figure, earning the brand of a quality TV drama that is enhanced by the sumptuous beauty of its settings. The imaginary Sicilian town of Vigata, sunny and colourful, with its baroque architecture, whitewashed Moorish houses and the translucent expanses of the sea, conveys the true magic of a Mediterranean 'sense of place' without degenerating into touristic triteness or folkloric stereotype.

Together with *Don Matteo* and the archetypical *all'italiana* police drama *Marshal Rocca*, *Inspector Montalbano* forms a trilogy of police dramas with individual protagonists; meanwhile the genre, as we shall soon see, has been veering towards 'choric protagonism'. The three series are furthermore united by the provincial setting, which, in addition to offering a local background, introduces a peculiar time perspective through scenographic details.

The protagonists of the three series are present-day characters, struggling with a phenomenology of crime that is recognizably inscribed in current events; in fact they live and act in a present that is constantly redolent of and filled with testimonies of the past. It is not the effect of some sort of 'backwardness' in the environment or a cloud of nostalgia or the characters' way of being, although some of their traits may appear to make them men 'of times past'. It is rather the architecture and landscapes, amply deployed in all three series, that communicate the sense of the past, testify to it, indeed:

Gubbio's monumental square and the Umbrian countryside in its seasonal changes (the seasons still exist) in *Don Matteo*, the town plan and the architectural remains of the medieval town of Viterbo in *Marshal Rocca*, the baroque façades, alternating with loggias, of the Mediterranean houses looking on to the sea in *Inspector Montalbano*. The purely decorative use of these scenographic components is not always avoided; but this does not prevent them functioning as iconic symbols, sometimes opening timeless visual horizons, of an ancient Italy that has survived into the present and makes it beautiful. The sea where Montalbano goes for his ritual morning swim is not only crystal clear (as it once was) but gives the feeling of physical and symbolic immersion in a timeless element.

Figure 5.3. Luca Zingaretti as the protagonist of the police series *Inspector Montalbano* (Raiuno, 1999–present). Courtesy of RAI.

Thus the pleasures of visual experience are added to the pleasures of the police drama, closely linked to the image – perhaps also conventional, but recognizable and resonant – of an urban Italy adorned with the living traces of her past and endowed with the pleasant resources of unspoilt countryside and seashore. The perceptible presence, within the narrative of contemporary crimes, of this patrimony of history, architecture and natural beauty, handed down over the years, makes *Marshal Rocca*, *Don Matteo* and *Inspector Montalbano* a heritage trilogy of police dramas.

Squads

Television 'plenty' in the 1990s coincided with an equally 'plentiful' era for the Italian police series. The genre flourished as never before, with a large number of new and returning series filling the schedules of public and private television channels. Additional signs of 'plenty' also emerged in the protagonistic arena, as the Italian police series progressed towards *choric protagonism* – meaning that the single hero or the detective duo began to make room for the ensemble cast of core characters.

At the start of the twenty-first century, first *La squadra/The Squad* (Raitre, 2000–2008) inspired by the English series *The Bill*, and immediately thereafter *Distretto di polizia/Police District* (Canale 5, 2000–) opened the way to choric protagonism. Just like the comparable American and European products, the two series are focused on a professional milieu – the police station on the outskirts of a city – and on the structure of functional and personal relationships between members of the squad.

This was not the start of a new phase, but a branching out from the preceding one that among other things led to the achievement of the 'mimetization' of the hero. Choric protagonism is a distillation of mimetic heroism, an advanced stage of the process of bringing down the status of the hero 'to our level'. Something resembling democracy or equality of heroic opportunities, as opposed to the hegemony of an individual hero, is achieved and recognized. There is no Inspector Montalbano or Maresciallo Rocca (those centralizing figures of ironic leaders) standing out against the background of police districts or *carabinieri* stations staffed by a micro-community of characters: these are horizontal groups where the central character, if there is one, does not assume the superior and privileged mantle of the 'soloist', but is *primus inter pares*. There is no longer any need to have recourse to ironic strategies in order to give credence to the human averageness of ordinary everyday heroes.

It is not by chance that these micro-communities sometimes end up developing links of mutual affection and familial-style relationships, thus assuming the shape of a work family. This is a family that is not based on blood ties or parental affinities, or on living in the same domestic space. But it is a family nonetheless – one whose unity is built on collegial and cooperative relationships, which tend to generate intimacy and affection between strangers who share the same workspaces, times and practices. In American

TV drama the work family appeared in the 1970s and functioned as an alternative to the 'true' family, an imagined island of affective and cooperative relationships within organizations where people could find refuge and relief from the growing tensions of family life (Taylor, 1991). In the Italian police drama the work family is more of a 'second family', a web of relationships that is not alternative but additional; or else, as often happens, areas (potential or real) are created between the 'work family' and the 'home family' that intersect and overlap each other, for example whenever a pair of lovers or a married couple is formed and contextualized in the professional setting itself.

Distretto di polizia/Police District (Canale 5, 2000–), the most successful and long-lasting police series produced by commercial television, is the paradigmatic example of this more recent evolution in Italian police drama. This ensemble series converts the professional milieu of the police station into a place where the creation and maintenance of personal relations extend far beyond the close collaboration that is normally practised between members of the same team. There are consolidated friendships, serious love stories and choric participation in life-changing events, such as the joy of birth and the sadness of deaths. Not unlike soaps, there is constant talk about the events and problems of private life, one's own and that of others, held in the workplace during working hours and re-echoing from one scene to the next and from one sub-group of characters to another. Indeed, the structural innovation introduced by *Police District* borrows from the continuous serial the paradigmatic complexity of the network of interpersonal relations (Allen, 1985) and the ensuing pre-eminence of conversation over action; it is through these conversational devices that individuals and their activities are systematically connected and brought back to the community. An accurate analysis (which cannot be done here) of the system of relationships in *Police District* would throw light on the truly communitarian nature of the links between the characters. In fact what exists between them (as Baumann recalls) is not the consensus that results from negotiations and compromises between diverse positions, but that understanding 'without words ... a reciprocal binding sentiment' (Baumann, 2001: 10) that can exist only between like-minded people, and that constitutes a community and keeps it together. Sheltered from endogenous conflicts, the micro-community of the inhabitants of the district is converted into an (ideal) extended family, a work family, which is surrounded and intersected by the natural families of the diverse components of the group.

The reversal of narrative agenda operated by the series – where the private dimension appears structurally superimposed on the professional dimension – produces as a corollary the displacement of the real enigma, the real investigative plot, to the inter-episode continuing story. In *Police District* the anthology plot (the storyline brought to an end within each episode) is relegated to second place and sometimes becomes a mere filler. Much more than a simple frame or a background, the running plot (the unresolved narrative unfolding from one episode to the next) is the central stage of the crime and the detection, calling for empathy and emotional participation, more so in that the continuing story systematically involves the protagonists as targets or victims of

Figure 5.4. Isabella Ferrari as the Chief Inspector Giovanna Scalise in the first season of *Police District* (Canale 5, 2000–present). Courtesy of Mediaset.

deadly threats. In pursuing its professional objectives of preventing crime and arresting criminals, along with safeguarding their own members, the squad gives the best of its ability and investigative effectiveness, reinforcing at the same time the inter-subjective bonds of affective solidarity that make up its structure.

The Girls with a gun

Hands clenched to grasp the weapon, arms motionless and tense, a young woman comes running forward in the opening credits of *Police District*: this is how the protagonist of the third edition of the series (2002) appeared on the scene, in the iconographic characterization of a 'girl with a gun' in action.

Armed women, of course in the role of legitimate possessor of a service pistol, are no longer a rarity in Italian TV drama. Indeed, policewomen and female *carabinieri* represent the advance guard of the fictional portrayal of the modern Italian woman, in her new areas of activity and her social protagonism.

It can be correctly asserted that within the large group of professions that are historically categorized as being for men, those practised in the so-called law and order organizations have been the most complicated to re-categorize culturally, and to reconvert in practice, into 'professions for men and women' – for a great many reasons that are connected among other things with the hold of arms, the pervading physical danger and the contact with crime and social disorder. In different times and at varying paces, the process of feminization has gone ahead in the 'armed professions' and the televisual police drama itself has begun to introduce female figures into its community of characters – without inverting the male-centric orientation of Italian TV drama.[3]

Outwardly, equal opportunities for male and female characters are assured. In Italian police drama the women are characterized normally by seriousness, ability and professional competence, virtues not unlike those accredited to the male characters. Just as trustworthy and dedicated, women police officers and *carabinieri* if anything exceed their male colleagues in fairness and sensitivity, putting the last quality at the service of interaction with other women who are victims of violence and abuse.

It should be added that female characters happen to play the most important dramatic roles and are by no means excluded even from the hierarchical roles of command, as we shall see later. Nevertheless, the world of the television police drama still has a masculine connotation. In the first place, even if it is true that female *carabinieri* or police officers play leading dramatic roles and are certainly not confined to the ranks of minor characters, they do not assume those outstanding roles that confer on a personage the status of unquestioned protagonist. Figures of great professional and human breadth such as Marshal Rocca and Inspector Montalbano, eponymous heroes of very popular series, have no female equivalent. In contrast, it is well known that in a television market not only geographically but also culturally close to Italy, such as France, the so-called recurring heroes protagonists in the most successful police series are very often females (*Julie Lescaut, Une femme d'honneur/A Woman of Honour, Femmes de loi/Women of the Law*).

In the second place, what feminist studies define as the 'male gaze' (Mulvey, 1975) continues to affect the women of television police series and, although it generally steers clear of insistent voyeuristic complacencies, loses no opportunity of giving prominence to the charm and seductiveness of the female body or certain types of come-hither female behaviour. Female police officers and *carabinieri*, what is more, often display the appeal of youth. Here we can see confirmed a standard feature of the portrayal of the female gender on television, which goes beyond the police drama genre and indeed lends itself to a range of controversial interpretations. In this specific case it can be observed that although the youth of the women intercepts their status as relative newcomers in the real and imaginary world of police organizations, it also favours the exercise of the 'male gaze' on the female body, as well as (and more programmatically) the play of inter-sexual relationships – professional, friendly and above all romantic – in the workplace. These relationships acquire without doubt an added value of stimulus and pleasure in the youth and charm of the female characters that are involved.

In short, the entry of women into the police and *carabinieri* squads in TV drama impacts both the structure of these professional communities – as is testified by the move from all-male groups to groups composed of men and women – and, even more, the system of their internal relationships: here, alongside pre-existing systems of belonging, working together and friendship, new bonds of a romantic and sexual nature take shape. With a few exceptions, all the female characters in the police drama end up sooner or later in some sort of romantic entanglement, correspondence or flirtation, or deep tie with a colleague in the same squad. Their presence opens doors for couples' experiences and liaisons, keeping them confined within the boundaries of the workplace.

The emergence of female characters in Italian police drama received a considerable boost from the entry of women into the 'armed professions' (the feminization of the police force, now substantial, and the inception of a similar process in the *carabinieri* and the army), the familiarization of the public with the armed heroines and warriors in Hollywood films and American series (*Xena, Nikita, Alias*), the legitimizing and reassuring effect of a profession serving law and order and the need to diversify within a genre that was fast expanding on both the sides of supply and demand; and not least, from the aim to lodge a typology of drama that was by convention 'macho' in the viewing preferences of the female audience.

But perhaps more importantly, the operation was made easier and relatively painless by the peculiar configuration of the Italian police drama; almost completely devoid of violence or conflicts, lightened by humour, open to the dimension of families and relationships, the domestic cop show engenders an ambience that is in itself welcoming, not hostile or insensitive, where the female presence can be introduced and naturalized with a minimum of culture shock. The modifications that a genre traditionally classified as male, or at any rate featuring a majority of male characters, undergoes when infiltrated with female figures are in turn reduced to a minimum. Although some cultural renegotiation of narrative genre and gender identity is always necessary in comparable cases, the Italian police drama creates the conditions for such reworking to be less complicated or controversial than has happened, and still happens, elsewhere. The masculinization of female characters, according to harsh and violent role models – a process feared and deplored by an entire feminist generation, and destined in all probability to come up against flat rejection by the general Italian public – is an example of a danger that is *a priori* ruled out for the female characters of Italian police dramas, where even the male characters share a style and a general air of gentleness and softness.

Beyond these specifications, it remains true that recent trends in the feminization of the Italian police drama, in tune with the advent of 'action heroines' in Hollywood films and in the production and consumption of televisual genres both in the United States and in Europe, amount to a very important turning point. Indeed, in popular imagination and culture[4] the armed woman – or, in the present-day version, the girl with a gun – has always had connotations of threats and social disorder as an incarnation of the subversive overturning of traditional gender roles and power relationships between the sexes.

If the cinematographic imagination can be allowed to rework this threat in terms of exaltation of the heroine (think of *Thelma and Louise*, Ridley Scott 1991), the televisual images offer a more domesticated and conciliatory version of it. In the Italian police drama the opposition between the masculine narrative genre and the feminine gender has been reconciled, and women's access to the armed professions has been made acceptable and normalized, through the shaping of a female figure for whom carrying out what was originally men's work in no way detracts from her traditional femininity (beauty, elegance, seductiveness, emotion, a desire for love and a maternal vocation).

Women on top

The feminine trend in Italian police drama initially took root by means of what could be defined as 'shared protagonism'. In other words, the heroine was not in the centre of the stage by herself, but was coupled with a partner. The duo of police officers or detectives is a classic formation, still very common in the international police drama; in the Italian version it was introduced by means of women, both because as newcomers in a male profession and milieu they were perhaps not considered sufficiently credible or acceptable as individual protagonists, and to exploit for dramaturgical purposes the dialectical play of contrast and attraction within a man–woman duo.

Female protagonism made its first appearance in police drama with the series *Linda e il brigadiere/Linda and the Brigadier* (Raiuno, 1997–2000); the title itself announced the sharing out of the principal roles. In a way that had great cultural significance, the first heroine of an Italian police drama arrived on the scene 'escorted', looked after by her elderly father, a retired policeman with whom the 30-year-old police inspector Linda Fogliani shared her home, like many Italian 30-somethings. Protective, sympathetic and a first-rate cook, the father acted as his daughter's helper and mentor at the start of her career with the police, and in practice solved the enigmas of the investigations on her behalf. However much the protagonist aspired in successive editions of the series to free herself and to show greater authority and professional independence, her exercise of a public role made only a marginal contribution to the definition of her feminine identity: this identity was in essence carved out by her private roles of the impatient yet loving daughter, the girlfriend who was troubled yet in love (with her boss), clad in the bodily form of a beautiful and seductive woman and often shot in scanty attire.

In this last respect, even though it was toned down in the televisual version, the series recalled a popular cinematographic trend that in the 1960s and 1970s was ahead of the times in staging much more dissolute female police officers and soldiers. The potentially disturbing impact of the unprecedented appearance of a female figure among the protagonists of police drama was thus softened in *Linda and the Brigadier* by the strategic appeal of the familiar and reassuring image of femininity armed with especially pleasing features and a desirable figure.

The protagonists of successive series (*Valeria medico legale/Valeria the Forensic Doctor* (Canale 5, 2000–2002); *Donna detective/Woman Detective* (Raiuno 2008–2010); *Ho sposato uno sbirro/I Married a Cop* (Raiuno, 2008–2010), almost always coupled with lovers, husbands or ex-husbands, seemed more well defined in their investigative role, though they remained characterized by the pre-eminence of their private lives. For example in *Lui e lei/He and She* (Raiuno, 1998–1999) the protagonist Giulia Romano – who in contrast to Linda displayed a well-harmonized androgynous corporeality, roaring around on a fast motorbike like a daring modern Amazon – endured the double burden of a childhood without a family and a painful deprivation of motherhood that made her a wounded and problematic young woman, rather than a police officer who was strong-willed if insecure. Entering a male profession seemed to be accompanied here by a sort of awkward femininity, expressed in the highest degree by the fact that the protagonist could not have children; the 'female problem' of her unsatisfied desire for motherhood was her personal burden.

At the beginning of the twenty-first century, it was precisely the mother status of the protagonist that was to mark an important turn in the process of feminization of the Italian police drama.

It was *Police District* that took a step forward in the concept of the armed woman by introducing for the first time the figure of a female 'boss': Chief Inspector Giovanna Scalise, widow and mother of two children. A twofold and complementary escalation of the politics of representation was undertaken by the series, which aimed at constructing the ambitious paradigm of full reconciliation between the male career of arms, carried out furthermore in a position of command, and the quintessential prerogative of female identity, motherhood, captured and followed in the topical stage of pregnancy and birth.

Police District is an ensemble series, as I have already said; therefore, Inspector Giovanna Scalise is not strictly speaking a protagonist with the same clear and unequivocal importance of a Marshal Rocca or an Inspector Montalbano. But as a district chief, she is the protagonist of a small earth tremor in the world of the Italian police drama: she comes on stage as a 'woman on top' figure in a male-dominated workplace. It is through her, and thanks to the standardization of the series' repetitive structures, that we become familiar with the character of a woman in charge: a woman who issues instructions, guides actions, uses the expression 'my men' and is consulted and listened to by them with respect.

The actress Isabella Ferrari's finely chiselled features and curt style of acting reverberate on the character of Giovanna Scalise – passionate and intense, subsequently physically softened by pregnancy – a certain austere and expressive sobriety that is rather unusual for a female figure in domestic TV drama. She is not the sort of assertive and ambitious woman in the style of Jane Tennison in *Prime Suspect* (1991–1995), capable of waging a concerted struggle against crime and sexism in the police force with an almost masculine determination (Creeber, 2001a): that would be an improbable figure in the Italian context and incompatible with the harmonious atmosphere in the district police force. On the contrary, the series manages to rapidly dispel the bewilderment engendered in the professional micro-community, and perhaps also in the public, by the initial impact of a character who appears rigid and stand-offish; and to reveal, behind this superficial appearance, an admirable female personality who is capable of managing the responsibilities and the tensions of both her professional and her family life in a sensible and balanced way.

Dedicated to her work to the extent that she is in her office the evening before giving birth, and very devoted to her children yet not to the point of allowing them to dictate her affective choices, an authoritative boss and at the same time a sympathetic colleague of 'my men', Inspector Giovanna Scalise epitomizes (maybe with a touch of affectation and an excess of programmatic perfection) the modern woman who is knowing and self-driven in public and private.

Obviously such an 'advanced' female character (in relative terms) needed to reach a tough compromise with more conventional modes and expectations of the portrayal of the woman. This operation of taming or normalization was carried out in the series by bringing into play two powerful catalysts of emotionalism and empathy: the threat of death and the procreation of life.

Like Giulia Romano in *He and She*, Giovanna Scalise carries a burden. She was present (in the opening scene of *Police District*) at the murder of her husband by the Mafia and subsequently helped with the arrest of the murderers. Her transfer incognito from Sicily to the police station in Rome is a security measure to save her and her two children from the revenge of the criminal world; but her hiding place is revealed by an informer and a Mafia boss starts to pursue her. Although the character Giovanna Scalise is not in the least like the stereotypical fragile victim and indeed gives proof in all circumstances of mental and physical courage, she is constantly haunted by the dark cloud of the threat of becoming an assassin's victim. That this should be an unlikely fate for a recurrent heroine is relatively unimportant; what matters is the double play of re-definition of the heroine, intended to lead the modern figure of the knowing and determined woman back to the more traditional *topos* of the woman in danger, and the figure of the leader to that of a lone person in need of protection by the squad.

When the heroine happens to expect a third baby, the love child of one of her collaborators, her transformation into the figure of a procreator of life intensifies her status and her recognizability as a woman in the full sense of femininity. And although this transformation makes her more precious as a person who is creating another, and therefore makes the threats to her safety more fearful and hateful, it also introduces an extreme tension at the emotional (and perhaps ethical) level between the polarities of life (identified with the woman and especially the mother-to-be) and death (which can strike her but which she herself can inflict as a person trained in the use of arms). This tension is destined to be relieved in the celebration of the protagonist as the creator of both the one and the other.

The motherhood of Inspector Giovanna Scalise in *Police District* is a typical instance of interpenetration between productive and narrative circumstances: in other words, the pregnancy of the actress in real life is reflected in the fictional character. The gentle and family-oriented world of the series does not place any obstacles in the way of such an interpenetration.

Therefore, after the seductive and desirable body (*Linda*) or the athletic and nimble one (*He and she*), a woman's reproductive body enters the scene of the police drama and installs itself centre stage with all the visibility of an advanced stage of pregnancy. Hospital series, set in gynaecological and obstetric wards, had of course already introduced pregnant women, but fleetingly and (above all) apparently faked. It is unquestionably emblematic of the radical rewriting of the genre in Italian televisual culture, and of the structuring of a consonant system of Italian viewers' expectations, that the tangible transformation of the female body affected by the generation of a new life should have found complete visibility and genuine protagonism in a police series.

And it is thanks precisely to the coincidence of empirical and diegetic reality, of the life circumstances of the actress and the character, that *Police District* could dare to shift, significantly, the frontiers of legitimate behaviour for a woman bearing arms, forward. Police officers in Italian TV drama, for a number of reasons that are easily guessed, make sparing and cautious use of weapons – we have heard Inspector Montalbano reprimand one of his men for shooting in the air to intimidate people during a police round-up – and the armed conflicts in which they happen to become involved seldom take the form of hand-to-hand fighting, a close encounter with an opponent. Engaging in eye contact with someone who may attack very soon, or being clubbed to death, in fact, constitutes a highly dramatic and dilemmatic existential test from which the characters, and the viewers, of an Italian police drama are normally shielded. Yet, the final episode of *Police District*'s second season put the female character, Inspector Giovanna Scalise, to this test. Heated and breathless, slow in her movements from the late stage of her pregnancy but determined to remain at her post until the end, the protagonist wanders round the rooms of the police station that have been emptied of police officers by a false alarm created by the Mafia boss who, by means of manoeuvres that gradually bring him closer, has at last managed to reach her. She will find him waiting for her in her office and confronting her, armed, from the other side of her desk. Like Thelma and Louise, Inspector Scalise keeps her pistol in a typically feminine place like a handbag, a sports bag of the holdall type, from where she extracts it, making the most of a moment of absentmindedness on the part of her persecutor, to shoot him dead at close range.

The invisibility of the gesture – we see only the consequences, in the male body that falls stiffly forward – and the just cause of legitimate defence on the part of a character who embodies at the same time state law and natural law serve to soften the initial shock that might be provoked by the death-dealing figure of an armed woman. But it is the immediate switch of this figure to her opposite image, her re-conversion from policewoman to mother, the act of giving life immediately after dealing death that makes up definitively for the shock. The protagonist barely has time to put down her pistol before she is struck by labour pains; we are introduced to the scene of the birth and witness the birth of her son.

The character takes her leave soon afterwards, allowing the series to bring to the end and to achieve, literally, the domestication of its armed heroine and of the first lady in charge of men. Now the mother of three children and with a new partner, Giovanna Scalise makes her choice and declares that she wants to dedicate herself to her family. Following in her footsteps, other 'top women' have made an appearance in Mediaset's police series in the 2000s: again in *Police District*; *Squadra antimafia/Anti-Mafia Squad* (Canale 5, 2008–2010); *RIS Roma/RIS Rome* (Canale 5, 2010).

Softening the elements of tension and conflict belongs to the pacifying approach of Italian TV drama; it therefore can come as no surprise that in police series little or nothing is disclosed concerning the greater or lesser organizational and relational criticalities, the perennial tensions in male–female relationships, the gaps in mindset and culture that generate dissent and lack of balance in professional settings where male domination is traditional.

In fact the Italian police drama, giving proof of its undoubted capacity for cultural mediation, has managed to advance the frontiers of an empowered female identity while at the same time keeping control of both the potential of the threat that is historically inherent in the figure of the armed woman, and the disturbing resonances and repercussions of the advent of women in men's professions.

From this there emerges a comforting picture of Italian society in which the male and the female are (or seem to be) fully reconciled in the welcoming and friendly world of working for law and order.

The merging of sailor's and peasant's storytelling

The trends of diversification that have more recently become manifest within the genre, also following the expansion of the textual corpus, do not prevent the domestic police drama from preserving some basic characteristics that ensure its typicality and recognizability:

i. A certain lightness, attributable to humour and the softening of conflict and violence. Italian police dramas may be melodramatic (though hardly ever intensely dramatic), but they do not fail to keep their promise of relaxing moments, raising a laugh or a smile from viewers (who for their part expect this), if not precisely or invariably the generous dose of humour of a 'dramedy'. The avoidance of action, especially in the sense of physical and armed clashes, is a logical behavioural corollary of the human profile of shrewd and even-tempered characters, inspired – whatever their heroic status may be – by an ideal of Italian mildness, sort of 'Italians good people' (see Chapter 8); but it is also an intentional modality through which the Italian police drama constructs its own identity, in contrast to the muscular and ballistic excesses (in other words, fights and shootings) that are regarded as stereotypical of American cop shows.

ii. A peaceful provincial atmosphere, rather than the burning wind of the big city; in urban landscapes, which for preference form the background to choric police dramas, it is hard to recognize the large modern city that has established itself from the start as the chosen milieu for the detective genre. 'Of this realization of a great city itself as something wild and obvious the detective story is certainly the "Iliad"', wrote Chesterton at the beginning of the last century (2008: 70). The Italian police drama finds it difficult to deploy a repertoire of stories and iconic identifications or other symbolic indicators in such a way as to restore the unmistakable flavour of the modern metropolis; it is better at evoking the shapes, atmosphere and image of the urban province, sometimes managing to transform it into a true emblem of Italianness.

iii. The pre-eminence of the characters and relationships over the plot of the detective story. Whether they concern individual crimes committed because of passion or self-interest or, as more often happens now, the various types of social crime (usury, domestic abuse, drugs, prostitution, illegal work, illegal immigration etc.), police plots and investigative proceedings are not exactly at the core of the narrative structure of Italian police dramas. The latter are more involved with working on the personalities, on the community of characters, on the web of relationships that form the structure of their public and private life and sometimes superimpose them on or merge them with the work family of the police station.

Let us return, in conclusion, to the analogy of the archaic tribes of the 'sailor' and 'peasant' storytellers. *Police District* and the new wave of *Italian-style* police series in the 1990s and 2000s seem to attest that the domestically oriented ('peasant') voice has never resounded as strongly as it does at present. In fact the Italian police drama has managed over the years to elaborate a genre that is consciously and proudly replete with features of 'national identity' and heritage – these include family, humorous understatement, mimetic heroes, small towns, soft tones, contained violence and relationships rather than action. However, as this shift to 'stories from the soil' has developed as part of a permanent intersection between the domestic and the foreign, it would be naïve to suggest that the interaction with extra-national elements and influences has not made a significant impact on contemporary Italian police series and the very Italian imagination of crime (as represented in television fiction).

Ulrich Beck (2003) suggests that the national paradigm can no longer work unless we recognize that national society and culture today have been inescapably trans-nationalized from within (albeit in different degrees) via their exposure to international flows and to the integration of both superficial and in-depth global processes and phenomena. Therefore, what we define as well-grounded national, domestic, local (storytelling or other) is no longer what it used to be in the past.

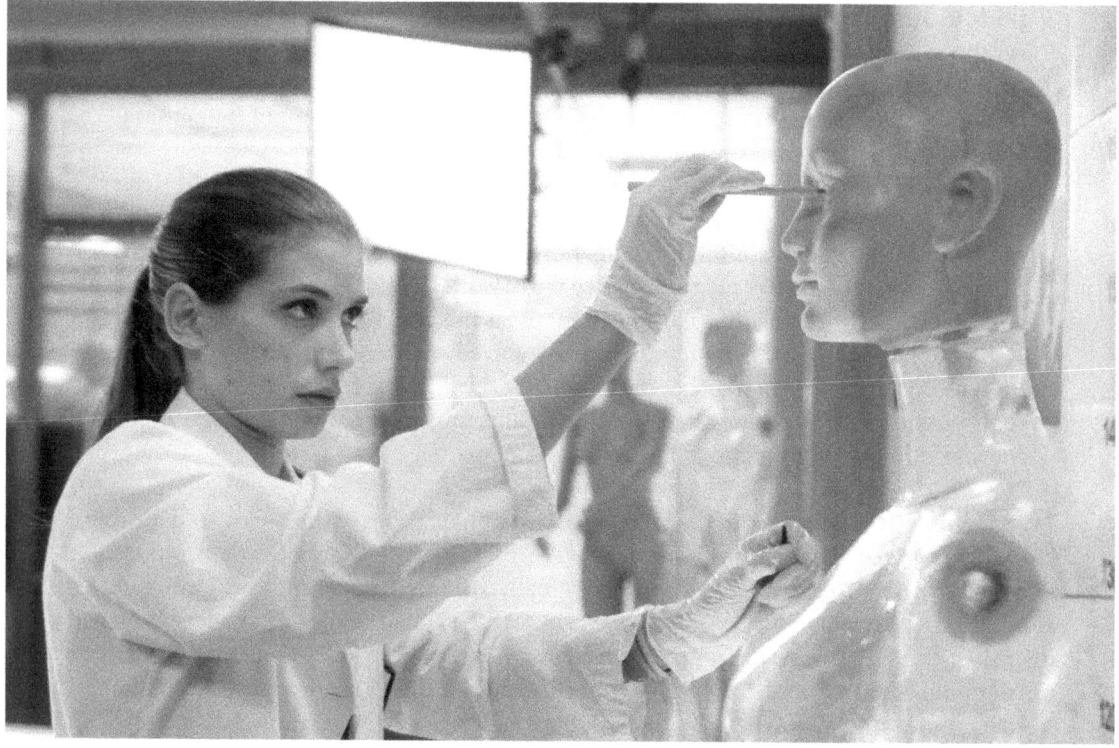

Figure 5.5. Giulia Michelini as the lieutenant Francesca De Biase in the forensic series *RIS. Imperfect Crimes* (Canale 5, 2005–2009). Courtesy of Mediaset.

That is certainly the case for the contemporary Italian police series. Whereas many elements of the genre were reworked so as to fit peculiarly domestic features, others – mainly pertaining to narrative structure, ensemble of characters, investigation procedures, shooting of scenes and editing — shifted towards the international canons introduced and established by foreign TV drama. *Police District* is recognizably Italian, but the innovative imprint of the multi-strand narrative first pioneered by *Hill Street Blues* (NBC, 1981–1987) is equally recognizable in the structure of the series. A similar trend can be seen in the emergence of the forensic investigation sub-genre. Though the *CSI* franchise has not managed to emulate in Italy the very high levels of popularity it achieved in France, where even domestic drama has been displaced from Sunday prime time to make room for *CSI: New York*, nonetheless it has played an important role in re-familiarizing Italian viewers with the new flow of contemporary American police series (*Law & Order: SVU, Cold Case, Without a Trace, NCIS, Criminal Minds*); and this time (unlike in the 1980s) with the blessing of the critics, who have now been won over by American 'quality drama' (Grasso, 2007). Following in the footsteps of the new course of scientific investigation introduced by *CSI: Crime Scene Investigation* (CBS, 2000–), Italian commercial television has for its part created a forensic series *RIS. Imperfect Crimes* (Canale 5, 2005–2009), which has been notably successful and – rather paradoxically, as it is the unofficial adaptation of an American concept – has generated an autonomous format, sold with variable results in other European countries. Although *CSI* is identifiable without a doubt as the original matrix of this Italian series – and it is sometimes even plainly exhibited through undisguised quotation or imitation practices, as if they wished to lay a proud claim to a prestigious ancestor – *RIS. Imperfect Crimes* cannot be dismissed as a simple, if very well made, Italian reproduction of a foreign original. There are in fact numerous differences between it and *CSI: Crime Scene Investigation*; and these differences form a greater part of the series' identity than the similarities. We need only think of the almost polar contrast between the lead characters, Gil Grissom in *CSI* and Captain Venturi in *RIS*: if Grissom's main trait 'is that of emotional disengagement/repression' (Pearson, 2007: 43), sometimes extending to an apparent insensitivity towards his colleagues, Venturi's initial *froideur* and composure soon melt away to reveal the sensitive temperament of a melodramatic character, prone to extreme gestures and a pursuit of the truth that is sometimes more obsessive than scientific. Nor does his status as a scientist shield him from fitting into the shape of the 'vulnerable hero', a familiar and easily readable cultural trope for Italian viewers, who recognize (and appreciate) in him the evidence of human frailty of the police drama hero. Venturi is not sheltered from the constant threat of becoming prey to and victim of criminal intent himself, and the suspense concerning his fate (and that of the woman he loves) drives the whole inter-episode narrative – a further structural difference from *CSI*.

We are not faced with mere imitative practices, but rather an appropriation and incorporation of elements from the trans-national television culture, which are indigenized (Buonanno, 2008) to become in turn an integral constituent of national models. Far from being a contradiction, or the cause of an inexorable clash, this mixture of local and trans-national is to be considered part and parcel of the current national specificity and renewed popularity of the genre. It seems as if the different narrative voices of the 'sailor' and the 'peasant' have ended up by merging.

This is not an unprecedented phenomenon. Benjamin himself emphasized that the mutual penetration between the stories of the 'sailor' and 'peasant' first happened in the workshops of medieval craftsmen, the site *par excellence* where the oral storytelling was once practised and raised to an art form.

Notes

1. In Italy, the crime story genre is called *giallo* i.e. yellow, which was the dust-jacket colour of the books in a very popular paperback series of detective novels that was inaugurated in the 1920s by the Mondadori publishing house. The 'giallo Mondadori' was distributed in bookstalls every week and is still a very successful series.
2. At that time, the hero of the police series was without exception a man. Female protagonists did not make their appearance until 1997.
3. The stories of Italian TV drama may be awash with saints, popes, civic heroes and ordinary everyday heroes, but they are traditionally sparing with female protagonists. If one had to rely on this sole corpus of texts to construct a map of gender status in Italy during the first decade of the twenty-first century, one would conclude that male domination was set in stone. It is indeed hard to contradict such an impression when faced with the predominance of male protagonists in contemporary televisual storytelling. Nevertheless, Italian TV drama is not suspected of misogynist inclinations, which would be incompatible with the general spirit of inclusivity and equality that pervades it, and made inadvisable among other reasons by the prevailing female composition of its audience. Yet, it must be acknowledged that although the availability of stories about women has always been (and in truth remains) limited in quantity as well as being barely incisive or meaningful at the symbolic and cultural level (in that it rarely manages to create popular and memorable characters), it has increased quite a lot in recent seasons. It should be added that the women of TV drama are in general positive and admirable characters: expert and effective in shouldering the burden of 'double presence' in the family and the workplace; sometimes – the younger ones – a little insecure but in any case never weak or submissive towards the opposite sex, capable of reacting with dignity to men's betrayals, abuse and small-mindedness but without losing sight of the value and purpose of a relationship that is based on the reciprocal and reaffirmed elective choice of the partners. In short, these are women who are determined but not feisty or aggressive (except sometimes in appearance) and who express a modern feminine subjectivity that is acceptable because it is not threatening.
4. The image of the armed woman, as an expression of a world that is disorderly and in breach of 'natural laws', was a widespread iconographic concept in the nineteenth century. In Italy, for example, a print was very widely circulated consisting of a series of boxed sections that represented 'the upside-down world' (Cocchiara, 1981). The boxed section dedicated to gender roles showed an armed woman in military uniform next to a man in women's clothes with a baby on his lap.

Chapter 6

In the Footsteps of *La Piovra*:
Twenty Years of Mafia Stories in Prime Time Drama

'Mob stories are always hot': a *tour d'horizon*

I concluded the chapter on *La Piovra* by defining it the 'protagonist of a lengthy season of the Italian imagination', but the deep impact made by this groundbreaking narrative on the national dramatic landscape has gone beyond its own huge popularity and long duration. In actual fact, *La Piovra* was also a powerful seminal work, opening the gates to a plentiful Mafia stories stream which, for at least two decades since the closure of the 'Cattani cycle' at the end of the 1980s, fuelled a substantial amount of the supply and demand in prime time domestic drama. I will take my cue from a strange but true episode in order to shed light, after a rapid overview of the international televisual scene, on the main characteristics of the twenty-year flowering of the Mafia Story genre in the field of Italian fiction.

At the end of November 2007 Italian news media and, even more prominently, the international press and Internet sites, announced the arrest of a Mafia boss hiding in the Zen district of Palermo. Even though he was regarded as a prominent figure in one of the most powerful Sicilian clans, the man was not of such high calibre as to merit the attention of the international media. But foreign observers were struck above all, and to some extent amused, by the circumstances of his capture. The wanted person, who was smart enough to have fled just a few weeks before a vast police operation that led to the arrest of the clan boss and his faithful followers, had been surprised in his secret hideaway while watching the final episode of *Il capo dei capi/The Boss of Bosses* (Canale 5, 2007). This was Canale 5's successful and critically acclaimed miniseries, which narrated the bloody ascent in the hierarchy of Sicilian Mafia power of the Corleonesi clan under the brutal command of Totò Riina. The final episode, broadcast on 29 November 2007, revolved around the capture of Riina; consequently, an effect of *mise en abyme* was created by the parallel event taking place in real life. 'Real life bursts into Mafia TV drama', ran the headlines of numerous news stories. In this particular case, the irruption was already an integral part of that very TV drama, which was inspired by true facts in crime news and law reports.

Bizarre though the event is, it nevertheless assumes an emblematic significance. First of all, it evokes the far from incompatible – on the contrary often coexistent and blended duality of – fact and fiction in the televisual Mafia story. Of course there is nothing new in this, since the crime story in general (suffice it to quote the police drama) is by its nature exposed and permeable to influence and inspiration from the news – although reworked in various ways and degrees, following the diverse national traditions and conventions of storytelling. A statement such as 'Real life bursts into Mafia TV drama' may however be equivalent to a sort of historiographic remark, assuming a more interesting meaning in the context of the present discourse, i.e. the identification of a new tendency that comes to light within the genre at a certain moment in time. We shall see later on that this is precisely the case with the Italian Mafia story.

In addition, this same event seems to provide incontrovertible evidence of the fascination with Mafia stories: they do not merely appeal to large Italian audiences but also manage to captivate even the members of organized crime. Portrayals of the criminal underworld in film and television are popular among the Mafia members who, in addition to taking an interest in the media's image of themselves and their own world, find in these portrayals – more often than is believed – models of behaviour and examples of lifestyles to follow. The young bosses of the Naples Camorra, as Roberto Saviano in *Gomorra* (2006)[1] confirms, see the characters in Mafia films as authentic role models and imitate their behaviour, styles of dress and even the architecture and furnishings of their homes. Just a few days before the mini-sensation generated by the circumstances of the arrest of the fugitive boss mentioned earlier, the *International Herald Tribune* of 19 November 2007 had published an article which, in referring to the success of *The Boss of Bosses*, did not fail to emphasize that Totò Riina himself, in his isolation cell, was one of the most assiduous viewers of the series.

No further anecdotes are necessary to agree with Christopher Moltisanti's statement in *The Sopranos* that 'mob stories are always hot'. In the comment quoted,[2] the character was reporting the opinion of his cousin Gregory's girlfriend, an assistant of Quentin Tarantino: thus, he referred to the cinema. But nowadays it is in television that the Mafia story seems to have found fertile ground, a potential often realized for excellent artistic achievement, and the right conditions for favourable reception from viewers and critics.

A brief *tour d'horizon* on the international televisual scene, past and present, will provide evidence of what John Cawelti recalled with greater authority: 'crime, particularly violent crime, has always been a sure-fire topic for the entertainment of the public' (Cawelti, 1976: 52). When this same scholar wrote about the phenomenal literary and cinematographic success of *The Godfather,* and how Mario Puzo's novel and Francis Ford Coppola's films had led to a profound modification in American crime mythology – by reconstructing this mythology around organized crime, rather than around the individual figure of the outlaw or the gangster – he ventured to make a prediction: 'Though no TV network has yet announced a series called "One Don's Family", I suspect that scores of producers and writers are racking their brains to figure out a formula that would be recognizably like *The Godfather*' (Cawelti, 1976: 51–52).

This was in the mid-1970s; and the author's prediction was destined to be simultaneously premature and far-sighted. Organized crime had previously been at the centre of the television series *The Lawless Years* (NBC, 1959–1961), which was rapidly obscured by the success of *The Untouchables* (ABC, 1959–1963). This in turn was said to have inspired Brian De Palma's film of the same title; both series were set in the roaring years of Prohibition. Despite its national and international success, *The Untouchables* remained a one-off phenomenon, perhaps also because of the controversy aroused by the scenes of violence that were regarded as excessive by the standards of the time, and of the dubious fascination that the gangster characters exerted upon young viewers.

More than twenty years later, two further series were to re-introduce the characters, settings and themes of organized crime. These too were set in earlier time periods: the 1920s and 1930s once again in the case of *Wiseguy* (CBS, 1987–1990), which received repeated nominations for Emmy and Golden Globe awards; and the early 1960s in the case of *Crime Stories* (NBC, 1986–1988), whose pilot episode was directed by Abel Ferrara. *Crime Stories* also provided ideas and narrative input for Martin Scorsese's film *Casino* (1995).

It may indeed be true that the genre of the Mafia story enjoyed a boost in popularity following the phenomenon of *The Godfather* (one automatically thinks of the films of Martin Scorsese, Brian De Palma and Abel Ferrara). Nevertheless, the Mafia theme in American television series and serials has tended to come and go; and it was barely in evidence for long periods of time before becoming very conspicuous and emerging as a phenomenon with huge popular appeal.

When this finally happened, on the verge of the twenty-first century, much had changed since the days of *The Untouchables* and the films of Coppola. With regard to the television system, subscription-based cable and premium channels had expanded and made the boundaries of what was deemed acceptable and representable in programme content (above all in relation to sex, violence and bad language) much more fluid. With regard to cultural mythologies, the grandiose vision of the power of organized crime – subject to the almost theocratic leadership of authoritative and revered bosses – had lost much of its evocative power on the collective imagination.

The series *The Sopranos* (HBO, 1999–2007), which began in 1999, did not merely bear the traces of these changes; it found in them the conditions of its own genesis and innovative character. Made for the paying public of premium cable HBO ('it's not TV, it's HBO', to quote the network's promotional slogan), *The Sopranos* engaged in the systematic deconstruction of the mythology of *The Godfather* (Francis Ford Coppola, 1972, 1974, 1990) – a mythology that fuels the vain nostalgia of the protagonist, Tony Soprano, for a sort of 'lost world of the "Cosa Nostra"' – through the narration, steeped in brutality and coarse language, of the complicated and depressing (actually causing clinical depression) daily life of an Italo-American Mafia boss, who is grappling with a family and a criminal organization at a high level of disorder and entropy.

The artistic excellence of the series, which is one of the greatest manifestations of that 'quality TV' (Jancovich and Lyons, 2003; McCabe and Akass, 2007) which in recent years has persuaded even the most obstinately suspicious and scornful critics of American TV drama to reconsider their standpoint, has easily managed to establish the Mafia story genre in contemporary American television. *The Sopranos* seems to have engendered a trend, no doubt also fostered by the intent to follow in the wake of the enormous popularity of the HBO series, which finally ended with its sixth season in 2007. Three years later, HBO has once again re-introduced Mafia issues and milieu (going back in time to the Prohibition years) in *Boardwalk Empire* (2010): a prestigious drama serial, awarded two Golden Globes, which boasts the master of the Mafia movie Martin Scorsese as the creative producer and the director of the first episode.

Nonetheless, the epigones of *The Sopranos* have not proven equally fortunate on the other networks. Showtime, another premium channel that in the same year as the start of *The Sopranos* broadcast the biographical miniseries *Bonanno: A Godfather's Story* (probably one of the last by-products of Coppola's saga), launched *Brotherhood* in 2006. The series received critical acclaim, but only a modest following of viewers. It shifted attention from the Italo–American underworld to criminal organizations from Ireland (the Irish mob), making it the backdrop for a story of an antagonistic relationship between brothers.

The Irish–American Mafia was also the protagonist in *The Black Donnellys* (2007); this series, despite boasting the prestigious author Paul Haggis, lasted for only one season on NBC. Undaunted, the network commissioned Lynda La Plante, a very talented and renowned English producer who has a particular commitment to stories of female empowerment (Jane Tennison of *Prime Suspect* is one of her creations), to produce a series called *Mafia Wives* about a seizure of power by a group of 'Cosa Nostra' women. In 1997 the same author had adapted her novel *Bella Mafia/Beautiful Mafia* for CBS: five widows of a Mafia family wiped out by a rival clan join forces to run business and avenge the massacre of their own families. But *Mafia Wives* got no further than the development stage.

Not surprisingly, macro-criminality inspires and provides material for television productions even outside the United States, if only sporadically. In Russia, for example, the mini-serial *Brigada* (RTR TV, 2002) was a great success with both critics and the public and reached the status of a classic. Set against the background of the collapse of the Soviet Union and the disorderly advent of the post-Communist era, *Brigada* – which pays homage to *The Godfather* trilogy in a number of quotations – depicted the fortunes over a ten-year period of a Muscovite gang involved in criminal activities with the various mafias that flourish in the country, including the one that infiltrates the bureaucracy and the political system. As a confirmation of the anti-mimetic belief that life imitates art, one of the most famous members of the Russian mafia produced his own series, broadcast on the local network of an Asian country, to counter what he regarded as the distorted picture of organized crime that was put out by *Brigada*.

Another mini-serial titled *Underbelly* (Nine Networks, 2008) shook Australian viewers and critics. Preceded by a promotional campaign without parallel and subsequently acclaimed as the best crime drama in the history of Australian television, the serial drew on press and literary sources to reconstruct the explosive conflicts within Melbourne's criminal underworld in the decade straddling the twentieth and twenty-first centuries.

Reverting to the issue of series with female protagonists, what did not succeed on the American NBC was in the end profitably achieved in Europe by Canal Plus. In 2006, this French pay-TV channel produced the series *Mafiosa/The Mafia Woman*, which is one of its most popular original titles. It focuses on the character of a young woman who unexpectedly, and against her will (like Michael Corleone in *The Godfather*), finds herself leader of a Corsican Mafia clan. *Mafiosa*, exported to over 60 countries, turned out to be one of French TV drama's greatest international successes.

A twenty-year cycle

We know enough to argue that stories about great criminals and great crime exert a powerful and almost universal attraction. The Italian public is certainly not unique in showing a keen appetite for organized crime on the small screen. Yet the Italian situation, without being as eccentric or folkloric as it may seem in the eyes of sympathetic but stereotype-bound non-native observers, is undeniably different with respect to the other countries I have mentioned. This difference lies in the unequalled abundance of Mafia stories offered by Italian television.

In fact, over a period of two decades beginning in the late 1980s (from *La Piovra* 4 onwards), exactly 100 TV dramas dedicated to the Mafia and, more generally, to organized crime were broadcast on the national public and private channels: this figure amounts to almost 10% of the total prime time offering in terms of number of productions. Such a large quantity, in all probability unequalled even in televisual markets that are more extensive and differentiated and endowed with a higher productive capacity, such as the American market, goes hand in hand with a continuity that despite peaks and troughs maintains the specific property of never reaching zero. That is to say, there has never been a television season from 1988 to 2008 in which at least one, but normally more than one, homegrown Mafia story has not made an appearance on the Italian screens.

It would be easy and to a large extent plausible to ascribe this abundance, truly reaching levels of excess in some seasons, to historical roots, the widespread pervasion in many areas and sectors of activity in Italy, the monopoly of violence, the huge scale of illegal trafficking: in short to everything that makes criminal organizations and cultures, whether or not related to the Mafia, a dramatic and unresolved problem of Italian society. For better (TV drama takes on the task of keeping the issue alive in the horizon of viewers' critical awareness) or worse (TV drama stimulates and indulges the 'perverse' taste for Mafia stories widely diffused in a country with a strong criminal tradition: the Mafia country par excellence, in the stereotype often taken for granted abroad), this kind of specular and referential explanation renders only part of the truth. It is opportune at this point to recall what Robert Warshow, an insightful critic of popular culture, wrote about the gangster movie in the 1940s: 'The importance of the gangster film, and the nature and intensity of its emotional and aesthetic impact, cannot be measured in terms of the place of the gangster himself or the importance of the problem of crime in American life' (Warshow, 2001: 100).

I shall revisit this topic later, but for now it is imperative to recall again the fundamental role of *La Piovra* in launching the Mafia story on the small screen, an influential role that is entirely analogous with that played by *The Godfather* in the American cinema. Although the Rai had already begun in the 1970s to produce some historical *sceneggiati* about organized crime – a biography of *Joe Petrosino*[3] (Raiuno, 1972), *Alle origini della mafia/The Origins of the Mafia* (Raidue, 1976) and *Storia della camorra/History of the Camorra* (Raiuno, 1978) – the huge popularity gained by *La Piovra* was a key factor in creating and maintaining the conditions for the plentiful flourishing of the Mafia story in the years to come.

After first discovering and exploring the narrative genre of organized crime, public television put twice as much productive effort into it as commercial television: two-thirds of the mob stories that I have examined have been produced by the Rai. Most of these are in the prestige format of the miniseries. Often enough, however, topics and issues regarding large-scale crime are incorporated into serialized productions, in particular into police and investigative series, for which these issues provide material either for some anthology plot or, more consistently and continuously, for the running plot. There is no recurring hero figure in an Italian police series who can avoid, sooner or later, tackling crimes perpetrated by one of the national or international mafias. From this perspective the Mafia story genre, although most often associated with miniseries and TV movies, has turned out to be and continues to represent an important pool for ideas and narrative material for short and long running series and serials.

In the course of this chapter I shall consider the corpus of the 100 titles as a unitary super-text, following the example set by George F. Custen in his pioneering and unique work on biopics (Custen, 1992; see Chap. 7). I shall accordingly not engage in analysis and critique of individual productions, but shall seek to identify, in the overall configuration of the corpus, the distinctive characteristics that make up the basic pattern of the Mafia story in Italian TV drama. In particular, I shall examine the typology of criminal organization, the sources of inspiration for the stories, the distribution of the roles of protagonists and antagonists and the articulation between the male genre and the feminine gender.

The centrality of Cosa Nostra

In everyday language, the word 'Mafia' has to a large extent lost its original meaning signifying a specific type of organization, culture and criminal power structure (historically known as 'Cosa Nostra') and has become a sort of generic umbrella word that can refer to any sort of macro-criminality. This semantic emasculation undermines the word's defining capacity but has the consequence of elevating the status of 'Cosa

Nostra' and extending its frontiers indefinitely by making it the emblem of all criminal power. For that matter, cinema and television have usually followed this same path, as the cinematographic and televisual Mafia story (even in a series free of all conventions like *The Sopranos*) has systematically chosen the Italo–American Mafia of Sicilian origin, that is to say 'Cosa Nostra', as protagonist.

Much the same happens in Italian TV drama where the Sicilian Mafia, regardless of the national or international setting of the story, is involved in more than half the plotlines. Organizations other than 'Cosa Nostra' receive less attention: less than one-third of the stories are concerned with the Camorra (macro-criminality centred in Campania) or the 'Ndrangheta (macro-criminality centred in Calabria).

The geography of criminal power has undergone significant restructuring in recent years. Campania's Camorra and Calabria's 'Ndrangheta have become the most powerful and terrible criminal organizations in present-day Italy. They have opened up and exploited new and lucrative veins of so-called sophisticated illegal activities (for example, eco-Mafia waste disposal, trafficking of arms and immigrants) without losing their position in more traditional sectors such as drugs and racketeering. The phenomenon of criminals turning state's evidence, the growing effectiveness of judicial investigations and police operations and the strengthening of other criminal associations have caused problems for the Sicilian Mafia. The 'Cosa Nostra' has witnessed a decline of its central role in the world of organized crime (La Spina, 2009).

TV drama may well take into account the defeats of 'Cosa Nostra' (the capture of the bosses Riina and Provenzano, for example, have been dramatized more than once); nonetheless in the fictional world the Sicilian Mafia remains pre-eminent as the incarnation of the devil, the epitome of criminal power and social evil to be fought. Although weakened in real life by competition with other criminal powers on the rise and by a series of successful police operations, in the past 20 years 'Cosa Nostra' organized crime has stood firmly at the centre of the televisual imagination.

Yet, the Mafia story is certainly one of the genres that make less appeal to the real-life experience of viewers. For the large majority of the television-viewing public – with the exception of those who live in regions controlled by the Mafia, the Camorra and the 'Ndrangheta – organized crime is literally fiction, in that it belongs to a world not directly experienced, or likely to be experienced, in the ordinary circumstances of daily life. TV drama and films, on the side of fiction, and newspaper reports on the side of facts, take it upon themselves to universalize, in the realm of the imagination, an experience that, in everyday life, is quite uncommon for the ordinary viewer. The Mafia story may be sensitive to the influences of the news and current affairs, as I have pointed out earlier, and may therefore incorporate elements and events that could have entered, if nothing else, into the viewers' horizon of consciousness; but the fact remains that, in its relationship with the public, it appeals primarily to a horizon of endogenous references, created from the genre itself in the course of its formation and development.

The impressive device of the return of the already known operates here, more than elsewhere, on a self-referential terrain – whatever is at stake: the sort of person, situation, the deeds, languages, landscapes and other things – whose truth claims, or more simply whose recognizability and credibility, rely to a remarkable extent on an already familiar repertoire, tried and tested through a previous corpus of stories, which help to orient the viewers' system of expectations towards the recurrence of similar or barely different experiences. '… Originality is to be welcomed only in the degree that it intensifies the expected experience without fundamentally altering it' (Warshow, 2001: 100).

It is precisely the rarity of real-life experience of the Mafia and, in contrast, the universality of the imaginary experience that can engender that effect of 'reality inversion' (Giddens, 1991) which takes place when fictional portrayals become the touchstone of reality. There was surprise, and perhaps even disappointment, on the part of the Italian public when the photographs of the boss Totò Riina published after his capture in 1993 showed the primitive face of a peasant, rough and brutal, in contrast to the image built up by so many TV dramas and films of Mafia bosses as romantically fascinating and charismatic characters, lords of crime and potentates of the earth.

'Cosa Nostra' has assumed in the collective imagination the position of a sort of criminal aristocracy that helps to keep it at centre stage. Consider for example how much more coarse, brutal and repulsive the figure of the Camorrista usually seems by comparison with the ruthless yet shrewd and sharp Mafia gangster, more often than not cultured and urbane, or how much more provincial the criminal underworld of Campania and Calabria seems when compared to the cosmopolitan horizons of the Mafia. The 'Cosa Nostra' leadership often turns out to be dramatically and aesthetically (which does not mean ethically) ennobled in TV drama. The fact that Totò Riina's merciless terrorist strategy in *The Boss of Bosses* could arouse horror and moral revulsion in most viewers does not prevent the character from assuming the (sinister) grandeur of the creator of an irresistible seizure of Mafia power. I could in addition allude to the glamour of the protagonist in *L'onore e il rispetto/Honour and Respect* (Canale 5, 2006, 2009), a character who aims for the summit of the Mafia with complete unscrupulousness and homicidally vengeful compulsion, accompanied if not redeemed by the elegant physique of a fashion model and the romantic air of a man with dark good looks (aesthetic endowment of the actor Gabriel Garko).

The article in the *International Herald Tribune* that I quoted earlier found it inexplicable that Italian viewers, normally ready to respond to the appeal of Mafia stories, should have deserted *The Sopranos*. But it is easily explained. By dispelling many myths about the Mafia and in particular by featuring a stressed-out and psychoanalysed protagonist, a husband and father and boss whose authority in both his blood family and his Mafia family is continually called into question, the HBO series fundamentally alters the expected experiences of the Italian public: these experiences are constructed on, and in turn are constitutive of, an image of crime that unceasingly feeds on the ambivalent myth – swinging between moral condemnation and secret admiration – of the supremacy of 'Cosa Nostra'.

Facts burst into fiction

The considerations that I shall develop from now on relate to a more restricted corpus than the total of 100 titles monitored over the 20-year period. The theme of macro-criminality in TV drama does not always carry the same weight in terms of plot. Sometimes it is to be found only in a subsidiary story line, or as part of the background, for example when it inspires occasional one-off plots in a police series or is used to spice up the passions and conflicts of a melodramatic tale. I have left aside these stories of lesser importance (although they are significant as indicators of the degree to which the genre pervades TV drama) in order to concentrate on the more numerous cases where the criminal phenomenon constitutes the true backbone, the focal theme, the main plot of the story. I am referring to a group of 69 titles (47 Rai and 22 Mediaset productions), which, as they coincide with crime stories in the full sense of the word, testify to a definitely substantial supply – even taking account of its distribution over a considerable time span of two decades.

It is particularly the second decade, starting with the 1998–1999 season, which witnessed a sizable growth in the supply of Mafia stories on Italian channels. There was an almost twofold increase in the total number of titles, whereas themes, plots and criminal worlds came to occupy even more often the centre stage in the narrative: the main plot of nearly 50 prime-time dramas revolved around organized crime, as against 21 in the previous decade.

This was no coincidence. These same years underwent accelerating growth in the productive capacity of the Italian television industry; and the privileged evening slots opened up as never before to homegrown TV drama. Hence the need to fill the prime time – where highly rewarding ratings are expected and normally achieved – with a surplus of new stories (variations on well-known themes and genres) and innovative stories (drawn from relatively unexplored narrative sources) – the latter certainly proving more difficult than the former to create and produce. In such circumstances broadcasters and producers typically prefer to put more trust in genres that have amply proved their worth and in narrative content that has well-tested appeal and effectiveness. There is no doubt that the Mafia story can be so described, with its added value of a strong Italian connotation; this was particularly valued in the climate of pride in national identity surrounding the rebirth of domestic TV drama (in embodying the Italian response to *Dallas*, *La Piovra* had been the first to endorse the distinctive and successful Italianness of the Mafia story).

The 21 productions of the first decade (1988–1998) were, with few exceptions, the prerogative of public television. In those years the Rai produced and screened six editions of *La Piovra* (from the fourth to the ninth), made some forays into the milieu of Calabrian crime, addressed the hitherto unbroached issue of criminals turning state's evidence, initiated the somewhat odd process of reconverting Michele Placido from the role of Inspector Cattani, the anti-Mafia hero *par excellence*, into a man of honour who experiences a crisis of conscience (*Un uomo di rispetto/Man of Respect*, 1993): a prelude to the total reversal of roles that was to take place when the same actor was asked to play the boss of bosses Bernardo Provenzano in *L'ultimo padrino/The Last Godfather* (Canale 5, 2008), a Mediaset production.

As for commercial television, in the same period the two editions of *Donna d'onore/Woman of Honour* (Canale 5, 1990 e 1993) stand out as the first attempt to tell the story of a career Mafia woman in a Sicilian–American setting (although the story was definitely oriented towards the 'maternal melodrama'). The top model Carol Alt, at that time an icon of fashion and beauty, lent her charm to the character of the female *consigliori*.

Figure 6.1. Massimo Dapporto as the anti-Mafia hero Judge Giovanni Falcone, followed in the picture by his bodyguards, in the biopic *Giovanni Falcone* (Raiuno, 2006). Courtesy of RAI.

In the subsequent decade (1998–2008) the substantial production of public television has explored the biographical variant of the Mafia story to tell the lives of the heroes–martyrs who fell in the fight against macro-criminality *(Brancaccio,*[4] 2001; *Giovanni Falcone*[5] and the remake of *Joe Petrosino*, both in 2006) and of the Mafia boss Provenzano (*L'ultimo dei corleonesi/The Last of the Corleonesi*, 2007). Further Rai dramas have reconstructed the complex investigative work leading to the discovery and capture of the murderers of Judge Falcone (*L'attentatuni/The Big Assassination*, 2001); or they have drawn inspiration from the news for stories of testimony and civilian courage against organized crime, and have cultivated a small-scale feminine trend, to which I shall return.

I have recalled how the crime genre, by its constitution, is permeable to the influence of news and current events. The real and the imaginary, fact and fiction, cooperate in an often inextricable interrelationship to create and narrate stories. Even the most highly imaginative and visionary Italian Mafia story – obviously *La Piovra* – never ceased to maintain a connection with crime and political news, evoking it through an astute and intriguing game of allusions (or indeed anticipating it, according to a certain mythology that flourished around the saga at the time of its maximum popularity). That said, it is always possible to distinguish between, on the one hand, fiction that develops purely imaginary plots, regardless of whether they are reminiscent of real events in a more or less overt way; and on the other hand, the fiction that recalls in an explicit, transparent and recognizable fashion, real-life characters and events of the present day or the past, regardless of whether they subject reality to a greater or lesser imaginative transfiguration.

Once you have split the textual corpus in accordance with this binary classification, most of the Mafia stories turn out to be (as could easily have been predicted) the fruit of the imagination: not infrequently a melodramatic imagination, with or without social pretensions, which subordinates the repertoire of conventions and stereotypes of the Mafia story to a dramaturgy of excesses that is all too typical of melodrama. By contrast, the role of the crime news as a source of narrative inspiration does not reach a proportion even of one title in four in the corpus as a whole.

Nevertheless, the move from the first to the second decade has coincided with a noticeable increase in the offer of docudrama, from only 3 titles in the period 1988–1998 to 15 in the next decade. The stories of anti-Mafia heroes and martyrs – the priest Don Puglisi, the judges Falcone and Borsellino,[6] General Dalla Chiesa[7] – and of the bosses Riina and Provenzano and their captors, also of ordinary men and women who were yet capable of standing up against Mafia power, are all based on facts.

The phenomenon, to which the Rai and Mediaset have contributed in almost equal measure, probably does not have the impetuous character or the dimensions of a true irruption; but it is undeniable that from the end of the 1990s the pre-eminence of the imagined Mafia story has been somewhat undermined by the advent of news-inspired stories, facilitated by the increase in productive capacity. Creating new stories and innovative stories entails a broader diversification of the inspirational sources and the devices of return of the already known; and the news can offer to this end an invaluable source of characters and events that, in addition to being already familiar to the public, bring the added value of an aura of truthfulness and of real life (Buonanno, 2007).

Not by chance, the TV dramas that refer to news and current events obtained by far the highest ratings within the genre. With *Ultimo/The Last*[8](Canale 5, *1998*) and *Paolo Borsellino* (Canale 5, 2004), for example, Mediaset achieved two of the greatest successes in its history, whereas the biopic *Giovanni Falcone* (Raiuno, 2006) produced by public television, was the most watched programme in the 2006–2007 season. From the perspective of its capacity to generate successes and to arouse strong resonances in public opinion, it is perhaps true that real life borrowed from the news irrupts into TV drama.

The stellar ratings achieved by *La Piovra* 4 (14.025) and *La Piovra* 5 (12.476) in the first decade clearly remain unbeaten. This in part corroborates the sensational power of the narrative imagination underpinning that seminal saga; but it is also a testimony to the era that has just ended, when the still unchallenged appeal of generalist television allowed the Mafia story to display in the highest degree its intrinsic and lasting appeal ('mob stories are always hot') to television audiences (Tab. 1).

Table 1. The top ten Mafia docudramas inspired by the news in 1998–2008.

Title	Season	Channel	Audience (thousands)
Paolo Borsellino	04–05	Canale 5	10.834
Ultimo/The Last	98–99	Canale 5	8.930
La vita rubata/Stolen Life	07–08	Raiuno	7.604
Giovanni Falcone	06–07	Raiuno	7.597
Il capo dei capi/The Boss of Bosses	07–08	Canale 5	7.284
Il testimone/The Witness	00–01	Canale 5	6.954
Brancaccio	00–01	Raiuno	6.935
Il coraggio di Angela/The Bravery of Angela	07–08	Raiuno	6.412
L'ultimo dei Corleonesi/The Last of the Corleonesi	06–07	Raiuno	6.360
L'ultimo padrino/The Last Godfather	07–08	Canale 5	5.926

Heroes and villains

In film critic circles, and among gangster movie fans themselves, there was a long-held conviction that a genre with such intrinsic ties to the big screen (like the western, to which it is often compared in histories and theories of the cinema: Neale, 2002) could not adapt itself to the aesthetic and ethical ambience of television without losing some of its fundamental characteristics, thus becoming something other than itself. One example of this is the renunciation of the intense expressionist colours of the photography, which were one of the aesthetic hallmarks of the genre. Furthermore, the transition from the big to the small screen was seen to require (deplored) adjustments that compromise and misrepresent the focal point of the narrative, namely the crime and the criminals as the protagonists. This so to speak purist position, however clearly it may reflect anti-television prejudice, rightly identifies rewriting in accordance with its own principles as a prerogative exercised by television in appropriating – in the double sense of making things one's own and making them appropriate for the new context – genres codified by the cinema, or by other cultural and artistic forms.

In fact in cinema tradition the protagonist of the gangster movie or Mafia story is normally the criminal: the individual or the organization. The cinematographic construct of a criminal mythology and a Mafia mystique has found an effective instrument and consistent support precisely in the prominence of the negative hero as the protagonist, whether an individual personality or a group. There is no need to postulate a necessary or inevitable coincidence between the leading dramatic role and the dominant narrative perspective; but it is true that the diegetic centrality of the negative hero – which arouses fascination and public controversy in equal measure – in principle offers fertile ground for mythopoetic dynamics. Not by chance, the genre itself in its classic film version has codified from its beginnings, as an antidote or barrier against the mythicization of the gangster figure, a narrative structure in the shape of one ascending and another, equally relevant, falling trajectory as the prelude to the tragic and fatal defeat of the negative hero. Consider for example the death of the protagonist in Raoul Walsh's *White Heat* (1949), a cult gangster film. As he is pursued by the police, he shouts from the top of a building his boundless pride at having arrived on top of the world; then an explosive burst of flame puts an end to his life and his conquest.

For reasons that are still largely valid (despite the disclaimer provided by *The Sopranos* with all the force of a brilliant exception), the television environment, especially in the context of a generalist system, remains somewhat resistant to the adoption of the cinematographic canons of the gangster movie. In particular, the domestic and everyday nature of the medium sits uneasily with the features of the tragic narrative, while family viewing, mainly during prime time, militates against an excessive emphasis on villains as protagonists.

In consequence, the Mafia story, ever since its first appearance (*The Untouchables*) on the small screen in the late 1950s, has turned into a televisual variant that prefers its protagonists to come from the world of law and order rather than the criminal underworld. And it is this variant that most Italian TV drama has adopted. Taken as a whole, the productions whose stories of macro-criminality put institutional figures of State servants at centre stage are four times more numerous than those centred on criminal individuals and organizations. Examples of the latter category are the two editions of *Woman of Honor* (Canale 5), *A Man of Respect* (Raidue) in the 1990s, *The Last of the Corleonesi* (Raiuno), *The Boss of Bosses* and *The Last Godfather* (both on Canale 5) in the 2000s.

Figure 6.2. The capture of the Mafia boss Totò Riina (centre of the picture, played by Claudio Gioè) in the miniseries *The Boss of Bosses* (Canale 5, 2007). Courtesy of Mediaset.

What I have defined earlier as the diegetic centrality of the negative hero has little impact on the Italian Mafia story. It goes without saying that even if they are not protagonists or characters with much depth, Mafia characters in TV drama must still function as effective ingredients of the stories with a strong and lasting emotional, cognitive, ethical and aesthetic impact. The basically one-dimensional character of Totò Riina in *The Boss of Bosses* does not make the tale of the bloodthirsty ascent of the Corleonesi to the heights of 'Cosa Nostra' any less captivating; nor does it remove from the protagonist himself that grim fascination, like it or not, which is greatly deplored by the many who fear

Figure 6.3. Gabriel Garko as Tonio Fortebracci, the protagonist of the melodramatic Mafia story *Honour and Respect* (Canale 5, 2006, 2009). Courtesy of Mediaset.

rightly or wrongly that Mafia stories in film or television run the risk (without knowing how to avoid it) of showing the bosses in a favourable light. And more romantic than grim, perhaps, is the fascination emanated by the simplistically ambivalent character of Tonio Fortebracci, the villain protagonist – already a mythical figure for the members of the numerous fan clubs that have flourished on the web – of the melodramatic Mafia story *Honour and Respect*.

If macro-criminality and its exponents seldom emerge as the true protagonists of these stories, this is because they fulfil the opposing and complementary function of antagonists in the distribution of the roles. In a well-tempered narrative, and in particular in the Mafia story where conflict is mostly an essential component in the genre, the antagonists are crucial figures for the development of the plot and for the deeds of the protagonists themselves (and it is quite common, especially in films, to encounter protagonists who are eclipsed by more captivating, better built and better acted antagonists, given also a certain predilection on the part of authors and actors for negative characters, who are regarded as more intriguing and interesting). In widely practising the displacement of the criminal underworld from the protagonist position to the antagonist front, Italian TV drama has done no more than adhere to conventions that were established, for the reasons mentioned earlier, by the televisual variant of the gangster movie. Nevertheless the peculiarities of domestic storytelling, notably the conventional tendency to dampen down the dynamics of conflict whatever the narrative's generic frame, apart from the Mafia story, end up by creating conditions that are themselves unique: in the sense that the Mafia story becomes perforce the narrative territory where the representation of fierce conflicts is concentrated, and the Mafia and in general organized crime and its exponents appear in the dramaturgy (and in the politics of representation) of Italian TV drama as the antagonists *par excellence* and by antonomasia. A consequence and at the same time an eloquent testimony of this is the fact that the repertoire of conflicts involving a criminal antagonist or organized crime spills over from the province of the true Mafia story and infiltrates narratives of a different genre – there were at least 30 such cases in the twenty-year period – where it serves, if need be, to spice up the plotlines and heighten tension. In this connection the lesson of *La Piovra*, which pointed to the Mafia system (built on the alliance among organized crime, politics and finance) as the social evil of Italy, is still alive.

Oddly enough, however, well-constructed antagonist figures, complex criminal personalities whose facets go beyond cunning and violence or other limited sets of stereotypical characteristics, are seldom encountered. Whether or not this is by deliberate choice, everything in the Italian Mafia story happens – with few exceptions – as if the antagonistic and adversarial nature of organized crime were so self-evident and so completely taken for granted that it could easily and convincingly be personified in stereotypes, simplified characters and conventional clichés. As antagonists, these personify and portray the power and criminal threat after the manner of masks rather than individuals. They are the recurring and recognizable avatars – not in the mystic religious sense of the word, but in its metaphorical meaning of iconic simulation of reality – through which the Mafia, Camorra and 'Ndrangheta reveal (or disguise) themselves in Italian TV drama.

A male-dominated genre and its exceptions

Having preferred to assign the protagonist roles to the forces of law and order and the judiciary, the Italian Mafia story has become a factory of anti-Mafia heroes. Whether the characters in the story are completely imaginary, like Inspector Cattani in *La Piovra*, or borrowed by TV drama from real life – such as captain Ultimo, judges Falcone and Borsellino, General Dalla Chiesa, the eponymous protagonists of biographical docudramas – a fair number of institutional anti-Mafia heroes have joined the circle of the characters who defend legality and justice.

Figure 6.4. Giorgio Tirabassi (right) as the anti-Mafia hero Judge Paolo Borsellino in the biopic *Paolo Borsellino* (Canale 5, 2004). Courtesy of Mediaset.

Real or imaginary, martyrs or winners, the institutional heroes of the Mafia story (policemen, soldiers, magistrates) make up a group that is almost entirely mono-gender (male), except for a negligible female presence in just a few cases in twenty years. There would be no need to emphasize something that, in large part, was to be expected – and one could even admit that a genre with a high level of conflict and violence is perhaps not the most appropriate forum for an equal opportunities claim on behalf of protagonists – except that this is how, by contrast, the deviation that is concealed within the last cluster of stories is stressed.

I am referring to the much less numerous (18 titles) but by no means irrelevant group of Mafia stories that elect as protagonists not men of the institutions but members of civilian society, ethical and courageous citizens who, without embracing the mission of servants of the State and thus finding themselves in the position of unarmed heroes, nevertheless show active and proven willingness to tackle the power of organized crime. From *Il coraggio di parlare/The Courage to Speak* (Raiuno, 1991) to *Una sola debole voce/A Lone Weak Voice* (Raidue, 1999) to *Il testimone/The Witness* (Canale 5, 2001) to *A voce alta/Out Loud* (Raiuno, 2006) and *Il coraggio di Angela/The Bravery of Angela* (Raiuno, 2008), this further declination of the Mafia genre runs through the whole of the twenty-year period, appearing more frequently in the second decade: in tune with, first, the growing tendency of Italian TV drama to celebrate the everyday hero and, second, the irruption of the news into the Mafia story. It should be said that with one exception, this variant centred on everyday heroes has been cultivated solely by public television.

Within this latest narrative trend, a phenomenon has taken shape that is quantitatively minor (no more than six or seven titles), but deserves to be highlighted because of one exceptional characteristic, to which I have referred earlier, i.e., the leading role of women as anti-Mafia heroines. The Mafia story is innately male, by reason not so much of its anthropological faithfulness to the macho centrality and masculine culture of 'Cosa Nostra', as the deep symbolic connections traditionally established between violence, power and money – the dominant themes in the Mafia story – and the social construction of masculinity. (In truth, it is not so unusual in present-day criminal organizations, especially the Camorra, for women to direct activities and to be in charge, even if only in a mostly supplementary role, legitimized by kinship with a male figure, father or husband or brother.) As a rule, then, the genre does not contemplate female protagonists either in criminal circles or, for specular reasons, in the institutional milieu of the fight against crime. There were volatile signs of change in some of the projects on American TV networks (to which I referred at the beginning) and, without going as far as America, in a single production on the French satellite channel (*Mafiosa*, Canal Plus). But to revert to Italian TV drama, in twenty years of Mafia stories there have been only rare exceptions to the rule of male protagonists on the opposing fronts of crime and the law.[9]

Yet outside the ambit of legitimate or illegitimate violence, it sometimes happens that women are protagonists in Mafia stories as exponents of a civilian society that is averse to crime and refuses to surrender to it; or as rebellious individuals who, from inside the

Figure 6.5. Lunetta Savino as Angela, a woman who dared to challenge the Neapolitan camorra, in the reality-based tv movie *The Bravery of Angela* (Raiuno, 2008). Courtesy of RAI.

criminal environments or milieux that collude with organized crime, to which they are bound by cogent family ties, develop motivations and summon the strength to break with the Mafia culture and system. The motivations and the strength of female refusal are triggered off and sustained most often by unbearably wounded feelings, by threats or the experience of the irreparable loss of 'important others' in the circle of family and friends, and not least by the maternal intent to keep their children safe.

Angela, who has lost her husband and elder son in a blood feud between Calabrian clans, refuses to embrace the role of vestal virgin of the vendetta cult that is assigned to women of the clan and faces up to the risks and sorrows of life on the run to save her younger son, barely in his teens, from the grip of a deadly culture of violence (*Un bambino in fuga/A Child on the Run*, Raiuno, 1990). In *Liberate mio figlio/Set my Son Free* (Raiuno, 1992), based on the true story of a kidnapping, another brave mother is the main instrument in freeing her son from ruthless imprisonment in a pit in the Aspromonte woods:[10] it is her intense appeal to the kidnappers' mothers, in the name of the universal feelings of maternal love for their children, that breaks down the barrier of *omertà* and brings the dramatic story to a happy ending.

By contrast *Non parlo più/I Shall Say No More* (Raidue, 1995), another TV drama inspired by a true story, starts with the loss of a father figure. The female protagonist turns State's evidence to exact revenge on the murderer of her Mafia father, whom she saw being assassinated when she was a child; then it is the meeting and rapport with a judge (in real life Judge Borsellino) that encourages the young woman's painful process of developing a civic awareness imbued with the values of legality and justice. Another tormented inner struggle is what induces the female protagonist of *Una sola debole voce/A Lone Weak Voice* (Raidue, 1999), an upper-class lady of Palermo who is faced with the unexpected discovery of her husband's involvement with the Mafia, to make the difficult choice of breaking with the codes of *omertà*, the marital pact and the particularistic protection of family interests and agreeing to testify against the Mafia in a trial. In *Donne di mafia/Mafia Women* (Raidue, 2001) the character Teresa, who married a Mafia gangster for love without initially knowing about his criminal activities, succeeds in her arduous purpose of convincing her husband to repent, after an indirect revenge wreaked on a family member brings into the open the violence hidden behind the reassuring appearances of a normal life. Finally *Il coraggio di Angela/The Bravery of Angela* (Raiuno, 2008) – a TV drama that echoes the true story of a female entrepreneur of Naples, nominated by *Time* magazine in 2005 as one of Europe's heroes – tells the story of an indomitable female character who emerges victorious from the battle against racketeering, thanks to high and firm ethical standards, the support of a united family and her inspiring mission to save the adolescent son of her cousin from the evil influence of his father, a Camorra boss.

These women are mothers, daughters and wives, whether or not aware of their husbands' Mafia involvement or collusion, who are spurred on by the trauma of a tragic event or a shocking revelation to repudiate and fight against the rules of an illegal or violent life system – for affective reasons or because of a burgeoning moral conscience or both. There are also women in these dramas who, belonging to lawful society and sharing its principles and values, refuse to surrender to blackmail and abuses on the part of organized crime. In both cases the anti-Mafia heroines of TV drama, whether they choose to escape the grip of the Mafia environment or rebel against being the victims of criminal power, are characterized by the firm intent (to different extents instinctive and reflexive) to revoke, withdraw and deny their consent to the universe of Mafia values and behaviour: TV drama thus entrusts to female characters the task of reminding viewers that not only the repressive actions of the forces of law and order (carried out by male protagonists) but also the loss and denial of consensus can help to undermine, both internally and externally, the cultural foundations of organized crime's power.

What renders these stories interesting and significant is not the central role *per se* given to female characters, as a male-dominated genre like the Mafia story must nevertheless always make room for women (if for no other reason than in consideration of female viewers of TV drama). More important is the radical reversal of the main cultural function effectively fulfilled by women in Mafia society as broadly understood (not only 'Cosa Nostra'). In fact, whether their importance is basically limited to the familiar roles of mother, wife and daughter – though these roles are the cornerstone of blood families – and to the function, performed in shadow and silence, of faithful ancillary support; or whether they play an active part in criminal enterprises as now happens even in the oligarchic organizational structure of 'Cosa Nostra': Mafia women are above all the custodians and agents of the crucial task of inculcating the Mafia codes and values of honour, *omertà* and vengeance into the younger generation, and the guarantors for the handing down of Mafia culture from one generation to the next.

It is within the power of the imagination to rework reality. This small corpus of TV drama does that by means of the inversion of reality, a device to which popular culture has traditionally had recourse when adumbrating imaginary worlds (Cocchiara, 1981). The civilian heroines of the Italian Mafia story – sometimes Mafia women in the true sense, sometimes not involved with organized crime but for some reason in a perilous relationship with it – seem not only committed to testifying that criminal power can be resisted, but also determined to break the inter-generational continuity of the criminogenic Mafia culture, by assuming the salvific role of the natural or vicarious mother. Equally, the more active leadership role taken by women in real-life criminal organizations, in a questionable process of emancipation or pseudo-emancipation (Fiandaca, 2007; Ingrascì, 2007) entirely internal and subordinate to the Mafia power system, is reconverted by TV drama into a process of female empowerment that instead purports to be one of total emancipation *from* this very power system.

Hence, under the banner of the male genre of the Mafia story, in the context of narratives that revolve around criminal worlds where women's possible access to decision-making and leading roles does not substantially modify their subordinate social status in relation to males, or their culturally conservative function in the bosom of the family, a feminine image has taken shape that is among the most significant that have been created by Italian TV drama in the past 20 years.

The Mafia is everywhere

At the end of the first decade of the twenty-first century there are signs that the presence of the Mafia genre in Italy's fictionscape is being scaled down. After 2008 the supply of mob stories has been reduced to one title per season on the commercial networks, whereas the drama department of public television has announced that 'over-exploited' themes such as macro-criminality would be included, but only to a minor extent, in production plans for the near future.

As the overview provided by this chapter demonstrates, the veritable goldmine of the Mafia story has indeed been intensively exploited by Italian TV drama for at least twenty years. But although broadcasters have good grounds for fearing, and therefore wish to forestall, the effects of saturating their viewers, it would be opportune to await more decisive and lasting evidence before pronouncing the decline or the end of the 'Mafia cycle' in television imaginary.

The fact is that the Mafia or the Mafias, but in particular 'Cosa Nostra', continue to exert a powerful mental and emotional grip on a great many Italians, predicated on the intriguing ambivalence between revulsion and scorn for a criminal system that is socially pernicious and morally condemnable, and the sinister appeal of a power system that epitomizes a success story, albeit a depraved one, in its capacity to make a name for itself, expand and command (Arlacchi, 2009). The serious and pervasive nature of the historic social problem constituted by the presence of large criminal organizations on Italian soil does not suffice, of itself, to explain the pre-eminent position occupied by the Mafia theme not merely in television, but also in the publishing business – where recently the *Gomorra* phenomenon gave the trend an extra thrust – and in documentary films and the cinema in general. Since World War II the Italian film industry has produced dozens and dozens of Mafia movies, some of them made by Italy's greatest film directors: Pietro Germi (*In nome della legge/In the Name of the Law*, 1949); Francesco Rosi (*Salvatore Giuliano*, 1962; *Le mani sulla città/Hands on the City*, 1963; *Lucky Luciano*, 1973; *Dimenticare Palermo/Forget Palermo*, 1990); Damiano Damiani (*Il giorni della civetta/The Day of the Owl*, 1968); Giuseppe Ferrara (*Il sasso in bocca/Stone in the Mouth*, 1970; *Cento giorno a Palermo/100 Days in Palermo*, 1984); Giuseppe Tornatore (*Il camorrista/The Camorrist*, 1986).

The twenty-year period embraced by my survey of TV drama coincided with an era that was very critical for Italy's film industry; nevertheless more than 30 Mafia movies were made in those years, over half of them in the 2000s.[11] Although a significant number of these films, certainly the most critically acclaimed, can be included in the category known in Italy as 'civic engagement cinema' – characterized by a dramatic structure, a realistic style and the purpose of conveying social and political criticism of the evils of Italy – it is interesting to observe that the cinema has been the first to perceive and exploit the peculiar flexibility of the Mafia story by putting it at the service of many other genres. Social drama, the detective movie, the biopic, the historical film, comedy, farce, *sceneggiata* (the cinematic transposition of a form of musical theatre that is typical of popular Neapolitan culture), spaghetti westerns: the plots and *topoi* of the Mafia story have been incorporated and re-framed within a wide range of genres, giving rise to mutual contamination whose outcomes have sometimes proved valuable in terms of originality (for example Roberta Torre's musical *Tano da morire/Tano Is to Die*, 1997; or Paolo Sorrentino's psychological thriller *Le conseguenze dell'amore/The Consequences of Love*, 2004). 'The Mafia is everywhere' is a leitmotiv in the everyday conversation of many Italians: such a statement of ubiquity can be considered to be largely true, as far as cinematic genres are concerned.

The same thing has happened in TV drama. Italian TV drama has for its part refashioned the Mafia story into the generic forms of maternal melodrama, social melodrama, heroic biopic, police procedural, prison drama and road movie, and has inserted it (if only in secondary or peripheral plotlines) wherever it might serve to add force, colour or pathos to a narrative. The years when the trend created by *La Piovra* stimulated the demand for and supply of Mafia stories coincided with the expansion of the Italian broadcasting industry, which gave impetus to the production and consumption of home-made drama. During this time organized crime and in particular, once again, 'Cosa Nostra' has been an invaluable source of inspiration for Italian televisual storytelling, functioning as a reserve of dramaturgic form and narrative material that was not only endowed with generic versatility and widely usable, but had the added value of legitimization deriving from the prerogative of dealing with, evoking and commemorating one of Italy's 'dramatic social realities'.

Over the years Italian TV drama has constructed, and gradually updated, a vast and multi-purpose repertoire which, though not the only one of its kind, has nevertheless been one of the main providers of the elements and narrative devices – protagonists, antagonists, plots and conflicts – which domestic fiction has interwoven into the tale of Italian society at the beginning of the twenty-first century. Does the repeated insistence on the 'dramatic social reality' of crime and the Mafia culture – addressed in sometimes fresh and unconventional ways, but more often predictable and stereotyped – serve to bolster the mythology of the Mafia? Or by contrast, does focusing the narrative standpoint firmly on positive characters help to shatter the fascination of evil by enhancing and honouring the heroes and heroines, real or imaginary, of the anti-Mafia battle?

There is no need to appropriate the insoluble dilemma that stirs up public opinion in Italy every time the recurring controversy about the Mafia story on television is re-ignited. It is enough to emphasize that the alternative offered by this dilemma depicts rather a coexistence of mutually attractive opposites, in other words a powerfully captivating ambivalence, on which is predicated the endless fascination of a large viewing public for Mafia stories on the small screen.

Notes

1. *Gomorra. Viaggio nell'impero economico e nel sogno di dominio della camorra* (2006)/ *Gomorrah. Italy's other Mafia* (2007), by Roberto Saviano, is a gripping and disquieting non-fiction novel that throws a harsh light on the ramifications of the power system of large-scale crime in Naples. *Gomorra* became an international bestseller and was listed by the *New York Times* as one of the most important books of 2007. It was the inspiration for a much awarded cinematic docudrama with the same title, made in 2008 by the director Matteo Garrone.
2. First season, episode 8 'The legend of Tennessee Moltisanti'.
3. Joe Petrosino was an Italo–American policeman who lived in New York at the turn of the nineteenth and twentieth centuries. He headed a special team ('the Italian branch') consisting entirely of Italians and led a relentless fight against the Mafia-type organizations (the Black hand) that had infiltrated immigrant communities. He was assassinated in March 1909 during an investigative mission to Palermo.
4. The miniseries takes the name of the district of Palermo where the parish priest Don Pino Puglisi was assassinated in September 1993. He was well known for his dedication to saving marginalized young men living in areas of urban deprivation from being 'conscripted' into organized crime.
5. See note 3, Chapter 3.
6. The name of the judge Paolo Borsellino is constantly associated with that of Giovanni Falcone; the two judges had worked together for a long time and finally shared the same tragic fate. Borsellino, who was fully aware of being a 'dead man walking' after the attack on Falcone, was in turn the victim of a Mafia killing in July 1992.
7. General of the Carabinieri Carlo Alberto Dalla Chiesa was primarily responsible for the capture of Red Brigade terrorists in the 1970s. In May 1982, he became Prefect of Palermo, where a fierce Mafia war was raging; he was assassinated in September of the same year.
8. Code name of Carabinieri captain Sergio De Caprio. He directed the operation to capture the boss Riina, who was arrested in 1993 after over 20 years in hiding.
9. However I should point out that from the 2008–2009 season, so just beyond the twenty-year period of my analysis, the Canale 5 series *Squadra antimafia/Antimafia Squad* (2008–) completely feminized the poles of conflict, attributing both the role of protagonist and antagonist to female characters (respectively the deputy police officer Claudia Mares, head of the anti-mafia squad in Palermo and Rosalia Abate, widow of a mafia boss who is to succeed him in the 'family' leadership).
10. A mountainous massif in the heart of Calabria, covered with thick woods where members of the 'Ndrangheta' on the run used to hide; here the victims of kidnappings were held prisoner. This was a lucrative criminal activity engaged in by Calabrian gangsters, especially in the 1970s and 1980s.
11. I list just a few of them: Marco Tullio Giordana: *I cento passi/One Hundred Steps*, 2000; Pasquale Scimeca: *Placido Rizzotto*, 2000; Paolo Sorrentino: *Le conseguenze dell'amore/The Consequences of Love*, 2004; Matteo Garrone: *Gomorra*, 2008; Marco Amenta: *La siciliana ribelle/The Rebel Sicilian Girl*, 2008; Marco Risi: *Fort Apasc*, 2009.

Chapter 7

Life Stories:
A Heroic Enclave and the Rise of the Religious Biopic

The rebirth of the biopic

The biographical genre, also known as the biopic, along with the Mafia story and the historical drama (see next chapter) has been a cornerstone of Italian television fiction, a fundamental component in its most recent phase of development.

Unlike the Mafia story, that only established itself definitively in supply and consumption in the mid-1980s, biography (like historical narrative with which it is often intermingled) has deeper roots in Italian television fiction. It actually dates back to the 1960s in the *sceneggiati* series dedicated to the lives of 'great Italians': *Vita di Michelangelo/ Life of Michelangelo* (1964), *Vita di Dante/Life of Dante* (1965), *Vita di Cavour/Life of Cavour* (1967), *La vita di Leonardo Da Vinci /The Life of Leonardo da Vinci* (1971) and many others. And it was television biography actually, which enjoyed the privilege of sporting a *cinema d'autore* visiting card when the direction of the philosophers' tetralogy in the 1970s – *Socrate/Socrates* (1971), *Blaise Pascal* (1972), *Agostino di Ippona/St Augustine of Hippo* (1972) and *Cartesius /Descartes* (1974) – was entrusted to none other than Roberto Rossellini, the world-famous master of neo-realist cinema.

From this early stage, imbued with the pedagogic fervour of the public service, a rather unflattering 'narrative image' (Ellis, 1992) emerged of television biography as a genre weighed down by its didactic armour, resorting too easily to pedantic tones and deploying the conventional and hypocritical modes dear to hagiography. It seems that television biography is always accompanied by 'low repute', as we shall soon see, and Italy is no exception to this. But although such an image should not be regarded, even today, as entirely without foundation – it gets churned out regularly by television critics who tend to show little goodwill towards domestic drama – the rebirth of the biopic, after a partial eclipse between the late 1970s and the early 1990s, does not seem to have suffered from its modest aesthetic status. In fact biography has played a significant role in domestic drama, over the last two decades. There is no doubt that 'an active interest in life-stories continues' (Anderson and Lupo, 2008: 50), in Italy as elsewhere. However, the choice of whose lives are considered worthy of biographical treatment tends to change: over time; according to geo-cultural space; and equally as important, from one medium to another.

My examination of the biography genre in Italian television fiction will begin with an overall discussion of the question I have raised earlier, i.e., *whose* lives are considered worthy of biopics at different times, and in different contexts and media. The theme will

Figure 7.0. Alessio Boni plays the great painter Michelangelo Merisi da Caravaggio in the biopic *Caravaggio* (Raiuno, 2007), whose visual style recalls the dramatic use of lighting introduced by the innovative and trasgressive artist.

unfold amidst the glittering cultural conceptions of heroism and fame, following in the wake of other, analogous changes in the historical evolution of the biographical genre and its transmigrations from one medium to another. Basically my purpose here is to shed light on the peculiar features observed in contemporary Italian biopics with respect both to trends emerging elsewhere – Hollywood movies, American television – and the corpus of biographies produced by Italian television itself in the early decades of its history.

As a preliminary step the supertext of life stories aired in the twenty-year period 1989–2009 will be divided into the different 'heroic typologies' of those individuals deemed worthy of biographical treatment. In providing evidence of the distinctive features of the Italian biopic, this typological approach will make visible a characteristic that is almost certainly unique: the very high number of biographies of religious personalities (saints, popes, biblical and gospel figures). Therefore, I will dedicate the last part of this chapter to the contextualized reconstruction of the rise of the religious biopic in Italian drama at the turn of the twentieth and twenty-first centuries.

Anti-heroic society

In tune with a typical intellectual tendency to conceptualize the times we live in as 'post-something', we are apparently living in an age that a recent book (Sheehan, 2008) has defined as 'post-heroic'. Proof of the advent of the post-heroic age in Western, mostly European, societies, can be found especially in the shift of collective attitudes towards war: today it is rejected, opposed as never before in history, but up to the 1950s it had been almost ennobled and exalted as the setting for heroic gestures and the achievement of hero status.

Whether or not you believe in the current transition to a post-heroic age, it cannot be denied that the pre-eminent identification of the hero with the warrior or military commander, handed down to us by mythology and classical and medieval (and other) epics, clearly contributes to the arousal of suspicion (and this is putting it mildly!) with respect to heroism, given the present-day pacifist Zeitgeist. Yet it seems that the supremacy of the armed hero had already begun to decline before the 'obsolescence of war' (Sheehan, 2008: XVII) in twentieth-century European history, according to an interesting and plausible hypothesis of the close correlation between heroic typology and the different ages of communication (Strate, 1994). To go back to the distinction between orality and literacy propounded by Walter Ong (Ong, 1982), the warrior hero figure flourished mainly in ages and cultures where the predominant means of communication was the spoken word. The prodigious deeds of heroes who were armed mainly with outstanding courage and physical strength were in fact endowed with a high degree of 'memorability', which is an essential requirement for oral cultures, consigned to the volatility of the spoken word, to be handed down from one generation to the next.

Writing, and especially the role of the moveable type printing in forming a 'lettered' society, went on to create the conditions for a different heroic typology, in which the criterion of outstanding and intrepid action (understood in the mental and intellectual sense, not only in the physical) remained paramount. Thus, ever since the arrival, many centuries earlier, of an age of printing (Eisenstein, 1993), the warrior figure had begun sharing his heroic status with scientists, inventors, explorers, creators and artists.

Heroes are not what they used to be; perhaps they just don't exist any more. In accordance with the concept of a post-heroic age, a number of scholars and commentators have maintained in recent times that the West has now become 'a world without heroes' (Roche, 1987). In the 'growing corpus of contemporary literature decrying the loss of traditional heroes' (Drucker and Cathcart, 1994: 3), the authoritative precursor should probably be identified as Joseph Campbell. In the closing pages of *The Hero with a Thousand Faces* (Campbell, 1993), a celebrated and influential study on the mythical hero originally printed in 1949, Campbell noted how far removed from the present day the symbolic universe was, that had produced the legendary heroes of ancient myths. Human society has become estranged from and inhospitable towards traditional heroes: they just don't live here any more.

Some time later, at the beginning of the 1960s, Daniel Boorstin – in a book (Boorstin, 1992) that is still capable nearly half a century later of illuminating our awareness of the cultural phenomena that are endemic in our present-day mediatized society – was to maintain that erstwhile heroes were being dethroned by 'celebrities' created by the media. I shall turn later to the theme of media celebrities; but now I just want to take my cue from some of the author's observations on the suspicious and disenchanted attitudes, sometimes demythologizing to the point of defamation, that inform our present-day sentiments and common opinions concerning heroes and heroism. 'We see greatness [of heroes] as an illusion', wrote Boorstin (1992: 51). Perhaps even as a burden on an imperfect and unhappy society, one might add – especially in the light of the exorbitant and persistent good fortune that continues to smile on the witty remark made by Galileo in Bertolt Brecht's play: 'Unhappy is the land that needs a hero' (Brecht and Bentley, 1994: 115).

Nevertheless, there is room for discussion concerning the advent of a post-heroic era. Clearly, we cannot deny the existence of gaps and discontinuities between the present and the past, as far as heroic conceptions and practices are concerned. Rather we should observe how the definition of the post-heroic era, limited to characterizing the present in terms of temporal succession and cultural eclipse in relation to a previous heroic age, completely sidesteps the true rupture, the turning point in the passing of an epoch. What truly characterizes the world in which we live is not so much the fact of coming later and leaving behind the heroic worlds of the past (as is implied by the prefix 'post'), but the existence of a particular set of conditions that have favoured, and continue to nourish, cultural trends of hostility towards heroism (which requires us to have recourse to the prefix 'anti').

In other words: however far they may be along the road to a possible eclipse, heroes (real or imaginary) still inhabit the present; and it is not such a rare occurrence to come across lives, deeds and personalities that are truly heroic, provided that one knows how to recognize them. Therefore, it is not entirely true that we live in a world without heroes. What matters is that the small or large amount of heroism, traditional or modern, that still exists in our times is exposed to the tensions of an anti-heroic critique, more strident and widespread than ever before. Intolerant and demythologizing elements have not been slow in the past in making their presence felt: Voltaire admitted to having little love for heroes ('ils font trop de fracas/they make too much noise'),[1] Ralph Waldo Emerson declared that 'every hero becomes a bore at last' (Gumpert, 1994: 61); but what we are seeing today is the apparently irresistible advance in public opinion of an anti-heroic rejection of huge collective proportions. Rather than post-heroic, the present age lends itself better to being defined as *anti*-heroic.

In a fine essay published at the beginning of the 1990s, Mike Featherstone did not hesitate to state that 'Western modernity ... has led to an *assault* [my italics] on the heroic life' (Featherstone, 1992: 173). One of the main 'assailants' he felt was feminism, with its critique of the masculine and male chauvinist values that were held to constitute the framework of heroic conceptions. But ultimately Featherstone, like Alvin Gouldner before him, maintained that if heroism had become a contentious concept in Western societies, this was due above all to the growing pre-eminence of everyday life, in conformity with the present-day culture of consumption and leisure. Everyday life and heroic life seem in fact like two poles of an antinomy that cannot be reconciled: it is not by chance that the legendary hero's journey ritually starts with his abandonment of the ordinary world. Everydayness is the province of ordinary existence, of common sense, regular habits and at the same time (and increasingly) the immanent horizon in which the search for well-being and personal self-achievement is carried out. As opposed to this, the heroic life is realm of unique experiences, of undertakings that are out of the ordinary, where great individual virtues responding to the appeal of transcendence are put at the service of objectives aimed at the common good. Furthermore, heroism demands courage, it entails suffering, it exposes one to dangers and exacts the supreme test of facing and overcoming the fear of death; whereas everyday life embraces aspirations for a happy existence, lightened by the pleasures of ludic and consumerist practices, rewarded by the satisfactions of loving relationships and sociable activity and above all sheltered as much as possible from the risky events that remind humans of their mortality – which, as we know, is intolerable. In the conception and modern experience of everyday life, therefore, there resides a potential for criticizing the heroic life, pointed out by Gouldner over 30 years ago: 'I have suggested repeatedly that EDL (everyday life) is a *counter*-concept, that it gives expression to a *critique* of a certain kind of life, specifically, the heroic, achieving, performance-centred existence' (Gouldner, 1975, quoted in Featherstone, 1992: 164).

However the many 'accidental heroes' (according to the superficial cliché reiterated by the media) who inhabit our world speak to us, among other things, of the ambivalence of everyday life: it is a polarity that can be alternative to, and critical of, the heroic life but also a potential humus of new typologies of heroes who are fused and confused with common people.

The most impressive among these new typologies is directly related to the presence and influence of the media in today's societies. I am referring again to 'media celebrities', those individuals whose fame is generated and nourished mainly by modern communication media, in particular by television. Media celebrities are the heroes of our times and have taken the place of traditional heroes in their function as role models for individuals, mainly for young people. As Mark Rowlands (2008) convincingly maintains, media celebrities testify to and benefit from a radical cultural shift in the concept of fame. Whereas at one time fame was a relatively scarce asset and constituted the acknowledgement of and reward for a special talent or an outstanding achievement, or a demonstration of excellence, it has nowadays become a commodity that is almost universally available and, above all, 'unconnected to any achievement or excellence in any recognized form' (Rowlands, 2008: 25). Daniel Boorstin had already in his day diagnosed the tautological nature of this contemporary variant of fame, the possessor being in most cases purely and simply 'a person who is known for his well-knownness' (Boorstin, 1992: 57). Only in an anti-heroic age and culture can those who are merely 'known for their well-knownness' rise to the rank of heroes and enjoy the benefits of fame.

The biography genre and the shifting definition of fame

Although it is not totally devoid of the anti-heroic influences of the present age, popular narrative is not short of heroes, and still nourishes our fantasy with stories of heroic lives and personalities, whether they spring from our imagination or from real life (Bechelloni, 2010).

Telling the stories of heroes should in no way be underestimated or trivialized, as it is crucial to their very existence. Nobody reaches the status of hero without fundamental support by a story (oral, written or audiovisual) that discloses his or her heroic action and value. 'Without the story and the storyteller there can be no fame, and without fame, individual acts, no matter how courageous, become part of the passing parade' (Drucker and Cathcart, 1994: 10).

We should take the opportunity here to bring in some remarks on the biography, the genre that is entrusted with the task of telling such stories. The narrative genre of biography suffers from a sort of 'imbalance of status', which affects its position not so much in the literary or historiographical sphere as in popular media communication: press, cinema and, of particular interest to us, television. The imbalance is to be found in the contrast between the relative pre-eminence that the genre has enjoyed in cinematic and televisual production and, parallel to this, in viewers' consumption preferences and, on the other hand, a seemingly widespread neglect[2] on the part of scholars and critics. In this connection, I might mention a number of authoritative contributors who entirely agree with one another, despite a distance of more than half a century between them. In the opening of his famous study on biographies in the popular American press in the first half of the twentieth century, Leo Lowenthal observed that 'surprisingly enough, not very much attention has been paid to this phenomenon' (Lowenthal, 1944: 109). For his part Steve Neale, in placing the biopic among the 'major genres' of Hollywood films, emphasized the lack of 'critical esteem' (Neale, 2000: 60) which, with very few exceptions – George Custen's (1992) study, to which I shall refer shortly – has been a constant feature of the genre's history. Finally, Dennis Bingham, in his very recent and impressive work, makes a point in the introduction, of emphasizing the 'low repute' of this 'respectable genre' (Bingham, 2010: 3).

In fact, apart from short phases of decline, biographies have regularly helped the Hollywood film industry to achieve outstanding success at the box office and prestigious recognition in the form of Oscars – nominations and awards. I need only recall *Lawrence of Arabia* (D. Lean, 1962), *Gandhi* (R. Attenborough, 1982), *Schindler's List* (S. Spielberg,

1993), *Amadeus* (M. Forman, 1984), *Erin Brockovich* (S. Soderbergh, 2000), *A Beautiful Mind* (R. Howard, 2001), *Capote* (B. Miller, 2005), *Walk the Line* (J. Mangold, 2005), *The Queen* (S. Frears, 2006), *Milk* (G. Van Sant, 2008), *La vie en rose* (O. Dahan, 2008), *The King's Speech* (T. Hooper, 2010). At the same time the biopic has been and still is, within and through the transformation of televisual systems, a resource of creativity and popularity for broadcasting networks and even more so for narrowcasting. In the United States, as part of the move to recover and reuse TV movie and miniseries formats as instruments of 'channel branding' (Lotz, 2009), basic and premium cable networks have started to invest regularly in the production of biographical TV dramas, for instance *Georgia O'Keeffe* (Lifetime, 2009), *The Reagans* (Showtime, 2003), *Johnny Cash* (A&E, 2005), *House of Saddam* (HBO/BBC, 2008), *Into the Storm: Churchill at War* (HBO/BBC, 2009), *Temple Grandin* (HBO 2010). In Great Britain, the new channels created by the BBC for terrestrial digital television, BBC3 and BBC4, are relying on biographies to expand the small niche audiences for narrowcasting (even at the cost of boring and displeasing the critics). For their part, the major British networks do not refrain from appealing to a genre that counts numerous classics, as well as contemporary masterpieces, of English television, from *I, Claudius* (BBC, 1976) to *Miss Austen Regrets* (BBC, 2008).

I have hitherto referred more than once to the notion of fame. In fact, this is exactly what we are concerned with: fame, and personalities who in a biography receive the seal and consecration of a renown already acquired by virtue of special talents, heroic deeds, entire lives that are exceptional to some extent. Fame is to be understood as a form of 'glorious renown', traditionally 'associated with respect, and not just respect but deserved respect' (Rowlands, 2008: 8). The biography genre is the only one whose very existence and *raison d'être* rests on exemplary courage, cultural acknowledgement and the social esteem of fame acquired by men and women, creators of great things and heroic achievements in the most diverse fields of human action.

George Custen was right in maintaining that 'publicly defining fame' (Custen, 1992: 215) is the 'cultural role' of the biography genre; just as it gives many viewers an accessible version of history, biography offers observers and cultural analysts privileged access to the shifting conceptions of heroism and fame that are expressed, at a given moment, in media texts and discourses. Leo Lowenthal, already quoted, was the first scholar to analyse biographies in this sense; and although his pioneering work relates to magazines, not cinema or television, it constitutes an indispensable reference point for illuminating and in part anticipating cultural trends that were destined to emerge in films and later in television. Lowenthal's study, carried out on a vast corpus of biographical articles published over a period of 40 years (1901–1941) in two popular American magazines, is too well known and I shall provide no more than a brief summary here. It is enough to bear in mind that the results of his research throw light on a progressive and decisive reconfiguration of the typology of the biographical subjects, who in the first twenty years of the twentieth century were chosen primarily from the political and military élites, professional people and businessmen, but were rapidly replaced in successive decades by popular figures of the world of art[3] and entertainment. In Lowenthal's definition, 'idols of production' – an aristocracy of individuals of outstanding qualities and virtues, inspired by and the potential inspirers of elevated ideals – have definitely given way to 'idols of consumption', emblematic figures of a society that puts leisure and entertainment at the centre of its own concerns.

It is not necessary to share Lowenthal's Frankfurtish disdain for 'mass idols' (or by contrast a certain idealization of 'idols of production'), to recognize his merit in having acutely diagnosed for the first time a cultural shift that was soon to leave its mark on the evolution of the biography genre in the creative and productive context of other media.

In Hollywood cinema, as we learn from Custen's study, biopics, up to the beginning of the 1940s, drew their subjects from the traditional élites: monarchs, famous politicians and businessmen, renowned personalities from the worlds of art and science. There was no lack of biographies of stars of stage and screen, through which Hollywood celebrated itself, but these were a relative minority. It was in the next twenty years that the shift, already detected by Lowenthal in popular magazines, became evident. In the course of the 1940s and 1950s the constant advance of 'idols of consumption' reshaped the 'fame agenda' of film biopics; the proportion of entertainers, initially fewer than 10%, rose to 28% of the total of biographies produced in the 1950s (Custen 1992: 169), drawing in their wake sports champions, while those representing decision-making and artistic élites declined in number, though they did not disappear altogether. A new élite was emerging that had created its own fame, pursuing careers in the world of entertainment.

But the advent of the new paradigmatic figure of contemporary fame did not itself alter the basic prerequisite, the necessary (if not only) condition that makes a life worthy of being narrated: the cinematographic biopic continued to require from its own subjects, whether political leaders or show business personalities, a certain dimension of greatness, a heroic inclination, admirable behaviour and, in short, evidence of a personality and existence at least partially outstanding, which have already received public acknowledgment in tributes made to their fame.

This condition started to fade, maintains Custen, when the biography genre (along with others) migrated to television in the course of the 1960s. Quite rapidly, in fact, television rewrote the biopic's rules, changing its main component fundamentally by completely overturning the fame agenda: those being fêted were no longer the people who were respected for having achieved great things in a particular field, but ordinary people, who became the protagonists of TV biopics – 'unremarkable' individuals who were suddenly and fleetingly pulled out of the anonymity of their everyday lives by some unexpected and disruptive event. It should be understood that ordinary people did not occupy all of the protagonistic limelight; show business celebrities still took up a lot of space and the biographies of famous people did not entirely disappear; but there is no doubt that through this form of apparent 'democratization' of a fame that is less and less predicated on excellence and heroism, the biography genre is transforming its own cultural role into fulfilling the mission – embraced by a large part of contemporary television – of giving everyone his or her 15 minutes of fame, as predicted by Andy Warhol.

Custen was writing in the early 1990s. His data, as well as his considerations on the televisual biopic, were influenced (though he makes no explicit mention of this) by the substantial presence of TV movies (Rapping, 1992) on American networks; these, often in the rushed form of the 'instant movie', brought facts and personalities from the newspapers to the screen, drawing narrative material from the sensational press. A case in point is the biopics produced by ABC (*The Amy Fisher story*, 1993) and CBS (*Casualties of Love*, 1993) on the so-called Lolita of Long Island.[4] Sometimes the sensational deed was related to a relevant social issue: *The Burning Bed* (NBC, 1984), starring Farrah Fawcett, focused on domestic violence and drew on the true story of a Michigan housewife who killed her abusive husband by setting fire to his bed.

As for more recent years, the information that we can gather from a range of sources – specialized magazines, the sites of TV networks, other online resources – confirms the 'demotic turn' (Turner, 2010a), as Graeme Turner defines the growing visibility of ordinary people on television, in the biographic genre. Lifetime, a cable network for mainly female viewers, continues for instance to tell cases of women who have survived breast cancer (*Why I Wore Lipstick to My Mastectomy*, 2006) and of girls who have mysteriously disappeared on tropical islands (*Natalee Holloway*, 2009). Yet there are no doubts about the overwhelming presence in today's television biopics of celebrities from the world of entertainment and show business: film and television stars, singers, ballet dancers, authors and performers of every musical genre. These personalities, famous examples of artistic careers that in any case demand some degree of talent and commitment for the gratifying benefit of fame to be bestowed on them, have more recently been joined by new celebrity figures who – although in all probability they are the source of a very restricted corpus of biopic – nevertheless indicate by their presence a significant change in the *modus operandi* of contemporary television. In fact we have here 'TV celebrities' in the true sense, belonging to the category of the person 'who is known for his well-knownness', to quote Boorstin; and, more precisely, known for having participated in some of the many reality shows through which television today produces its own ephemeral celebrities, or 'celetoids', according to Chris Rojek's definition (quoted in Turner, 2010a: 14). Like 'factoids', which are inauthentic facts, fabricated by sources of information, 'celetoids' are sham celebrities, fabricated by television in the absence of prerequisites for genuine fame. 'The individuals with no particular talents that might encourage expectations of work in the entertainment industry, no specific career objectives beyond the achievement of media visibility ...' (Turner, 2010: 14) acquire in this way an ephemeral notoriety that might mean some of them get to join the ranks of those individuals who merit a biography. Witness *The Fantasia Barrino Story: Life is Not a Fairy Tale*, about the winner of an edition of *American Idol* (Lifetime, 2006).

Entertainment programmes now occupy an enormous amount of space in the networks schedules of multi-channel environment schedules; their pervasive presence and influence on consumption patterns make entertainment the dominant genre on television. Although it provides only a tiny fraction of the immense corpus of programmes on today's television, the biography genre helps to sanction our entry into the 'age of entertainment' (Turner, 2010) by remodelling its own agenda accordingly.

A heroic enclave

The long roundabout path that has brought us thus far has also provided us with those strands of knowledge that were required to place the Italian case in a comparative context, so as to discern similarities and differences between the Italian biopic and international trends. I shall not here be concerned with the production values or artistic quality of Italian biopics (often disparaged by the critics, who find them hagiographic and didactic); nor do I wish to deal with their greater or lesser fidelity to the 'true lives', which they claim to recount truthfully, or which they more prudently say were only a source of inspiration. We can be content to agree with Custen that 'biographies are real not because they are believable. Rather, one must treat them as real because ... [they] are believed to be real by many viewers' (Custen, 1992: 7). Some of whom, it should be added, know no other way of acquiring an awareness, even a distorted one, of the 'human interest story'. My concern relates primarily to the biographical typology. Who are the personalities whose lives Italian TV drama has deemed worthy of narrating during the past 20 years? The question is not about their distinctive individuality; it concerns the fields in which they displayed their excellence and in consequence earned their fame (Tab. 1). And what changes in the hierarchy of the cultural values that (consciously or otherwise) preside over the 'bio-worthiness' as it were, are likely to be observed in present-day types, compared to the biopics made by Italian television in the past?

Table 1. Subjects of biographies (1989–2009).

	RAI	Mediaset	Total
Religious figures (saints, popes, priests, biblical and Gospel figures)	29	15	44
Rulers, politicians, entrepreneurs	10	4	14
Heroes–martyrs (anti-Nazism, anti-Mafia ...)	9	4	13
Creative artists, scientists and inventors	8	3	11
Entertainers and sport champions	5	3	8
Criminals	–	2	2
Others[5]	4	2	6
Total	64	33	98

The pre-eminence of religious figures – saints, popes, the blessed, catholic priests, characters from the Old Testament and the New – in the corpus of biopics in the last 20 years may come as a surprise to anyone who is not acquainted with Italian TV drama. A religious trend has in fact made its way through the biography genre, offering it a wide repertoire of subjects. Altogether, the religious, Biblical and Gospel figures account for 44 out of 98 biopics; in other words, more than 2 out of 5 television biopics were dedicated to people who could be defined as 'faith heroes'. This topic will be more extensively dealt with later on.

I take from Lowenthal the definition (though in truth it is not entirely convincing) of 'idols of production', in order to single out the category of political and entrepreneurial élites, which is much narrower than the previous one (14 biographies). We find great historical figures in this group: rulers, lawmakers, conquerors (Caesar, Augustus, Charlemagne), political leaders and trade unionists of republican Italy (De Gasperi,[6] Moro,[7] Di Vittorio[8]) and innovative entrepreneurs (Ferrari,[9] Mattei[10]). These personalities are not infrequently controversial; but the fascination of power gives them an aura, and the fame that surrounds them is nourished and sustained by the admiration and respect engendered by their influence on the history of the world, and indeed of Italy.

The third group of biographical subjects (13) concerns those men and women who have proved their exceptional courage in the service of great ethical and civic ideals, by fighting the twentieth century's political evils incarnated in Fascist and Nazi totalitarianism, and Italy's social evils, identified in the culture and criminality of the Mafia: personalities such as Giorgio Perlasca,[11] Salvo D'Acquisto,[12] Ada Sereni[13] (anti-Nazi heroes), and also the judges Falcone and Borsellino, General Dalla Chiesa, Don Puglisi (anti-Mafia heroes). These 'heroes of freedom and justice' were very often hero–martyrs, following in the wake of a tradition of heroism (from Christian martyrology to the martyrs of the Risorgimento and beyond), which is rooted in Italian history and culture.

The group comprising creative artists (Michelangelo, Caravaggio, Puccini and – rightly – a revolutionary couturier like Coco Chanel), scientists and inventors (Maria Montessori[14], Einstein, Meucci[15]) is slightly smaller (11 biographies). They are individuals who have in common some sort of 'gift' or talent, a flair, an out-of-the-ordinary intellect that has allowed these 'heroes of art and science' to tower above others in their own field.

Greatness is also the prerogative of some sporting champions (Coppi, Bartali, Carnera)[16] who along with well-known personalities in pop music (Dalida, Gaetano)[17] make up the category of 'entertainment heroes'. With only 8 biographies, entertainment occupies fifth place among the Italian biopics, proving itself much less important than elsewhere as the 'reservoir' of celebrities who may become the subjects of biographies.

The mission and testimony of religious faith, the responsibilities and conquests of power, the ideals of freedom and justice, the expression of creativity and geniality: over 80% of biographies created by Italian TV drama in the past twenty years were drawn

Figure 7.0.1. Paola Cortellesi plays the world famous scientist and pedagogue Maria Montessori in the biopic *Maria Montessori* (Canale 5, 2007). Courtesy of Mediaset.

from these exacting arenas, where people who can legitimately be regarded as exemplars and inspirational models of human greatness earned their fame in the course of recent and distant history.

A similar heroic penchant has characterized Italian TV drama from its very beginnings. But it is interesting to compare contemporary biographies with those produced over a time-span of more than 30 years, from the early days of television in Italy to the second half of the 1980s (Tab. 2). In fact, a significant analogy with the present – that is, the centrality of the 'traditional' élites, by no means threatened by the new élites of 'heroes of consumption' – can be found in this older corpus, and at the same time a marked divergence in the construction of the agenda of fame, which in the first period gave pride of place to the group of writers, artists, thinkers and scientists. The 'heroes of art and science', who inspire just 11 of the contemporary biographies, were the protagonists of half (25 out of 50) the televisual biopics produced during the whole period of public television's monopoly and in the first decade after the advent of commercial television.

Table 2. Subjects of biographies (1954–1988)	
	RAI
Creative artists, scientists and inventors	25
Rulers and politicians	15
Religious figures	5
Heroes–martyrs	2
Entertainers and others	3
Total	50

By aiming at fostering the formation of a cultured and literate society (typical of an age of writing, as I have suggested earlier), that agenda was fully consistent with the ideals of a humanistic and literary culture, as well as with the pedagogic mission of public television in the past: just as the sub-group of figures of the Risorgimento, within the more comprehensive category of political personalities, helped to speak for the process and the protagonists of the 'birth of the nation'.

In contemporary biographies, by contrast, we find scarce consistency, indeed a 'felicitous disharmony', with the advance of an age of entertainment – to which Italian television itself is by no means impervious or averse in regard to a substantial part of the contents of its programming.

The corpus of biographies of the past twenty years is quantitatively unimpressive, a drop in the televisual supply ocean, which is undergoing an exponential proliferation in the multi-channel environment. It should nevertheless be acknowledged that Italian TV drama has created and cultivated, in the midst of the entertainment age and in the context of an anti-heroic age, a small, resilient enclave of 'heroic' television.

The Bible Project

Biblical figures (*Abramo/Abraham, Mosè/Moses, Giuseppe/Joseph*), Popes (*Papa Giovanni/Pope Giovanni, Karol un uomo diventato Papa/Karol a Man who Become Pope, Giovanni Paolo II/John Paul II, Il Papa buono/The Good Pope, Papa Luciani/Pope Luciani*), the saints and the blessed (the thaumaturgical *Padre Pio/Father Pius*, the adolescent virgin

Figure 7.1. John Voight as Karol Wojtyla in the religious biopic *John Paul II* (Raiuno, 2005). Courtesy of RAI.

Maria Goretti, the elderly nun *Madre Teresa/Mother Teresa*), the divine figure of Christ (*Jesus*), the Apostles and the Evangelists (*San Pietro/Saint Peter, San Paolo/Saint Paul, San Giovanni.L'apocalisse/Saint John.The Apocalyps*), and many others, adding up to a corpus of 44 titles over a span of two decades. The re-emergence of the biographical trend in contemporary Italian fiction has been accompanied by – and has received a vigorous, decisive impulse from – the rise of the religious biopic in the production (and, as we will see later, in the consumption) of domestic drama.

The surge of interest in religious arguments and personalities that began to emerge on the threshold of the third millennium does not seem to be an exclusively Italian tendency. Questions of faith, spirituality, religious visions of life have been embodied and explored in the narratives of many American prime time series in recent years, from *CSI* to *Battlestar Galactica, Lost, Big Love* (Winston, 2009); whereas the expansion of themes and figures taken from Christianity (*The Passion of the Christ*, Mel Gibson 2004; *Kingdom of Heaven*, Ridley Scott, 2005), which has occurred in Hollywood movies has made 'films about religion and religious figures [...] a significant part of popular culture' (Grace, 2009: 2) in the early twenty-first century. Nonetheless, the large number of religious biopics and the wide-ranging cluster of 'heroes of the faith' (Christian-catholic) to be found in Italian fiction stories in the last two decades is something of a phenomenon which, in terms of its remarkable range and duration, might be considered unique in today's international panorama.

This pervasive religious presence in Italian televisual storytelling often arouses reactions in foreign observers, which swing from a surprised amusement, as if face to face with a bizarre manifestation of local folklore and a half-concealed condescension (shared what is more, by many of our critics and intellectuals) with respect to a phenomenon that seems to emanate from – and prosper in – the humus of a traditional religiosity, from a society still working towards secularization. But in both cases people usually end up adhering to a simple explanation, which establishes a direct, taken-for-granted connection, between the religious culture of *the* catholic country *par excellence* – not by chance, the home of the Pope – and its televisual collective imaginary.

Of course, the existence and (in certain circumstances) the influence of religious factors ingrained in the historical *longue durée* of Italian society and culture should not be denied or underestimated. Italy in fact stands out from other catholic countries by the persistent and majority-held sense of belonging to the catholic faith, seen and perceived by most Italians as a fundamental part of their collective identity as well as their national history.

The greater sensitivity of Italians with respect to religious issues, as opposed to people in the other industrialized countries, the high percentage (between 75 and 85% according to the statistics) of those who claim to be believers, the gender and generation gap between believers and non-believers narrower than elsewhere, the minority but still consistent nucleus of practising Catholics (around 30% or more, depending on the indicators): all these emerge systematically from international comparative research and induce

Figure 7.2. Jeremy Sisto and Jacqueline Bisset as Jesus and his mother, Mary, in the religious biopic *Jesus* (Raiuno, 1999). Courtesy of RAI.

religious phenomena analysts to speak of an 'inherent religiousness' of the Italians.[18] We might add that national territory is more than any other rich in historical religious memories, whose visible traces are scattered throughout the land in numerous places of worship, art galleries, towns and villages and in literature. A 'catholic imagination' springs to life from this, populated by saints, statues, churches, cathedrals, stained glass windows, paintings and nativity scenes, which contributes to symbols, icons and religious hallmarks being profoundly rooted in Italians' collective imagination and is in all probability not unrelated to their lasting catholic sentiment.

Figure 7.3. The dead Christ (played by Jeremy Sisto) across the knees of his mother, Maria (played by Jacqueline Bisset), in the position inspired by Michelangelo's Pietà, in the religious biopic *Jesus* (Raiuno, 1999). Courtesy of RAI.

However, the inherent religiousness of the Italians and the robust roots of a catholic sentiment that is reflected in, among other things, the profound religious connotation of the scenery itself of daily life, constitute a necessary but insufficient pre-condition for the explanation of the rise and mass appeal of the religious biopic in today's dramatic landscape. In the first three decades of television history, religiosity and the sense of belonging to the catholic Church were by no means less profound and widespread among Italians than they are nowadays (just the opposite!). Furthermore, as I stressed in the first chapter, public television was for a long time subject to catholic-oriented government influence. Yet, within a relatively large corpus of biographies – 50 titles produced between the 1950s and the end of the 1980s – only 5 of them were religious biopics,[19] far behind the heroes of the art of science and the idols of production.

Indeed, the advent – and the success – of religious fiction at the end of the century and the beginning of the new millennium have to be traced back to a number of factors, among which the most important are: the initiative and vision of an influential television producer; the propulsive function of important though contingent events within the catholic church; processes of transformation that have influenced and reconfigured in a significant and complex fashion the relations between the sacred and the secular, plus the characteristics themselves of religiosity in Italian society. I will go further into this later on.

The origins of the religious trend in the domestic drama can be dated back with precision, to the creation – in 1992 – of the production company Lux Vide. Soon to be a major player in the national television industry, Lux Vide was founded by Ettore Bernabei, who had been Director General of the Rai for more than a decade, in the public monopoly period (see Chapter 2) and is considered by all one of the great figures in the history of Italian television. Fervent Catholic, Vatican insider, proponent of value-oriented quality television, Bernabei immediately launched the company into the ambitious project of producing a large collection of miniseries and TV movies on the books and major figures of the Old and New testaments: the Bible Project, whose scope was to conjugate cultural relevance, artistic value and great popular appeal in the narration of religious stories taken from the sacred scriptures of the Christian tradition.

The prestige and glamour of the cinema, the substantial resources channelled by co-productions, large-scale international circulation: we see here the triad of strengths on which the Bible project was built and developed over a decade, from 1993 to 2002. With very few exceptions – among which the chapter on Genesis directed by the Italian Ermanno Olmi: a sober, contemplative, art film that gained the lowest ratings of the entire series – the titles of the collection were directed by non-Italians (Joseph Sargent, Roger Young, Nicolas Roeg and others). Many of the actors, mainly leading actors were in turn recruited from among the great Hollywood stars, from Richard Harris in the role of Abraham and St. John the Evangelist, to Ben Kingsley as Moses, Paul Mercurio as Joseph, Oliver Reed as Jeremiah, F. Murray Abraham as Mordecai in *Esther*, Gary Oldman and Jacqueline Bisset in *Jesus*; whereas the natural scenery and the impressive scenographic reconstructions of an enormous set mounted in a desert oasis in Morocco provided the settings for the shooting. Considered the largest international co-production in the history of television, the Bible Project – over which the Italian producer always held complete creative and organizational control – brought together a number of European broadcasters and also American networks (TNT, CBS). Thus, the titles of the collection were able to benefit from distribution on a worldwide scale, and won important international awards (the Emmy for *Joseph*, for example).

In Italy the 12 biopics of the Bible Project, all broadcast on the first Rai channel, right from the beginning had a great deal of success – though uneven (Tab. 3) – which reached a peak with much awaited and controversial history of the life of Christ (of which I will talk later).

Table 3. Audience figures for the Bible Project

Title	Season	Average audience (in millions) and share	
Abraham	1993–1994	9208	31.7%
Jacob	1994–1995	7725	25.9%
Joseph	1994–1995	10553	35.9%
Moses	1995–1996	10536	36.1%
Genesis	1995–1996	4122	18.2%
Samson and Delilah	1996–1997	8128	29.6%
David	1996–1997	7827	28.6%
Salomon	1997–1998	9049	32.2%
Jeremiah	1998–1999	7925	27.6%
Esther	1998–1999	6659	23.4%
Jesus	1999–2000	10806	37.1%
St. Paul	2000–2001	9087	31.4%
St. John. The Apocalypse	2002–2003	8262	29.7%

Source: Observatory of Italian Fiction

The fact that the Bible Project (and above all its creator and producer) had known how to intercept the vague demand for religiosity and spirituality, which was beginning to resound in the *air du temps* towards the end of the twentieth century, is a reasonably plausible idea. However, it is more accurate to say that the chapters of the television Bible were able to capture an emerging trend of collective sensitivity as much as they created and fuelled within Italian TV drama a new, vigorous biographical/religious genre, which built its success on the shrewd mixture of an appeal to the universal figures and values of Christianity, together with the visual splendour and production values of Hollywood-inspired cinema. Thus the Bible Project set the standards for religious drama as a great television event capable of satisfying at the same time the profane pleasures of sumptuous spectacularity – a resource seldom seen in the productively modest panorama of domestic fiction – and the intimate demand for spiritual nourishment. Furthermore, being programmatically conceived and realized taking into account an international public,[20] made up of believers of different Christian confessions and also non-believers, the television stories from the Bible both favoured a biblical reading from an inter-religious dialogue viewpoint[21] and adopted a biographical approach that was concerned with the human dimension – and vicissitudes – of the characters. Though undiminished in their status as heroic biblical figures with a great destiny, the latter underwent, however, a remodelling, since they had to appear as exemplary embodiements of a common (and in certain ways modern) human condition[22].

'A mix of biblical tradition and insistent humanizing' (Gates, 2001: 218) has characterized the different chapters of the collection. But this mix was never (or never appeared) quite so biased towards the humanizing and modernizing side as when, in the miniseries *Jesus* the Bible Project had to face up to its most difficult challenge, by recounting the life of the one who, for Christian believers is the Son of God, made man (and even for many non-believers too, one of the great characters of history). Jesus was the most awaited and publicized chapter of the series, and the reasons were not only those inherent to the almost universal attraction of the personage. In the months leading up to the programming, envisaged for Christmas 1999, the press had released repeated anticipations on the unusual, non-canonical, indeed transgressive nature of the figure of Christ as recounted by the miniseries. And further revelations were circulated after the preview organized two weeks before airing on television for top political and religious leaders in the capital city. The press book distributed on this occasion, for example, explained the order of priorities of the story in these terms: 'The miracles, the prayer, the passion, the path followed, *but above all, the man*' (my italics). In addition, the producer Bernabei explained in the interviews how the choice to focus above all on the human nature of the Nazarene matched the intent to appeal to a larger than usual television public, that of the year 2000, made up of not only the believers, but also the indifferent and the absent-minded. In turn, journalistic accounts directed the attention of readers to the unprecedented and repeated presence, in *Jesus*, of a modern Satan dressed in Armani clothes, and insisted upon describing in detail the denim outfit worn by Christ in the final scene. Great space was equally dedicated to the political correctness, which had led to the inclusion of rapid but explicit references to atrocities at different times in history in the name of Christianity (Crusades, witch and heretic hunts, wars of religion) and a reconstruction of Jesus' death sentence in which, for the first time, the Jews were absolved.

These potential activators of additional curiosity and interest for a version of the life of Jesus, which had been announced in advance as new, audacious and 'in tune with the times', merged with a climate of expectation made more fervent by the symbolic meaning given to the special temporal placement of the televisual event. The latter had in fact been scheduled to air close to Christmas 1999, two thousand years after the birth of Christ – his two-thousandth birthday, in the homespun language of certain newspapers – and, just as important, coinciding with the opening of the catholic Jubilee year, 2000, which was to celebrate the arrival of the third Christian millennium.

Aired over two evenings in early December, the miniseries did not disappoint expectations. The story of a Christ refulgent with earthly beauty,[23] joyful, who does not refrain from taking part in dances at weddings, who reveals some sentimental penchant for Mary of Bethany, who cracks jokes[24] – and who nevertheless resists a modern Tempter armed with cynical dialectical skills and virtual technology, and fulfils with the tragic sacrifice of his life his mission as Saviour – attracted an average audience of almost 11 million viewers (13 million in the final episode). When the Italian television audience reaches this large size, we can be sure that the assorted components of the entire national population – well beyond the 'hard core' of practising Catholics, those who for example follow televised religious ceremonies (Martelli, 2003) – are in fact represented in the viewing public, in proportions that are not too biased in respect of the real statistical distributions.

Obviously, seeing is not necessarily agreeing. As for the reactions on the part of viewers, we have to content ourselves with anecdotal evidences. On the one hand were the hundreds of faxes of thanks, expressing approval, received by the Rai from all over Italy (it seems, for the first time in its history); and on the other hand, the negative comments arriving at the catholic daily *Avvenire* via the telephone (as many, it seems, as the positive opinions – and by members of the clergy as well) (Calvini, 1999). Clearly, it should not surprise us that an unconventional miniseries on the life of Jesus – judged severely by Pamela Grace in her work on the religious film, as 'disjointed, contradictory and profoundly cynical' (Grace, 2009: 45) – should have generated such lively debate in the country, centring above all on the humanity of Christ and on the shift undergone by the television version away from the Gospel interpretation. What might seem more surprising is the observation that the many negative reviews and remarks on *Jesus*, coming from secular circles of opinion and criticism, contested the modernist claim to reconvert Christ into a character who is 'human, all too human', while actually deploring the absence of a powerful religious dimension (sacredness, mysticism, transcendence), which had been sacrificed to a fashionable New Age spirituality. 'For those who believe, Christ shouldn't be a contemporary, a trendy character, it should be the believers who raise themselves to his level …' (Grasso, 1999: 1).

On the contrary, those unconventional and controversial features that upset people the most in *Jesus* were in fact defended by catholic sources (though negative reactions by conservative Christian sources were not lacking). For example *Avvenire*, a daily catholic newspaper, taking in equal consideration both the appreciation and the criticism expressed by its own readers, welcomed what it saw as a work capable of arousing interest and discussion in the public about religious themes. In turn Cardinal Paul Poupard, president of the Pontificio Consiglio della Cultura, in an interview given to *Corriere della Sera* welcomed the humanization of Christ in *Jesus* as the courageous reversal of a thousand-year-old cliché: 'For two thousand years, only what is divine in this story has stood out, as if the human aspect was only appearance' (Cesarale, 1999: 30). Finally, in *L'Osservatore romano*, the official Vatican organ, the cinema critic, though he was somewhat uneasy with the 'Christology from the bottom' perspective adopted in *Jesus*, recognized the 'singular visual efficacy' (Patruno, 1999: 14) of the work and established parallels with the Christian tradition of a catechesis by images very popular in the United States.

Therefore we have:

A biography of Christ, made by a production company with overt catholic sympathies, basically taking liberties, as it were, with Holy Scripture – though in form rather than in substance – on account of those millions of people who, to quote Cardinal Poupard 'have only a very vague idea of who Jesus was' (Cesarale, 1999: 30).

A domestic audience that rushes *en masse* – its heterogeneous composition being that of a generalist public – answering the call of a religious biopic that has been labelled in advance as somewhat 'non-canonical' with respect to traditional Christological representation.

A series of different reactions, ranging from enthusiasm to reprehension and passing through intermediate positions, within the viewing public, which in any case displays a high degree of interest and involvement in the narrative of *Jesus*.

The apparently paradoxical inversion of roles between, on the one hand, a secular opinion supporting, we might say, a sort of intangible sacredness of the sacred; and on the other, the catholic side – including the higher ecclesiastical authorities – welcoming with (moderate) benevolence the modernizing and humanizing interpretation of *Jesus*, acknowledging how attuned it was to contemporary cultural and religious sensitivity.

This ensemble of factors, emerging from the case of *Jesus*, might help to illuminate the state of Italian religiosity at the beginning of the third millennium, and the phenomenal rise of the religious biopic in the supply and demand of domestic TV drama in Italy.

A plural catholicism

We are not dealing here with a phenomenon of resurgence of traditional religious sentiment in a still backward catholic country undergoing secularized modernization. No one denies the existence in Italy of those forms of belonging to a faith and feeling Christian/catholic, which are deeply rooted in an ancient popular tradition or founded on an equally deep adhesion to the ecclesiastical institutions and their dogmas and precepts. But this is just one of the components of religiosity in contemporary Italy where, during the last twenty years, we have witnessed a pluralization in how to interpret and experience catholic sentiment, the emergence of diversified (albeit not incompatible) conceptions and expressions of faith (Garelli, 1991), the growing individualization of religious beliefs and practices, together with a widespread non-observance of ecclesiastical precepts concerning sex, procreation and matrimony. Italian catholicism has become 'a plural catholicism' (Garelli, 2003: 817), in which different modes of understanding the sense of belonging and being a catholic (quite often 'each in his/her own way') find their place and coexist, within the same horizon of Christian/catholic references. 'The Italians have learned, in this way, to be religiously modern, to combine cultural loyalty to catholic sentiment and autonomy in believing' (Pace, 2003: 828).

The Church itself has not stood still and, in leading the way for a process of renewal that began with the Vatican II council, has opted for 'a modern way of "*being a church*"' (Pace, 2003: 826) developing an elevated level of tolerance for diversification in religious practice. As a result, ecclesiastical institutions have relinquished their claim to a hegemony founded prevalently on doctrinal and normative appeals of the catholic religion, preferring to assert their authority by calling, among other things, upon the communicative efficacy of a religious message that speaks the language of charity, stating human and spiritual values forcefully and offering constant inspiration about life's deeper meanings (Garelli, 2003).

Thus, the religious biopic emerged on the TV drama scene alongside processes of modernization, which were modifying the religious field in Italian society. The traces of such transformations were already clearly visible in the updated and negotiated versions of the Bible Project stories, realized and marketed in full awareness of the diversified socio-religious geography of the national (and international) context of reception. What also forms part of a 'modern way of being a church' is the careful and often benevolent appreciation of the ecclesiastical hierarchies for television works, thanks to which – apart from the differences in degrees of critical judgement – supply and demand of a Christian/catholic 'religious product' is in any case achieved.

The success of the religious biopic is to be considered also in relation to the phenomenon of de-secularization, which appeared in different forms on the social scene in Italy and elsewhere in the years at the end of the century and beyond (Berger, 1999; Martelli, 1990). Interacting in a complicated fashion with the environment of a secularized modernity, the de-secularizing trends have significantly contributed to a reawakening of religious sentiment – understood here in the admittedly vague sense of a widespread demand for spirituality, an aspiration towards the sacred, which may have little or nothing to do with belonging to a church, a nebulous search of sources of values and meanings of existence.

In actual fact, this is not so much an awakening or a return; it is rather the surfacing of new, heterogeneous forms of religiosity, often of a clearly subjective nature, nourished by emotional reactions rather than faith, sensitive to the call of immanence rather than the transcendent; but in the end, they are still manifestations of a new ferment in the religious sphere, a confutation of that definitive eclipse of the sacred envisaged by the old theories of secularization.

Italian fiction has found a place in this tendency since it first manifested itself, 'and at the same time has succeeded in fuelling and channelling it' (Cappello, 2003: 125) towards the consumption of narrativized and more or less spectacular forms of religiosity. Biographies of great figures belonging to the Christian/catholic tradition have secured high chances of success thanks to the fact that, despite the growing individualization of forms of belief, most Italians have a bond, albeit subterranean, of cultural loyalty with, and even an emotional attachment, to 'the religion we are born into'; and although no longer thinking of it as the repository of absolute religious truths, consider it a source of meaning and certainty to draw from if need be.

And finally, worth mentioning is the Jubilee celebrated by the catholic church at the beginning of the third millennium. If the incidental nature of the event – officially concluded at the end of the year 2000 – means we cannot explain the success of religious

Figure 7.4. Sergio Castellitto as the 'secular, complex, tormented' protagonist of Canale 5's religious biopic *Father Pius* (Canale 5, 2000). Courtesy of Mediaset.

fictions for years afterwards by appealing to the 'Jubilee effect' (Cappello, 2003), it is undeniable that it left its mark in the evolution of the religious biopic in Italy. The production of this type of drama has not only greatly increased since the Jubilee, it has also become more catholic-oriented and the biographies of popes, saints and the blessed of the catholic church have prospered, finding themselves among the greatest success stories of the noughties (Tab. 4).

Table 4. Religious biopics among the 30 most watched dramas in 2000s

Title and placement in the ranking	Season	Channel	Format	Audience (millions)
1. *Papa Giovanni/ Pope Giovanni*	2001–2002	Raiuno	Miniseries	13180
2. *Padre Pio tra cielo e terra/Father Pius between heaven and hearth*	2000–2001	Raiuno	Miniseries	13123
3. *Karol un uomo diventato Papa/ Karol a man who became Pope*	2004–2005	Canale 5	Miniseries	12832
5. *Padre Pio/Father Pius*	1999–2000	Canale 5	Miniseries	11660
6. *Giovanni Paolo II/ John Paul II*	2005–2006	Raiuno	Miniseries	11329
8. *Jesus*	1999–2000	Raiuno	Miniseries	10806
9. *Madre Teresa/Mother Teresa*	2003–2004	Raiuno	Miniseries	10600
12. *Il Papa buono/The good Pope*	2002–2003	Canale 5	Miniseries	9982
14. *Maria Goretti*	2002–2003	Raiuno	Tvmovie	9896
16. *Papa Luciani. Il sorriso di Dio/ Pope Luciani, the smile of God*	2006–2007	Raiuno	Miniseries	9598
25. *San Paolo/Saint Paul*	2000–2001	Raiuno	Miniseries	9097
30. *Lourdes*	1999–2000	Raiuno	Miniseries	8693

Source: Observatory of Italian Fiction

Figure 7.5. Michele Placido as the humble but combative, totally devoted to God and the suffering people, protagonist of Raiuno's religious biopic *Father Pius between Heaven and Earth* (Raiuno, 2000). Courtesy of RAI.

In a cultural goods market like television, with its structural uncertainty about audience results, religious drama in the noughties has proved to be reliably predictable in terms of popular success. A religious tale has seldom disappointed the broadcasters' expectations of a fair return in terms of viewing figures. Commercial television itself, which in the twentieth century had decided not to compete with the Rai on this terrain, later went on to produce a number of religious biographies (*Karol, un uomo diventato papa/Karol, a Man who Became Pope, Il Papa buono/The Good Pope, Sant'Antonio/Saint Antony, Francesco/Francis, Rita da Cascia*), some of which were very successful.

The relevance assumed by the religious biopic in the early years of the twenty-first century can be seen in the singular way it stirred up competition between public and private television. Three times the Rai and Mediaset have confronted each other on the biography of the same religious figure: Padre Pio da Pietrelcina, and popes John XXIII and John Paul II.

To conclude, I will briefly mention the two biographical miniseries about Padre Pio produced and aired by Rai and Mediaset during the Jubilee year (Bechelloni, 2010). The miniseries were dedicated to the figure of the Franciscan friar beatified in 1999 (and subsequently proclaimed saint in 2002) who, during his life, in virtue of the stigmata, the gift of foresight and great achievements in favour of the sick and the suffering had become an object of infinite popular devotion in Italy. Even today, the places associated with the life and works of the charismatic friar are the annual destination of millions of pilgrims, coming from all over Italy and the rest of the world.

Canale 5's biopic was aired in spring, that of Raiuno in the autumn; both took advantage of an intense advertising campaign designed to build up viewer expectation, and further amplified by journalistic insistence on cross references, comparisons and controversies. Both of them attained a (miraculous, it was said) share of 45%. The double biopic was seen by many as an extreme demonstration of low profile, merely imitative, copy-cat competition between the Rai and Mediaset: a 'war of the stigmata' according to the newspaper headlines. This is really too simple an interpretation, as it was in fact an enormous challenge that, in the favourable context of the jubilee, saw the Rai and Mediaset competing in the demanding reconstruction of a figure deeply rooted in the popular tradition of the religious practices and beliefs of the Italians.

Both public and private television, acknowledging drama as a cultural form worthy of this ambitious project, turned the biographies of Padre Pio into the arena of a challenge on the religious dimensions of the Italian identity. Each television offered a different interpretation, each intended to stress its own cultural identity. Canale 5's fiction was a stylistically innovative work, shifting between realistic and fantastic tones, a sort of psychological detective story, introspective and philosophical, based on a mystical character embroiled in the struggle between good and evil and the drama of sufferance and the mysteries of the sacred in the human condition. The main character was brilliantly interpreted by Sergio Castellitto, an icon of the Italian 'modern' hero. 'We could have painted a conventional portrait, a *santino*[25]; our Padre Pio instead is *secular* (my italics), complex, tormented', Angelo Rizzoli, the producer, declared (Fumarola, 2000: 57).

The Raiuno fiction, produced by Lux Vide, opted instead for a visual and narrative style of great simplicity, that of a popular tale. Padre Pio was represented as a suffering but not mortified character, a humble man raised to sainthood by total devotion to God and the earthly project of alleviating the physical and moral suffering of the sick. And the metaphysical conflict between good and evil was replaced in this biography by the dispute between science and faith, which had long exposed the miraculous friar from Pietrelcina to the strict inquisition of the Vatican hierarchy, suspicious of his supernatural gifts. This time the part was entrusted to Michele Placido, an iconic symbol of a more traditional Italian hero-type, combative and potential martyr. Finally, whereas the Canale 5 biography ended with the death of Padre Pio, that of Raiuno exploited documentary material of the beatification ceremony in St Peter's Square, wishing to stress the immortality of a saint of the catholic church.

Radically different, equally successful, the two biopics about Padre Pio – the fruit of the competition between public and private television – further testify to the pluralist Catholicism of contemporary Italy as fertile ground (in the presence of other conditions) for domestic religious drama.

Notes

1. 'J'aime peu les héros, ils font trop de fracas' ('I don't care for heroes, they make too much noise') is the beginning of a letter in verse sent by Voltaire to Frederick II of Prussia on 22 May 1742; cited in E. Cassirer, (1973: 304).
2. If not intolerance. On 29 January 2010 an article appeared in the English daily paper *The Independent* with the eloquent title 'Bored with biopic' (http://www.independent.co.uk/arts-entertainment/tv/features/bored-of-biopic-1882227.html, accessed on 29 January 2010).
3. Lowenthal is at pains to distinguish between the 'serious arts' (painting, music, dance …) and the popular arts; and he notes the progressive disappearance of the former from the spheres of activity that provide the heroes of periodicals.
4. Amy Fisher earned notoriety by attempting to kill the wife of her lover Joey Buttafuoco in 1992.
5. This also includes female personalities whose private life is closely intertwined (as lovers, wives and daughters) with that of rulers and politicians.
6. Alcide De Gasperi (1881–1954), founder and leader of the Christian-Democrat party, was one of the founding fathers of the Italian Republic, and the European Union as well.
7. Aldo Moro (1916–1978), president of the Christian–Democrat party, five times Prime Minister, was kidnapped and killed by the Red Brigades.
8. Giuseppe Di Vittorio (1892–1957) was a charismatic leader of CGIL, the trade union confederation close to the Italian Communist Party.
9. Enzo Ferrari (1898–1988), the eponymous founder of the world famous automobile industry and racing stable owner.
10. Enrico Mattei (1906–1962), head of the Italian state energy company after World War II, died in a plane crash, the accidental nature of which has been disputed.
11. Giorgio Perlasca has been called the 'Italian Schindler'. A livestock dealer and a former Fascist, he saved thousands of Hungarian Jews in the winter of 1944–1945 (under the false identity of a Spanish diplomat accredited to Budapest), from being exterminated by the Nazis. Perlasca and his 'heroic imposture' remained unknown in Italy for nearly half a century, until his story was reconstructed in a book and later in a very successful television biopic (*Perlasca. Un eroe italiano/Perlasca: An Italian Hero*, Raiuno 2002). Perlasca has been recognized by Yad VaShem, the Holocaust Martyrs and Heroes Remembrance Authority, as a 'Righteous among the nations'.

12. Salvo D'Acquisto (1920–1943), staff sergeant in the Carabinieri, sacrificed his live to save a group of civilians from a Nazi reprisal.
13. Ada Sereni (1905–1997) was, in the late 1940s, the organizer and commander of the operation that helped thousands of Shoah survivors to emigrate to Palestine.
14. Maria Montessori (1870–1952), physician and educationalist, founder of an innovative educational method based on acknowledging and supporting the natural development of children's potentialities.
15. Antonio Meucci (1808–1889), Italian immigrant in the United States, was the real inventor of the telephone, as recently recognized by a resolution passed by the US House of Representatives in 2002.
16. Fausto Coppi (1919–1960) and Gino Bartali (1914–2000) were the greatest Italian cyclists from the 1930s to the 1950s; the rivalry between the two champions has for years been one of the most debated issues in the sport milieu and among cycling supporters. Primo Carnera (1906–1967), world heavyweight champion in the early 1930s, was an almost legendary figure because of his exceptional height and physical strength.
17. Dalida (1933–1987), Italian singer, naturalized French, achieved immense popularity on the international pop and disco music scene between the 1950s and the 1980s. Rino Gaetano (1950–1981) was an original and innovative singer and musician, who died prematurely in a car crash.
18. See for instance Religion Monitor, 2008, carried out by Bertelsmann-Stiftung (http://www.bertelsmann-stiftung.de/cps/rde/xchg/SID-E6EB323B-9FCA3A5F/bst_e ngl/hs.xsl/bildzoom.htm?, accessed December 2010).
19. *Francesco d'Assisi/Francis of Assisi* (1966), *Agostino di Ippona/Augustine of Ippo* (1972), *Mosé/Moses* (1974), *Gesù di Nazareth/Jesus of Nazareth* (1977), *State buoni se potet/Be Quiet if You Can* (the biography of San Filippo Neri, 1983).
20. I do not wish here to take up once more an issue I have covered in depth in previous chapters. I will limit myself therefore to pointing out here that once more we are in the presence of processes, concerning national fiction, of 'internationalisation from within'.
21. Exponents of different Christian and Jewish schools of biblical exegesis provided the Bible Project with constant research backup.
22. I offer as small anecdotic proof, from among the many that we might cite, the comment by Barbara Hershey, who played Sarah in *Abraham*, that the film was above all a 'great love story' (Cervone, 1993).
23. The character of Christ was played by the young, well-set American actor Jeremy Sisto, who was in fact very different indeed to the ascetic traditional iconography of the Redeemer as portrayed in previous cinema and television works.
24. For example, in response to his mother's statement 'your father would be proud of you', Jesus replied, smiling, 'which, of the two'?
25. A *Santino* is a small painted image of a saint printed on cardboard; in Italy the word is also used as a metaphor for 'saccharine perfection'.

Chapter 8

The Re-Enactment of the Past and the Politics of Memory and Identity in Contemporary Drama

The temporal turn

The previous chapter about television biopics has provided some premises of the arguments I will be dealing with in the following pages. The subjects of the many biographies realized by Italian television, though belonging to different 'heroic types', share an identical characteristic: they are all from times gone by. Perhaps they lived thousands of years ago like Christ or during the twentieth century like Padre Pio: but they still all belong to the past. And some of them – in the group of those I have defined 'heroes of freedom and justice' – were participants in, or witnesses to, crucial moments and events in the history of the twentieth century (Fascism, Nazism, World War II).

In this final chapter I will be concerned primarily with the temporal turn, which, at the beginning of the third millennium, has fostered, in televisual storytelling, a widespread and prolonged trend of a 'return to the past', contradicting, apparently, a Calendarial passage suffused with the mythical aura of the advent of a new era, the dawn of a future world. I will mention the different ways and genres through which this temporal turn has manifested itself and discuss in greater detail the strand of fictions in a true sense historical, re-enacting events and processes in Italian history and in particular the history of the 'short twentieth century' (Hobsbawm, 1995).

The return to the past does not seem to contradict only the idea of an entrance into a future tied to the dawn of the twentieth century, but a more general as well as conventional perception of the relations that the televisual medium maintains with the different temporal dimensions. As regards television, most people have their own firm convictions; one of these is concerned with the presentness of the medium, its being totally in tune with the here and now, without history or memory of the past.

Clearly it cannot be denied that most television contents and genres – news broadcasts, entertainment, TV drama itself – are primarily oriented towards the narration of the present (sometimes live and in real time): it is the stuff of our daily experience and, furthermore, provides one of the main reasons for the medium's appeal. But evidence is not infrequently blinding, in the proper sense of obscuring one's vision; and in this case it conceals the fact that of all televisual genres, drama is the one that is most suited, equipped and also accustomed to working with the sense of the past, history and memory.

Almost 40 years ago in a book that is now regarded as the founding text on television studies, Horace Newcomb (1974) identified the three basic components of televisual aesthetics as intimacy, continuity and history. Newcomb argued that TV drama can be historical in different and unsuspected ways: for example, through the long duration and the evolving temporality of serials, which unfold over a period of years and not only build up their own story but also capture and memorize social history, while the viewers' lives run their course in parallel. TV drama can also be historical because of the evolution of the genres; this is testified to by the coexistence, in television schedules, of old and new programmes that constantly compare the past and the present; or, more specifically, when it takes its inspiration from people who really existed, or from events that really happened, performing in such a way (and in its own way) the role of 'television as historian' (Edgerton 2001: 1). More generally, TV drama is historical when it recounts stories, true or imaginary, that are set in some period of the recent or distant past.

Italian TV drama was intensely and primarily historical – in this last sense – in the first 20 years (from the 1950s to the 1970s) of the public television monopoly, with protracted but decreasing instances of drifting in subsequent years. The productions of that time preferred to revisit the past through the mediation of national and European works of literature, or through biographies of great Italians or the reconstruction of events of the Risorgimento (the building of the nation in the nineteenth century). This was the era of the *sceneggiato* (see Chapter 1). The second half of the 1970s saw a process of 'presentification' of domestic TV drama, which reached its peak in the course of the 1990s. But television and televisual genres often function in cycles, closings and resumptions, runs and re-runs. We witnessed a return to the past in Italian drama production during the first decade of the twenty-first century.

The temporal switch of TV drama from the present to the past is a feature that has spread beyond Italy. To a different degree, and never to the extent of undermining the dominance of the present in the discursive regime of television genres, drama production in all the largest European countries was affected in the early years of the twenty-first century by a process of 'de-presentification', if not of true historicization. From the reconstruction of daily life during the Franco era in the Spanish comedy of manners *Cuéntame cómo pasó/ Tell Me What Happened* (TVE, 2001–) (Rueda Laffond, 2011) to the reinvigoration of historical and biographical *feuilletons* on the French channels (Bosseno, 2010), to the new intensive British costume drama season (Nelson, 2008), and the unusual exploration by German television of mythological (the Nibelungen) and political themes (the attempted assassination of Hitler, the biography of Albert Speer, Hitler's architect and confidant): all over Europe television storytelling has taken to cultivating what, according to Paul Ricoeur (2004: 16) could be defined as 're-enactment of the past' in contemporary narration.

We are facing here an occurrence that is at least in part the expression of a more general structure of collective feelings; contemporary observers and analysts (philosophers, sociologists and historians) have drawn attention to the perceptible presence and numerous signs of this sentiment. The philosopher Emmanuel Kattan focuses in a particular way on the reviving of the past with reference to more or less distant traumatic events, the so-called memory of trauma or 'wounded memory': for example, he speaks of the 'predominant place [occupied] in public space by concern with the past, in its different manifestations' (Kattan, 2002: 14). 'In this end-of millennium, Europeans ... are obsessed with a new cult – the cult of memory', Zvetan Todorov writes (2001: 60), thus noting the risk of 'compulsive worrying about the past' (2001: 61).

In any case, European TV drama has taken to working on the re-enactment of the past, breaking up (without subverting it) the almost exclusive symbiosis with the present that could have been seen only a few years earlier. Nowhere can one find more compelling evidence of this temporal volte-face than in Italian television. In other European countries the re-enactment of the past in all its forms, to be classified under the inclusive heading of 'period drama', is concentrated in a limited number of works, thus indicating a symptomatic but not extensive cultural trend. In Italy, on the contrary, period drama provided in the first decade of the twenty-first century no fewer than 112 prime-time domestic dramas.

As I mentioned at the beginning of the chapter, the temporal turn towards the past has affected different narrative genres, which shared the same penchant for the telling of stories set in historical periods before the present. Biographies have had the lion's share (55 productions) followed by literary adaptations (21 productions), fictions of historical reconstruction (20), costume dramas that situate wholly invented characters and events in the temporally exotic scenario of a pre-contemporary society (16). In fact the dividing line between these narrative typologies seems eminently fluid, as the distinction between literary adaptations and costume dramas resides only in the authorial sources of the former, and above all because most of the biographies are inseparable from, indeed constitute a primary vehicle for, reconstruction of events and processes in a true sense historical. In fact, the life stories are very often double-sided, or rather they are generic hybrids where the portrait of the protagonist stands against the background, or is placed in the midst, of the historical events and circumstances that characterized his/her times. Fascism, Nazism, World War II, and the genocide of Jewish people, for instance, have much more than a marginal place in the biographies of Pope John XXIII and John Paul II; and, just to mention a single but eloquent further example, they are the basic narrative material of the biopic about Giorgio Perlasca, the Italian Schindler (See Chapter 7, note 11).

Literary adaptations, biographies, history: the temporal turn of the noughties has acquired, for Italian fiction, the added meaning of a self-referential return to its own past, the years of the *sceneggiato*. Clearly, the comparison between the two periods brings to light major differences; the stories of the past constitute a key component of the contemporary dramatic landscape but they do not monopolize it, as it happened in television at the beginning; and the century to which contemporary storytelling returns again and again is no longer the nineteenth – i.e., that of the birth of the nation – but the twentieth, when national cohesion was seriously challenged by authoritarian regimes, world conflict, civil war. The period dramas on plentiful offer nowadays on Italian television channels may go back in time to the romantic nineteenth century (*Cime tempestose/Wuthering Heights,* Raiuno 2004), to a fantasized eighteenth century (*Elisa di Rivombrosa/Elisa from Rivombrosa,* Canale 5, 2003 and 2007), to the seventeenth century of Manzoni's *The Betrothed* (*Virginia, la monaca di Monza/Virginia, the Nun of Monza,* Raiuno 2004), to the ancient times of the

Roman empire (*August*, Raiuno 2003; *Nerone*, Raiuno 2004). In most cases, however, the historical dramas focus on the years and the tragic events of the Fascist regime, World War II and its immediate aftermath; or sometimes they shorten the distance from the present day, setting the scene in the era of the 1950s and 1960s that witnessed the migration of so many Italians within and outside their country, and the 'economic miracle' that turned a peasant society into an affluent, industrialized nation (*Marcinelle, Il grande Torino/The Great Torino, Raccontami/Tell Me*: Raiuno, respectively 2003, 2005, 2006–2008).

Nonetheless, certain similarities remain between the period dramas of yesteryear and those of today, especially as far as literary adaptations are concerned: in 2000s too, those taken from foreign novels outnumbered the adaptation of works of Italian literature. And though the latter obtained good placements in the top ten of the decade (Tab. 1), a classic of English literature like *Wuthering Heights* proved capable of summoning a somewhat larger audience than *Virginia, la monaca di Monza/Virginia the Nun of Monza*, based on the greatest novel in Italian literature *I promessi sposi/The Betrothed* (see Chapter 2).

Table 1. The top ten literary adaptations in the 2000s

Title	Channel	Season	Average audience (in millions)
Cime tempestose/Wuthering Heights	Raiuno	2004–05	8942
Virginia la monaca di Monza/ Virginia the nun of Monza*	Raiuno	2004–05	8625
La cittadella/The Citadel	Raiuno	2002–03	8557
Rebecca la prima moglie/ Rebecca	Raiuno	2007–08	7711
Cuore/Heart: a School-Boy's Journal*	Canale5	2001–02	7705
Assunta Spina*	Raiuno	2006–07	7576
Resurrezione/Resurrection	Raiuno	2001–02	7118
Piccolo mondo antico/The Patriot*	Canale5	2000–01	7026
Francesca e Nunziata*	Canale5	2001–02	6959
Le ragazze di Sanfrediano/ The Girls of Sanfrediano*	Raiuno	2006–07	6730

Source: Observatory of Italian Fiction *adaptation from Italian novel

The return to the past may assume more elusive, albeit not irrelevant, forms. In this connection it is worth pointing out the emergence, in the current dramatic landscape, of a form of visibility of the past unrelated to the temporal dimension of the story – it can actually accompany the period drama as well as drama set in the present – whose peculiarity resides in a lived and, as it were, embodied modality. It is manifested in the physical shape, marked by the unmistakable traces of the passage of time, of elderly actors and characters. The age of the characters is hardly ever revealed, but we know or can guess the age of the actors; yet there are roles that bear witness to the amount, if not the burden, of the years: parents of grown-up children, grandfathers and grandmothers, couples who

Figure 8.1. Bianca Guaccero as the protagonist of the literary adaptation *Assunta Spina* (Raiuno, 2006), set in Naples in early twentieth century. Courtesy of RAI.

Figure 8.2. Alessio Boni as Prince Andrej Bolkonskij in the literary adaptation *War and Peace* (Raiuno, 2006). Courtesy of RAI.

are getting on in years, groups of pensioners, 'venerable' old people and so on. People advanced in age, usually in supporting roles but sometimes as main characters, appear in quite a few recent fictions; and elderly people, the grandparental figures who are the incarnation of the past and its roots, have become the pillars of the family in Italian TV drama. *Un medico in famiglia/A Doctor in the Family* (Raiuno, 1998–), the most popular and long-lived of the contemporary family series (see Chapter 4) has pioneered this trend, rendering the elderly character 'granddad Libero' – the only stable moral and educational anchorage or point of reference in a multi-generational household that is constantly undergoing change – an acknowledged and loved national icon.

The Re-Enactment of the Past and Politics of Memory and Identity in Contemporary Drama

This phenomenon is doubtless related to some extent to the demographic structure of a star system in which there are plenty of mature actors, with a great deal of experience, thus well-tried and well-known: stories and characters are often created and tailor-made for them. But the fictional image of a population that includes a number of elderly people, conveyed by the visibility of many aged figures in TV drama, is by no means improbable or distorted. Italy's rate of longevity is among the highest in the world, having a life expectancy of over 80 years. Television audiences and especially viewers of domestic drama are to a considerable extent made up of senior citizens.

Figure 8.3. Vittoria Puccini as the bourgeois Elisa and Alessandro Preziosi as Count Fabrizio Ristori in the period drama *Elisa di Rivombrosa* (Canale 5, 2003). Courtesy of Mediaset.

It can be said that characters that are advanced in age fulfil the function of witnesses of time in two senses. First, they are witnesses of the existence of a past – to be sure, a fairly recent past and inscribed in the span of a human life, albeit a long one – which they have experienced and kept alive in their memories, and where their values come from: values that are marked more often by a vital and dialogical tradition than an outmoded and non-communicating traditionalism. Usually, elderly people in TV drama, especially fathers and grandfathers, represent the living roots of the adults and children, the bonds of solidarity between generations, the permanence of the past within the present. This is doubtless an idealized vision, yet it draws on the real-life experience of inter-generational relationships that are notoriously much more intense and closely knit in Italy than in other contemporary societies.

In the second sense, they are witnesses of time – and in this instance I mean the present day – because, with rare exceptions, the elders in TV drama bear little resemblance to the stereotypes of fragile and inactive old people, who are perhaps valuable for their resources of experience and affective generosity, but deprived of any chance for social protagonism. They are rather the sign and proof of the emergence of new stereotypes, related to the redefinition of generational identities and to the perception and self-perception of a new lease of life that takes shape while ageing. In TV dramas set in the present day, elderly people are energetic, hard-working and enterprising. And when, as quite often happens, they are the protagonists in historical or biographical TV drama, they stand out as towering figures on the horizon of history.

Past and present

Roger Silverstone has perceptibly observed that literary adaptations, costume dramas and biographies 'offer a continuous diet of times past as pastime' (Silverstone, 1999: 132). There are periods, one might add, in which this diet is enriched by a particularly intensive supply of times past, as we see in the Italian dramatic landscape at the beginning of the twenty-first century. Thus, it would make sense to try and ask ourselves about the possible reasons, conditions, intervening factors that have favoured and still sustain the temporal turn of televisual storytelling.

I would like to begin by dismissing the enlistment – as facile as it is hasty – of the trend of returning to the past under the insignia of an 'Operation Nostalgia'; likewise the ill-considered assumption that by following this path one is trying to escape or flee from the present. It can hardly be denied that the past, simply by virtue of being behind us and having existed already, delivers the reassuring vision of a stable and settled landscape that offers itself as an alternative to (but not necessarily a refuge from) a fickle and uncertain present. Michael Pickering and Emily Keightley, in an essay aimed at freeing nostalgia from the imputation of being a unilaterally anti-modernistic sentiment, acknowledge for example that 'uncertainty and insecurity in present circumstances create fertile ground for a sentimental longing for the past ... and the media help to fill this ground' (2006: 925). Nor can we rule out *a priori* the risk, pointed out by Todorov, that anxiety about the past generates those 'blessings of the good conscience' (2001: 63) that end up by relieving people of anxiety about the present.

Nevertheless, the fictional representations tend in many ways to incorporate the present in the re-enactment of the past; thus period and historical dramas do not refrain from speaking of our days. They do it by treating the past in accordance with the criteria of present-day judgement, choosing personalities and events that are more in tune with modern sensibilities, staging the problems, feelings and not infrequently the lexicon of today in the world of yesterday and, not least, entrusting the performance to actors whose faces and body language are unequivocally contemporary.

But insistence upon these details is unnecessary to uphold the statement that the return to the past in itself speaks to us of the present. If nothing else it tells us or it suggests that the world in which we live has become (and is perceived to be) confused, complicated and indecipherable. We inhabit this world seeking to come to terms with feelings of confusion, insecurity and disorientation about the future. Thus, the past, at a backward glance, assumes the reassuring contours of protected and safe territory; as this is where we come from and we take comfort in remembering, and being reminded, that our roots lie deep in this firm soil. The twofold spirit, firm and flexible, of individual and collective identity is sometimes evoked in cultural studies through the metaphor of the tree, anchored to the ground by its roots and at the same time waving in the air by virtue of its branches and leaves. It is never more necessary to trust in one's roots as when one's branches and leaves are taken by storm.

It is probable that stories about the past narrated by TV drama offer the antidote of renewed firm anchorage and links of continuity, to the uncertainty that emerges from the contemporary structure of collective feelings. Re-establishing links to the past may, in fact, help to revive our awareness and our confidence that we are not without resources when faced by the challenges of the hard times in which we find ourselves living.

As we emerge from a twentieth century that, through two World Wars, totalitarian regimes, massacres and genocides, has stored up an accumulation of wounds in the archives of the collective memory – to draw on Ricoeur (2004) – our entry into the third millennium, marked almost immediately by a deadly attack on a living symbol of Western modernity, that of the Twin Towers in New York, in all probability constituted a fertile breeding-ground for 'subtle anxiety on account of the end of an era' (Cavicchia Scalamonti, 2001: 9) and a sense of alarm at the threat to our security and identity, or that which is so perceived. Such sentiments can generate grave uncertainty about the present and how it will turn out in the future; they can trigger a drive, even a compulsion, towards rediscovery and acknowledgement of the past in an attempt to find reassurance, or inspiration, or simply something to take one's mind off the pressing worries of the here and now.

But beyond the climate of anxiety due to the passing of an era, which even in other countries – although to a lesser extent than in Italy – has inclined television storytelling towards times past, it is possible to identify an alliance, or at any rate a concurrence, of other conditions that have probably favoured the emergence of such a marked and persistent tendency. For instance, what Edgerton calls the 'big business' (2001: 2) of history on television should be taken into account. Period drama, in its various sub-genres, has given proof of its popularity, and in an industry whose guidelines are (to some extent inevitably) mapped out by previous experiences of failures and successes, the latter do not merely 'prolong' the stories – by generating continuations and repeats – but also 'multiply' them – by promoting the production of other stories of the same genre, laden with expectations of an analogous capacity to succeed.

Furthermore, the past, historical and literary, sacred and secular, still constitutes an immense reserve of material from which a wealth of narrative inspiration can be drawn. Historical events, heroic and exemplary lives, literary tradition and much else offer a further twofold advantage. They put at authors' disposal narrative material that is dense in dramaturgical potential, and allows the creation of works that benefit from the promotional value embodied in the notoriety and popularity of the original subjects (saints, popes, novels, events and historical personalities). Or at any rate they benefit from the curiosity aroused by the recurrence of names and stories that re-echo and resound in the common memory, even if only by hearsay. The past, in short, possesses the prized added value of 'a built-in promotional resource'; and, perhaps less prized but still capable of attracting audiences, the value of the visual pleasure of costumes, furnishings and manners of times past: the 'small pleasures' (Caughie 2000: 211) offered by the decorative details of an era.

And moreover, the return to the past fits into the logic of distinction by means of which fiction responds to the intrusive and competitive presence of light entertainment programmes, reality shows in particular. In terms of time dimension, there is no doubt that reality shows are also characterized by an extreme emphasis on the present. This is expressed and testified to by the access they provide to the voyeuristic scrutiny of 'life on live television' and to the minute-by-minute monitoring of what happens in the most diverse places: the houses of *Big Brother*, the academies of music talent shows, the desert islands of survivors. Although even the most addicted and inquisitive fans watch no more than snippets and fragments of this permanent surveillance, the conception and consumption of the latest generation of reality shows are unquestionably related to the idea of the uninterrupted monitoring of daily life, here and now, of a group of our contemporaries.

Much Italian TV drama – most of it indeed – favours the time dimension of the present. But it is no coincidence that TV drama should in very recent years have begun, more assiduously and frequently than ever before – at least not in the post-*sceneggiato* era – to narrate stories set in the (more or less) distant past: the drama does this, as we have seen, by reconstructing biographies (saints, popes, great figures of the twentieth century), drawing from ancient and modern history (the Crusades, the Roman Empire, the Nazi occupation), recalling hard news stories (murders, kidnappings, the search for and eventual capture of Mafia bosses). Whereas entertainment formats tighten their grip on the immediate present, the logic of the distinction between competing genres contributes to switching fiction towards the past. The abundant flow, still streaming, of stories of the distant and not so distant past, thus finds the conditions for its existence in a whole set of plausible reasons and intervening factors.

And finally, it is worth pointing out the divergent way in which the past and the present are dramatized and portrayed. Starting from the format – the miniseries, with its prestige, its high production values and well-established craftsmanship – the stories of past times and the worlds they narrate benefit from an over-valourization and also an assumption of quality that are not so easily ascribed to contemporary stories – these latter being for the most part consigned to serial narrative formulae, which are less highly regarded in Italy and are in any case not so lavish or so attractive, and as a rule are less skilfully handled. Thus a dichotomy of 'narrative images' (Ellis, 1992) is created, according to which the past – to put it very sketchily and in the awareness that it is a generalization – is productively and scenographically rich and dazzling, when compared with a present that is more faded and unadorned. Or in addition, the past is eventful, in the sense of being staged like a 'television event', whereas the present is mundane and routine.

There is a magnitude gap between the present and the past in the nature of the stories narrated, the heroic status of the characters, the relevance of the issues that are dealt with, the dramaturgical intensity and still other things, that again, and more importantly, end up by creating two separate worlds. On the one hand, there is the world we have lost, inhabited by great civil and religious personalities and amazing indomitable female figures, a world fraught with larger than life passions as well as tragic collective events. On the other hand we have the world where we live now, which perhaps also because of its complexity and incomprehensibility is rendered by much of TV drama in the abridged and minimalist versions of a small ship in the protected and protective waters of families and work families; a world where there is certainly no lack of heroes, but who are mostly 'common everyday heroes'; where the dilemmas and problems of present-day conditions are not exactly lacking, but as a rule they are only hinted at, alluded to or overlooked. Therefore, in the different forms of its re-enactment, the past (and the characters who incarnate the past and bear witness to it) somehow shines brightly in relation to the more modest modalities of narrating the opaque present.

Television as historian

From here on I will be focusing my discussion on a specific subgroup within the corpus of period dramas, i.e., those fictions, which, in that they re-enact real events and processes of evenemential and social history of Italy in the 1900s, can be defined as 'historical' (from the perspective of a popular historiography I will refer to a little later). We are dealing with a group of more than 20 titles – including of necessity the biographies of anti-Nazi heroes and pre-eminent figures in the royal family and Mussolini's family during the Fascist regime – and would come close to 30 units if we add the many biopics of religious and secular characters whose personal stories entwine significantly, to a greater or lesser extent, with facts concerning great events in history.

Exception made for three fictions *(Come l'America/Like America, Marcinelle, Il grande Torino/The Great Torino)*, which draw upon the social history of internal and international migration of Italians during the 1950s, the years and events coinciding with World War II, its antecedents and its consequences, provide the temporal and thematic fulcrum of the bulk of the stories.

In giving itself the role of narrator of the history of the 1900s, TV drama has in a way taken up the baton – and enlarged considerably the audience pool – of programmes of historical popularization, which public television, later imitated by the private networks, had begun to broadcast on the third channel Rai3 in prime time, starting in the late 1990s (Anania, 2003). Those documentary series had in turn privileged topics related to Fascism, Nazism, emigration and – with respect to the standards of a 'minor' network, with a modest market share – achieved a reasonable success among a selected audience: adult, male, educated viewers. Although not yet a big business, to say it with Edgerton, history had given significant proof of its potentialities in this sense.

The displacement from the documentary to fiction achieved the objective of broadening the horizons – with the introduction of historical issues, in a dramatized version and more or less shaped by imagination – of a generalist audience, which, in most cases, responded favourably, at times *en masse* (Tab. 2) to the appeal of what was on offer. Though a certain number of dramas registered mediocre audience results and although the range and intensity of the big successes of the historical genre remain in any case below the extremely high standards of religious dramas (see Chapter 7), the re-enactment of the twentieth-century past succeeded in corroborating – in both supply and demand – the role of television (drama) as historian.

Before I examine the Italian case in further detail, it is probably worthwhile to expand upon some considerations concerning the role of television in re-enacting the historical past. *Pace* those who maintain that television spoils the memory and erases history by obdurately sticking to the present, phenomenological observation and an ever-growing corpus of studies bear out convincingly the assumption that 'television is the principal means by which most people learn about history today' (Edgerton, 2001: 1). 'Television', confirms Lynn Spigel, 'serves as one of our culture's primary sources for historical consciousness' (Spigel, 2001: 368). Michael Pickering and Emily Keightley, for their part, state that 'uses of the past in contemporary media contribute to a historical imagination' (2006: 930). More critically, Silverstone observes that the media 'claim historical authority in drama and documentary' (1999: 127).

Table 2. Audience figures of the historical dramas in 2000s.

Title	Channel	Season	Av.Audience (in millions)
Perlasca.Un eroe italiano/ Perlasca. An Italian Hero	Raiuno	2001–02	12205
Come l'America/Like America	Raiuno	2000–01	9377
Maria Josè	Raiuno	2001–02	9160
Il cuore nel pozzo/The Heart in the Pit	Raiuno	2004–05	8831
Al di là delle frontiere/Beyond Frontiers	Raiuno	2003–04	8961
Edda	Raiuno	2004–05	8290
Marcinelle	Raiuno	2003–04	8102
La guerra è finita/The War is Over	Raiuno	2001–02	7777
Il grande Torino/The Great Torino	Raiuno	2005–06	7687
Storia di guerra e d'amicizia/Story of War and Friendship	Raiuno	2002–03	7336
Cefalonia	Raiuno	2004–05	7199
Mi ricordo di Anna Frank/ I Remember Anna Frank	Raiuno	2009–10	7021
La fuga degli innocenti/Hidden Children	Raiuno	2004–05	6938
Salvo D'Acquisto	Raiuno	2003–04	6837
Il segreto di Thomas/Thomas's Secret	Canale 5	2003–04	6836
Exodus: il sogno di Ada/Exodus:Ada's Dream	Raiuno	2006–07	6120
I figli strappati/Abducted Children	Raiuno	2005–06	5196
Mafalda di Savoia/Mafalda of Savoy	Canale 5	2006–07	5115
Questa è la mia terra/This Is My Land	Canale 5	2005–06	4979
Il sangue dei vinti/The Blood of the Defeated	Raiuno	2009–10	4957
Senza confini/No Boundaries	Raiuno	2001–02	4784
La buona battaglia di don Pietro Pappagallo/ The Good Battle of don Peter Pappagallo	Raiuno	2005–06	4092
Fuga per la libertà/Escape to Freedom	Canale 5	2007–08	4089

Source: Observatory of Italian Fiction

Figure 8.4. The wedding of Mussolini's daughter Edda (played by Alessandra Martines) and Galeazzo Ciano (played by Massimo Ghini) in the biopic *Edda* (Raiuno, 2005). Courtesy of RAI.

Documentaries and programmes that are historical in the strict sense, broadcast on thematic or educational channels such as the History Channel, may respond to the demands of experts and enthusiasts (there are more of these around than one might think, as is also demonstrated by the current widespread diffusion of popular historical literature); but most people get to know national and international history, and come into contact with the events, personalities and customs of other times, mainly if not exclusively by means of television programmes, drama included. The recent European and Italian tendency to re-enact the past in TV drama is based on a televisual aptitude for history: an aptitude that is deployed and realized in diverse ways in a range of genres and is vulnerable to alternating emersions and submersions, following the cyclical trends in many televisual phenomena, yet it unquestionably exists and should be acknowledged in opposition to the anti-history and anti-memory stigma that is conventionally and reductively applied to the medium.

To recognize television as a primary source of historical awareness for the majority of individuals today is not of course the equivalent of according television the status of an appropriate, reliable and truthful source. 'Television as historian' is a contestable and contested subject, still more so where (as in the case of drama) it makes room for an irruption of narrative imagination that reinvents and rewrites everything: not only when the relationship with an external reference is declaredly ephemeral or elusive (TV dramas vaguely or remotely 'inspired by') but also when the strategic ritual of scrupulously followed documentary evidence and expert advice is deployed.

The truth is that TV drama and television in general militate, as it were, in the field of popular historiography and popular memory; in such a role, they are more concerned with simplification than with accuracy, more committed to creating the conditions for emotional involvement than to pursuing the objective of analytical knowledge. From this point of view, one can better understand what is often attributed to period and historical drama as a presentist error: that is to say, a screening and staging of the past that is openly informed by the perceptive and evaluative frameworks of the present. The criticism may in general be well-founded, but its target is not so much an error as a prerogative or a characteristic; it is entirely appropriate for historiography and popular art forms to revisit the past and offer versions of it that have been reworked in the light of contemporary sensitivities and problems. As John Caughie nicely said with regard to the reappearance in the 1990s of the tradition of English period drama: 'History becomes the present in costume' (2000: 211); and in a sense the past proves useful, lending itself to be exploited for the benefit of the present, as problems, dilemmas and controversies are taken out of a contemporary context and transferred to a temporal elsewhere.

Furthermore, official, academic and popular historiography should not be regarded as irreconcilable antinomies: they rather represent the two polarities of a continuum along which one can move towards and cooperate with the other. 'There is no unambiguous divide between the historical and the popular representation of the past', to quote Silverstone once more (1999: 128). And it is probably true that 'history ... is not just something to be left to historians', according to an academic historian who is unusually sympathetic towards popular historiography (Susman, quoted in Edgerton: 6). Nor are we obliged to respect the rigid boundaries that academic orthodoxy has for years imposed to raise between history and memory (and the militants of this disjuncture are still around!) considering only the first worthy of full citizenship in the realm of science based on the objective, rational search for truth and dismissing the second as unreliable, emotional, contradictory. In fact – and not only in the representations of the media – history and memory tend 'to overlap in too many ways to be considered as pure categories ... [they] infuse each other' (Winter, quoted in Foot, 2009: 5). I am of course aware that I am dealing too hurriedly with a controversial and still largely debated question in historiographical circles as well as in the growing scholarship of memory studies. Just to clarify the sense in which I speak of historical drama, this admittedly cursory account should suffice.

Divided, denied, shared memory

I have already mentioned the specific temporal selection carried out by most historical fictions; they privilege, within the twentieth century, the period, 20 years or so, between the advent of Fascism and the end of the World War II. But looking closely at the selection, we see that it is even more restricted, as most stories have their temporal fulcrum in the early 1940s, in the final phases of the conflict and in its immediate aftermath. For example:

The hugely successful and acclaimed *Perlasca un eroe italiano/Perlasca an Italian hero* (Raiuno, 2002) tells the story of a Fascist businessman turned saviour of thousands of Jews during the Nazi occupation of Budapest in the winter of 1944.

Salvo D'Acquisto (Raiuno, 2003) recalls the generous sacrifice of the young carabiniere officer who, in September 1943, took the blame upon himself for an attack against German forces near Rome, to save a group of innocent civilians from the reprisal;

Based on a true story, the narrative of *Al di là delle frontiere/Beyond Frontiers* (Raiuno, 2004) revolves around the passionate and convention-breaking love story between an anti-Fascist Italian woman and a basically decent Wehrmacht officer, who ends up sharing her ideals of freedom and democracy, and contributing to the liberation of Venice, participating in negotiations between the Resistance and the German troops.

This too inspired by a true story *La fuga degli innocenti/Hidden Children* (Raiuno, 2004) narrates the mobilization of a small community in north Italy to help a group of Jewish children, in their flight from Germany, to get to Palestine.

Il cuore nel pozzo/The Heart in the Pit (Raiuno, 2005) is set on the Eastern border, which saw the tragedy of the *foibe*, the much contested – denied even – massacre of thousands of Italians, perpetrated by bands of Yugoslavian partisans at the end of World War II.

Cefalonia (Raiuno, 2005), reconstructs the tragic events concerning the annihilation of the Italian 33rd Infantry Division *Acqui* on the Greek island of Cephalonia, just after the Armistice of 8 September 1943; the events in Cephalonia inspired Louis de Bernières' *Captain Corelli's Mandolin*, which was made into a sentimental film of the same name (Jon Madden, 2001).

Exodus (Raiuno, 2006) is dedicated to the exodus to Palestine of the Jews surviving the Shoah; it is the biography of the courageous Roman Jewish woman Ada Sereni who just after the war managed to organize the departure from Italy of more than 20,000 survivors coming from all over Europe;

Mafalda di Savoya/Mafalda of Savoy (Canale 5, 2007) narrates the destiny of one of the daughters of King Victor Emanuel III. The fact that she belonged to a royal family, and that she was married to a German aristocrat, was not to save her, after the armistice of 8 September 1943, from internment, then death in a Nazi concentration camp.

On the other hand, it is not so often that fiction goes back in time to explore the history of the 20 years of Fascist rule in Italy, as in the two female biographies, *Maria José* (Raiuno, 2002) and *Edda* (Raiuno, 2005). The first is dedicated to the wife of Umberto di Savoia, the last king of Italy (only for the month of May 1946); known for her disapproval of the Fascist regime and her aversion for the Italian–German alliance, Maria José offers a perspective – from within the court and at the same time open to the anti-Fascist opposition – from which to observe the history of Italy from the aftermath of World War I to the end of the monarchy. *Edda* reconstructs the twenty-year trajectory of Fascism through the biography of Mussolini's favourite daughter, following the public and private events in her married life with the foreign affairs ministry Galeazzo Ciano – the Duce's heir apparent – up to his arrest and execution for treason in January of 1944.

The latest studies of the politics of memory in post-war Italy have speculated on the singular effect of the memory blurring concerning the Fascist regime, stemming from a process of public memorialization, which, up to fairly recent times, has greatly favoured the short 1943–1945 period, so as to construct on the anti-Fascist resistance the founding myth of democratic, Republican Italy. '… with the monumentalization of the *biennio* (the two years between the fall of Mussolini on 25 July 1943 and the insurrection of 25 April 1945), the Fascist *ventennio* was effectively marginalized in the memory … and virtually obliterated from the official history of the Italian postwar Republic' (Fogu, 2006: 149).

We cannot apply to fiction such a clear-cut historiographical evaluation; in the historical dramas under consideration here – as in a series of other fictions with a historical setting, a variety of religious biographies for example – phases and characters of the Fascist regime, political climate, aspects of daily life during the years of the dictatorship, are in any case present or evoked, perhaps fitfully, or in the sketchiness with which Italian fiction gladly tends to comply – and usually, to be honest, observed from a perspective of perhaps conventional but unambiguous critical distancing and condemnation. However, although not strictly limited to the 1943–1945 two-year period, the temporal dimension within which historical fictions in the 2000s move freely is short and significantly situated in the dramatic final phases of the regime and the war. This temporal placement is directly linked to the thematic agenda – the synthetic summaries provided earlier give us an idea of the subjects dealt with – in which it is possible to single out the elements of a specific politics of memory.

First and foremost is the intention to create a 'common memory' concerning personalities and events that not only belong to an undoubtedly crucial phase in Italian history in the twentieth century – but were also ignored, marginal or repressed in the collective memory or in the forms of public and institutional memorialization. In present society, memory in common (Jedlowski, 2005) is typically a product of the media, the deposit left by a shared experience of consumption of the same media contents – obviously open to interaction and tension with pre-existing individual and collective memories and likely to contribute to creating new ones.

Therefore, the purpose of building a common memory has presided over the narration of stories relatively little known by the Italian public. The story of Giorgio Perlasca, for example, remained in obscurity for more than 40 years after the war, before being discovered and popularized in a biography (Deaglio, 1991); the television version brought it to the attention of 12 million people. And again: forgotten for years was the story that inspired *La fuga degli innocenti/Hidden Children* (Raiuno, 2004), that of the policeman Giovanni Palatucci (*Senza confini/No Boundaries* Raiuno, 2001) who after his efforts at saving Jews was deported to Dachau where he died, as well as the commitment of the Roman priest don Pietro Pappagallo – one of the victims of the Fosse Ardeatine slaughter – for the victims of Nazi–Fascism *(La buona battaglia di don Pietro Pappagallo/ The Good Battle of don Peter Pappagallo*, Raiuno, 2006).

Delivering from oblivion people and events worthy of being remembered, and digging up past events, forgotten not because of unawareness or indifference but because a heavy silence of repression and denial had fallen – their highly 'uncomfortable' and controversial nature being the reason: those were the major intents pursued by the historical drama. In response to the second objective *Il cuore nel pozzo/The Heart in the Pit* (Raiuno, 2005) and *Cefalonia* (Raiuno, 2005) were produced; one, via a story of imagination situated in the historical–geographical context of real events, the other with closer attention to the historical reconstruction of events, these fictions measured themselves against the evocation of two appalling slaughters perpetrated on thousands of Italian civilians and soldiers at the end of World War II.

Historical memory is often conflictual: for reasons pertaining to civil wars and deep politico–ideological fractures that have characterized Italian history and life since unification, 'Italian memories have often been divided' (Foot, 2009: 1), and 'markedly different and often conflicting strands of memory' (Perra, 2010b: 4) have clashed and still clash about 'the legitimate version' of historical facts. The events narrated in *The Heart in the Pit* and *Cefalonia* are among the most controversial, both in the collective memory and in historiographical interpretation; on both, public discourse has been reticent, embarrassed, totally absent indeed for much of the time.

This is especially the case with the so-called slaughter of the *foibe*, narrated in the fiction *The Heart in the Pit*. The *foibe* are deep natural chasms to be found in the north-east of Italy on the border with Yugoslavia. An unknown number of Italians living at the time in this area, annexed to Italy after World War I, died in the *foibe* or in mass graves following summary execution by Yugoslav communist partisans after the armistice of 8 September 1943, and again at the end of the war. The number of victims, estimated to be in their thousands, is itself open to dispute; in fact the historiographical and above all

Figure 8.5. Giorgio Perlasca (played by Luca Zingaretti) rescues a Jewish child from deportation in the biopic *Perlasca. An Italian Hero* (Raiuno, 2002). Courtesy of RAI.

politico–ideological debate was split between two different interpretative readings of the *foibe* slaughters (crudely ascribable to opposite political alignments: left-wing or right-wing). Should they be considered war crimes, reprisals in response to other war crimes, equally ruthless, perpetrated by the German and Italian armies, plausibly also deriving from deep anti-Italian resentment, as the result of repression exercised by the Fascist regime; or rather genocide, ethnic cleansing, intentionally pursued by the Yugoslav authorities after the re-annexation of the ex-Italian territory which had to be 'reslavized' and purged of potential objectors to the new communist regime. Behind this second interpretation is the fact that violence and expulsions of the Italian population continued long after World War II, leading to a mass exodus lasting many years.

Much more than divided, the memory of the *foibe* was a memory denied in Italy for more than half a century. The oblivion that descended like a curtain upon these tragic events served to remove a mnemonic encumbrance, which constituted for many, and in many ways, a source of embarrassment and unease. It evoked a dysphoric image of defeat and sufferance, which most of the country was unwilling to come to terms with after the war. Those on the right like those of the left tended to minimize or deny responsibility and guilt: Fascists blamed communists and vice versa in the *foibe* slaughters and in any case they saw no advantage in sustaining a memorialization, which would have meant opening that Pandora's box of crimes committed by both parties. Italian governments, in turn, did not wish to irritate Yugoslavia, which the West had decided to treat with kind gloves, especially after Belgrade had left the Soviet orbit.

It was not until the end of the 1990s that the curtain of silence began to lift. In 2004, during the second Berlusconi government (2001–2005), Parliament approved a law with a large majority which, echoing the 'Day of Memory' already instituted in 2000 to honour the victims of the Shoah, established the 'Day of Remembrance' in honour of the *foibe* slaughter. The beginning of a process of public memorialization did not, furthermore, coincide with the elaboration of a shared memory, capable of conciliating the different and conflicting strands of memory of the *foibe* – which in the reactions to the drama *The Heart in the Pit* found a further occasion to come to light.

Interviewed on the set, during the shooting in the summer of 2004, the director Alberto Negrin said he was aware of the controversy that the fiction might trigger although he insisted upon stressing the non-political angle, the emotional aspect of the story, centred upon the human drama of a small Istrian community fleeing a ferocious persecution. *The Heart in the Pit* narrates in fact the march to salvation, under the guidance of a priest and the protection of a few adults, of a group of children; following them is a Yugoslav partisan with his men, seeking his child, who he had never seen, the result of the rape of an Italian woman. Along the way the group witnesses the ferocious methods of extermination of the civil population carried out by the Yugoslav partisans; one of the children discovers the bodies of his own parents at the bottom of a chasm; the Italian mother of the disputed child ends her life by throwing herself into a chasm to escape her persecutor. In the end, the children will be taken to safety, while a long slow column of refugees announces the beginning of the exodus.

The line followed by fiction is one of political prudence, which entails making choices that are, to large extent, negotiated, and adopting elusive approaches to the historical material. The script, for example, contains no spoken reference to communism, says little about Fascism and though it stresses mostly the ethnic motivation of the massacre as opposed to the hypothesis of a 'rendering of accounts' of wrongs undergone, it seems to attribute at least partially, the anti-Italian hatred of the partisan chief to a personal obsession. Strong emotional involvement as well as a certain lightening of the tones of a sombre tragedy, is assured by the protagonistic presence of the children – an aspect that children-centred Italian culture is notoriously sensitive about.

The Re-Enactment of the Past and Politics of Memory and Identity in Contemporary Drama

Figure 8.6. Civilians rounded up and brought to the foibe by Yougoslav partisans in *The Heart in the Pit* (Raiuno, 2005). Courtesy of RAI.

The Heart in the Pit was aired in early February in 2005, at the time of the first anniversary of the 'Day of Remembrance' and was seen by a huge audience, which came very close, on average, to 9 million viewers. The preview and the press conference held the previous week were the object of full journalistic coverage, which had prepared the ground in depth, in terms of expectations. The newspapers had spoken in advance of the plot and reported the declarations of the head of drama at the Rai on the commitment assumed by public television in constructing a 'shared memory', and above all they had given space to the controversy that had immediately been triggered. The left-wing press, for example, denounced the attempts at exploitation of the fiction by right-wing parties (Nove, 2005: 1), and advanced the suspicion that behind the 'shared memory' lay the snare of an obliteration of the irreducible differences between Fascism and anti-Fascism

(Bucci, 2005: 15); readers were also informed of the accusations of the Serbian press concerning 'the cinematographic vendetta of Berlusconi against Tito' (Gallozzi, 2005: 21). In turn the right-wing and centre–right newspapers ironized about 'those nostalgic of the ... partisan version of national history' (Di Lello, 2005: 1) and did not fail to evoke the responsibility of the Italian Communist party in 'spreading a veil of lies and hypocrisy' (Cervi, 2005: 1) over the truth behind the *foibe*; an authoritative commentator emphasized the absence of any clear imputation of guilt on the part of the Yugoslav communists, and the 'human and sentimental traits' (Veneziani, 2005: 1) attributed to the brutal partisan chief.

Figure. 8.7. The former alpine soldier Ettore (played by Giuseppe Fiorello) helps a group of children to escape capture by Yugoslav partisans in *The Heart in the Pit* (Raiuno, 2005). Courtesy of RAI.

This politico–ideological polemical vein gained strength during and after the airing of *The Heart in the Pit*. However, as against the contrast between the accusations of historical falsity – an 'anti-Semite inclination' even (Germani, 2005: 16) – on the one hand, and the smugness on the other because finally 'the wall of silence has been breached' (Fragalà, 2005: 21), other arguments came into play: the celebration of a success beyond expectations, the reviews of television critics, the comments of certain historians. Television critics were fairly concordant (which does not always happen) in recognizing that the dramaturgical choice of looking at an immense collective tragedy through the eyes of children, though of undoubted efficacy in kindling intense sentiments of commotion and pity, distracted the authors from committing themselves to a serious historical contextualization. '*Il Cuore nel Pozzo* represents too limited a point of view, too intimist, too personal with respect to a scenario sinisterly conceived by an ideology of ethnic purification', said the critic of *Corriere della Sera* (Grasso, 2005: 33). Others expressed the same opinion: 'The historical and ideological component ends up having less substance than the sentimental' (Levi, 2005: 36), 'This forgotten, or rather obscured tragedy, remains inevitably in the background of the story of its little protagonist' (Messina, 2005: 53). In a similar vein, in the declarations of historians, the appraisals of a fiction that clearly contributed to 'letting us know', alternated with criticisms about the weakness of the narrative of *The Heart in the Pit* in 'helping us understand' the facts concerning the *foibe*: in the absence, above all, of a more complete and balanced account of the violence undergone as well as the violence inflicted by the Italians in the historical atmosphere of Fascism and the War (see in particular Bidussa, 2005).

The heated debate, triggered by a highly disputed narrative material and the criticisms about the dramaturgical and historiographical treatment – whose limits partially derive from the simplifying canons of popular historiography practised by TV drama – did not hinder *The Heart in the Pit* from proving itself one of the most efficient instruments of a politics of memory, aimed at redeeming from oblivion what had been repressed in recent Italian history. Historical understanding and shared memory of the facts brought to light and offered to the collective awareness are naturally another story entirely. No longer denied, the memory of the *foibe* remains still today a deeply divided memory.

'We are not like them'

The case of *The Heart in the Pit* is highly emblematic of the attempt to reveal and reconcile conflicting historical memories but is at the same time rather atypical, to the extent that it renders an image of the Italians as defenceless victims of an extermination carried out by a ruthless and victorious enemy. Usually, the historical dramas under consideration tend to present and represent Italians not as victims but as heroes: hero–saviours of other human beings threatened with slaughter, persecution, denial of rights (*Perlasca*, *No Boundaries*, *Hidden Children*, *Exodus*); hero–martyrs, willing to sacrifice their lives to save the innocent and the persecuted (*Salvo D'Acquisto, The Good Battle of don Pietro Pappagallo*); war heroes, fallen on the scene of a mass execution, confronting their destiny consciously, defiantly and not as defenceless victims but as soldiers, adamant in their refusal to surrender their arms to an enemy force (*Cefalonia*).

Heroes, almost always; victims, sometimes. In any case, the protagonists of historical fictions are meant to represent those who in the most tragic and sombre moments of twentieth-century history – and according to different feelings and actions, by reason of different personal stances and motivations, and the specific set of circumstances behind their choice, decisions and behaviours – have testified to the dissention and resistance of Italians to regimes of violence imposed by Fascism and Nazism. What many fiction stories narrate, indeed, is the widespread form of civil resistance – acknowledged by recent historiography too – enacted by Italians independently of their political alignments or other factors of differentiation and division. Members of the aristocratic elite, exponents of military institutions faithful to the monarchy, catholic priests, Jewish women and even functionaries of the Fascist police (Giovanni Palatucci) and volunteers in the war effort Fascism had claimed (Giorgio Perlasca): an assortment of characters occupy the protagonistic limelight of historical dramas, which staged and enhanced the civil resistance of the Italian population, thus contributing to the emersion of a phenomenon that had for long been obscured by the all-absorbing myth of the partisan resistance as the only and determinant form of anti-Fascist and anti-Nazi opposition. We can see here another founding element of the politics of memory pursued by the historical drama of the noughties.

Predictably, all this has aroused controversy. Especially the biographies of Giorgio Perlasca (*Perlasca: An Italian Hero*) and Giovanni Palatucci (*No Boundaries*) – both of them with a militant Fascist past, both saviours of thousands of Jews and therefore recognized as 'Righteous among the nations' – have induced certain commentators to speak of a 're-legitimization' of Fascism, carried out via the re-conversion of contradictory individuals into symbol–figures of an heroic Italy (Perra, 2010a). This is not my interpretation, nor that of other analysts (Bechelloni, 2010). The thematic (and political) option of the historical drama in favour of civil resistance, like the muting – equally denounced by the critics – of the crimes, which in that same historical phase the Italians were responsible for, are clearly not devoid of meaning or without scope. On the contrary, they constitute an integral part of a politics of memory strictly correlated – as always with memories, individual and collective – with a project of identity construction or reassertion.

The purposeful placement of the historical drama in a horizon of identity references, which were intended to be shared and therefore unifying, has entailed a selective memorialization, above all committed (at least the intentions, not necessarily the outcomes) to avoiding, or leaving in the background, that which might be traced back to divisions and fractures, urging an identification of an internal enemy, corroborating the idea of a splitting of the Italians between 'us' and 'them'. Although the hypothesis of re-legitimization of Fascism appears to those who know Italian fiction entirely conjectural, there is no doubt that the historical drama has made its choices according to a logic of national reconciliation hinging upon the recognition of a common identity matrix and belonging. As regards reconciliation, it was not by chance that one of the first in the long series of historical fictions produced during the 2000s happened to be called *La guerra è finita/The War Is Over* (Raiuno, 2002). *The War Is Over* narrated the deep friendship between two young men, both in love with the same woman, who ended up fighting on opposite sides in the war, one in the partisan resistance, the other in the Fascist formations of the Italian Social Republic (a puppet State headed by Mussolini in northern Italy between November 1943 and April 1945). Though ideological hatred had led them to extreme gestures and the cultivation of sentiments of revenge, at the end of the war they agree to comply with the exhortation of the woman – who in turn has loved both men – to depose all the reasons for the conflict between them regaining, albeit in the diversity of their destinies, the fraternal value of friendship, which united them as youngsters.

In wishing to appeal to a shared sense of Italianness, of being Italians, the historical drama has not invented anything new: it had at its disposal, and made use of, a preexisting identity construct endowed with an elevated potential of recognizability and shareability, already widely used in other narratives (for example cinematographic) of self-representation of the Italian people. I refer to the construct – to a certain extent, a mythical one and thus, like all myths, not without some foundation in truth – of 'italiani brava gente' (Italians good people) or the 'good Italian' (Bidussa, 1994; Del Boca, 2005; Perra, 2010b). This colloquial expression, now commonplace, condenses a set of virtuous traits that are presumed to characterize the behaviour of Italians and shelter them from abandoning themselves to or from consenting to the ferocity of man against man: a marked sense of humanity, a tolerant nature, generous impulses expressing solidarity even at the risk of personal danger, this latter an inclination liable to overlap with heroism should the need arise. In short, a kind of 'inherent goodness' in Italians, which comes to accompany the 'inherent religiousness' mentioned in the previous chapter. We should add that in a range of variants from the most to the least stereotyped, the model of the 'good Italian' presides over the construction of most heroes in domestic fiction. And undoubtedly, it is incarnated in the characters whose brave and noble deeds – saving people's lives, self-sacrifice, civil resistance – historical dramas have narrated, thus leading them back to a common matrix of Italianness, which goes beyond all differences.

Every identity needs to confront an otherness to recognize itself and find confirmation of its own constitutive distinction. As is easy to predict, in the dramas being analysed the pole of otherness is usually occupied by the evil figure of Nazis, above all (but not only) in the guise of persecutors and exterminators of Jews. Within the historical drama the narrative strand centred on the Shoah found ample space for a number of reasons. Above all, this is a consensual issue, which can count upon an almost unanimous condemnation of the genocide carried out by the Nazis. The annual celebration of the Day of Memory, inaugurated in the year 2000 to honour victims of the Shoah, was a further incentive, offering the chance to broadcast, in coincidence with the anniversary, a 'topical' fiction. It is true also that many Italians, at home or elsewhere in Europe (for example in Hungary, as in the case of Perlasca) were generous in their commitment at the time to help Jews avoid arrest and deportation. Thanks to this network of civil solidarity, the survival rate of Italian Jews was very high.

The narrative of the Shoah has provided fertile ground (but I should repeat, not the only one) in a confrontation between an identity and an otherness, in which the inherent goodness of the Italian character stands out, confirmed as an unmistakable marker of difference with respect to the 'other' (German, Nazi) and at the same time an element of national communality. The proud awareness of the ethical distinction conferred by this specific prerogative of Italianness has never been so clearly expressed as in the drama *Cefalonia*. I have already mentioned that *Cefalonia* reconstructed what is considered one of the most appalling war crimes committed by the German army during World War II: the slaughter of thousands of the Acqui Division, which, after the armistice of 8 September 1943, refused to hand over its weapons to its ex-ally and current enemy. In the fiction, the soldiers who survive the mass shootings join the Greek partisans and a year later defeat the Germans remaining on the island. The insurgents capture and are about to shoot the German officer who had commanded the firing squad; but an Italian non-commissioned officer (who is a protagonist in the story and in fact represents the point of view of the narrative) intervenes to impede the execution of the prisoner, and in response to the excited reactions of the others who are protesting 'but *they* did it' replies calmly and clearly 'but *we* are not like *them*'.

On this clear-cut binary opposition between us and them, a harmonized interconnection has been established between the politics of memory and identity in the Italian historical drama.

Conclusion

The convocative power of mainstream drama

As I have outlined in my introduction, the main aim of this work is to bring to light an all-important component of Italian TV landscape and culture: namely, TV drama as an instance (among many others, ranging well beyond the Italian case) of 'invisible television' on the international scene of contemporary media studies. In so doing, the preceding chapters have focused on the most popular genres, on the most successful fiction programmes of Italian TV. In this connection, I will offer here some integrative comments concerning the success achieved by home-grown drama in the latest phases of its development, during the 1990s and the 2000s that have coincided with 'the passing of an era' in Italian national broadcasting. Brief conclusive remarks will be provided in the last section.

As hitherto mentioned several times, since the mid-1990s the Italian TV drama industry has gone through a phase of expansion, which, by jointly involving production, supply and consumption of domestic drama, has resulted in a sort of 'golden age' of TV storytelling. The production of fiction, which in the 1980s and early 1990s had dramatically decreased under the impact of foreign imports, increased significantly in a relatively short span of time. Thus a plentiful supply of home-grown drama came to fill the schedules of TV channels and, taking advantage of being aired in prime time when most of the viewers gather before the screen, managed to attract the largest possible audiences. In fact this period has witnessed an uninterrupted series of well-received and highly rated dramas; in other words, over these years the harvest of success has been rewardingly rich.

Of course, such an achievement should not be traced back solely to the re-launch of a production system, or to editorial strategies and scheduling policies aimed at enhancing and promoting national TV storytelling. This would mean forgetting, or at any rate overlooking, that what is seen at work when huge audiences gather is the cogent 'convocative power' (Trupia, 2002) displayed by this or that TV show. The convocative power, besides obviously being predicated on the intrinsic requisites of attractiveness and craftsmanship and to further ingredients that might strengthen and widen the product's appeal, often transcends them: indeed, a primary factor in making this power effectual lies in the external references of a broader social and cultural context, in structures of feelings, climates of opinion, states of mind and other components of the Zeitgeist that help to orientate and shape the choice and preference models of TV viewers.

Therefore it is worth recalling that in the recent years the 'cultural proximity' factor (Straubhaar, 1991, 2007) – the audience's eager preference for home-grown contents – has proved itself to be a guiding light for TV consumption, presumably also as a counterpoint to the processes of globalization that were widely perceived as threatening to strip national and local communities of their own native identities. The call of cultural proximity, infused with the flavours and taste of 'home', endowed with the special resonance of the sense of place, fuelled a more pressing demand than in the past for Italian storytelling and created an extensive pool of viewers of TV drama who were ready to respond to the captivating appeal of home-grown supply. This wider horizon of demand and expectations for national storytelling has provided fertile soil for an impressive series of big hits: whose interest lies, first, in the very nature of drama as narrative and second in the temporal location that goes hand in hand with a dramatic process of change in the TV environment.

As regards the first point, it is sufficient to recall both the role of broadcasting TV as a 'central storytelling system' (Newcomb 1988: 88) and the purpose of narratives to dramatize society and structure and develop the dramaturgy by which a society represents itself (Buonanno, 2008). As a maker of genuine 'social tales', TV drama unfolds stories on screen, whether well-crafted or otherwise at the artistic and technical level, which are the fruit of 'interpretative practices' of reality. It hardly needs to be said that these stories tell us at least something about the social world and the cultural climate within which, at any time, our daily life is situated and runs its course; and it is entirely plausible to ascribe a special eloquence to very popular stories, those that prove the most effective in convoking a large following of viewers, who 'listen to' them and possibly, to a greater or lesser extent, recognize themselves and their life-worlds in the narrative.

Of course, we need to be wary of the mechanical application of any 'circular' hypothesis to justify success; this would lead us into the error of regarding every most-watched programme as being loaded with a resonant wealth of meanings. Nevertheless the success and wide popularity of domestic drama, insofar as they are indicators of the extent to which national TV storytelling is able to gather the largest possible audiences around the same stories, deserve to be seriously considered from the perspective of a cultural analysis aimed at reading reality through fiction. They should be regarded as the most paradigmatic expression of the eminently 'choric' nature (Newcomb and Alley, 1983: 31) of television drama in the context of broadcasting TV. In the metaphor of the chorus as a collective narrative voice, intended to bring into accord and blend the polyphonic diversity of multiple voices, the TV drama that we usually define as 'mainstream' can be distinctly recognized. Mainstream drama is the core of any system of popular narration, the primary generator of the highest viewing figures and phenomena of true popularity; and it is still today the main component of the dramatic landscape in Italy.

Ascribing the connotation of mainstream to the most watched fictions can hardly come as a surprise or give rise to much controversy; indeed, exceptions apart, these stories would not occupy top positions in drama ratings if they did not deploy a range of features, issues and treatments endowed with compelling and inclusive attractiveness with respect to heterogeneous components of the audience, or if they did not draw on a broadly shared social imaginary and common repertoires of sense-making frameworks and resources (which they also help to create, maintain and modify). Here precisely lies a major strand of interest of the mainstream fiction, since it allows us, as time flows on, to grasp the emerging configurations, the persistence and transmogrification of what, at a given moment in time, seem to coalesce into a widely diffused commonality of vision, imagination, feelings and taste that is embodied in and articulated and addressed by popular TV narratives.

Mentioning the passage of time introduces the second order of considerations. In the same temporal arc that witnessed the vibrant revival of the domestic TV drama industry, when the fruits of a conjuncture of favourable circumstances originating within and outside the TV world were harvested in the guise of intense and widespread success, there has been a move in the TV system towards a post-broadcast multi-channel environment: first barely perceptible, but now progressing at a faster pace and making an impact that can clearly be observed and assessed.

There is no need to adhere to the extreme and improbable prediction – longed-for or feared, depending on diametrically opposed viewpoints – of broadcasting TV threatened with marginalization by the advent of narrowcasting, to agree on the outstanding transformative capacity of the multi-channel environment. To confine my remarks to the aspects that are strictly pertinent to the present discourse: the tenfold or even a hundredfold multiplication of networks and the consequent expansion of content supply and therefore of the range of choices, have brought about a redistribution of TV viewers, who – being scattered into many segments, though very unequal in their size – inevitably give rise to instances of erosion, depletion and contraction. We are now faced in Italy with unmistakable evidence of falling ratings for generalist channels, even in the presence of praised and widely watched programmes.

It is highly probable that the most recent years, marking the close of an era of almost unchallenged domination by broadcasting, were the last, or nearly the last, to preserve the necessary conditions that allowed Italian TV drama to enjoy a period of great, indeed outstanding, success. Let me be clear about this: there is no reason to maintain that high ratings now belong to a TV world that we have lost, or will soon be lost forever. The Italian market today is, and for some time will be, in an initial phase of audience fragmentation which, according to Denis McQuail, corresponds to the 'central-peripheral model' (McQuail,1997: 137). At this stage, although the multiplication of channels makes it possible to enjoy a wide range of TV programmes both outside and on the edge of the mainstream, the generalist networks continue to occupy centre-stage on the TV scene and to attract a majority share of audiences. But in a mature multi-channel environment the largest possible audiences, who still gather round and will continue to gather round the most appealing stories, will not be the same: neither in their size, which will be reduced by a little or a lot, nor in their internal composition, which will tend to be less pluralist and less – as it were – ecumenical.

I have introduced terminology into this discourse that current language has borrowed from the vocabulary of agriculture: harvest and fruits. What makes these words unexpectedly pertinent in relation to the successes of TV drama is the common premise of the seed. The word 'broadcasting' in English originally meant 'casting or scattering (seed) in all directions'; and as John Durham Peters (1999) argues in a profound and persuasive fashion, generalist TV – in that it is aimed indiscriminately at heterogeneous components of the population, like the seeds scattered by the farmer all over the ploughed land – has adopted and put into practice a dissemination model of communication. It is not a better or a worse model than any other, but simply distinct and specific. Its peculiarity rests in its non-selective character, in a sort of inclusive attitude that predisposes it to working on what can unite and hold together (if only for the short duration of a TV programme) the different fractions of an assorted aggregate of viewers. Its achievement is measured by the equivalent of a rich harvest: a vast viewing public, and hence audience ratings escalating to the highest peaks. That is what the Italian TV landscape witnessed during the 1990s and early 2000s, predictably the last period when the unifying communication model of broadcasting expressed itself with all the intensity and effectiveness of the mainstream drama's convocative power.

The ambivalent criminal Mafia – both social evil and success story, when it comes to making money and rising to power – and those, either state officials or common citizens, who are engaged in the endless fight against it. The life stories of the many Italians who had attained great heights in different fields of the human endeavour, their uncommonly heroic stature being complementary to the mimetic or ironic ordinariness of the police heroes. The stream of the religious biopics that have drawn on the deep-rooted (albeit far from unchanged or homogeneous) Catholic sentiment of the Italian population. Finally the history of the twentieth century as a crucible of experiences that were traumatic and at the same time healing, in which the national unity was put to hard test and asserted itself yet again in the confrontation with the 'other'. All these components steeped in the variegated tapestry of Italian society, culture, historical memory and national identity have fed the narrative that flowed within and through the most successful and popular TV dramas during the period under consideration.

Obviously to resort to the components of the multifaceted (and in many instances contradictory and even fractured) prism of culture and national identity is more than just routine practice of TV drama in every country: it is an all-important device for communicating a strong sense of place and 'our-own-ness' and arousing in viewers the pleasure of recognition, the latter being in turn a condition of popularity. Therefore the question that really matters is not so much whether TV dramas, especially the successful ones, bring into play aspects related to specificities of national culture and identity, but rather which elements they resort to, which issues they address and how these change over time.

A more wide-ranging exploration of the current dramatic landscape would enable us to identify a whole repertoire of features that bear the unmistakable mark of Italian-ness; suffice it to mention, for example, the family, or on the visual side the urban and natural scenery. The peculiarity here, however, lies in the circumstance that the major genres that have hegemonized the contemporary drama scene in Italy – indeed, the most prolific and favoured genres, which have engendered hundreds of stories and the bulk of the top-rated TV dramas – have worked together to shape and maintain a vast area of the storytelling environment that can be regarded as almost unique in terms of the unequalled density and salience of the Italianness-related narratives (Mafia, religion, the homeland's history, national real-life heroes, fictional heroes embodying the national character at its height). In spite of differences concerning genres, subject matters, modes of address and much more, the similarities with the long-past epoch of the *sceneggiato* are overtly perceptible: hence, something of a circularity emerges between the dawn and the (initial) demise of the broadcasting TV, as far as the engagement of domestic drama with the nation and the national audience is concerned.

It nonetheless remains true that, from the 1990s to the early 2000s, Italian TV drama has experienced a period to be regarded as unique, not so much owing to the lack of comparable precedents in the past as because it is most unlikely to occur again in the future. The kind of TV dramas that were produced and eagerly watched over those years are not necessarily on their way to extinction; but even if they are destined to last, they will have trouble in the years to come in matching the outstanding audience size of the latest seasons.

Thus, broadcast TV in the last stage of its hegemony has offered home-grown drama, in the phase of its renaissance, the opportunity – unlikely to recur – to narrate stories of Italian identity to the largest possible national audiences.

Visibility for what?

More than a decade ago, a landmark scholarly work convincingly highlighted the need to 'de-westernize media studies', pointing out that most interest and attention in western academic circles had all too long been concerned with just 'a tiny handful of countries' (Curran and Park, 2000: 3), while the rest of the world remained overlooked, under-researched and forgotten. I have no intention of discussing if and to what extent such an indisputable recommendation has been received and put into action; in fact, scholarly voices have continued to question the parochial assumption that the patterns of change experienced in the widely studied anglophone markets should automatically fit into the mostly uncharted TV landscapes of non-western countries (Turner and Tay, 2010). Instead, I am at pains to remark how reliance on, and international circulation of knowledge about just a handful of countries, even more restricted perhaps when it comes to TV drama, has resulted in the uneven dichotomy between what counts as the West – a *totum pro parte* denomination in this case – and 'the rest of the West', this being in turn a substantial part of the invisible or forgotten rest or the world. Without dismissing the efforts of de-westernizing media studies, filling the void or rather widening the scope of the West in the same field of studies seems to me a scholarly endeavour that is both necessary and worth undertaking. The present book on Italian TV drama is intended to take a step in this direction.

A primary task of TV scholarship today – speaking from the point of view of a media scholar steeped in sociology – is to illuminate the features and especially the peculiarities which characterize different TV landscapes (with regard to storytelling or whatever else might be concerned), setting them in the context of the long-duration historical processes and factors and the localized conditions and contingencies that contribute to their formation as well as to their transformation. Present-day TV studies find themselves confronting the challenge of a huge expansion of the horizons of media change, which makes it more important than ever before to have at one's disposal maps and charts of the many diverse territories where these processes of change are taking place – at variable paces, following different sequences of steps and heterogeneous patterns of development. Otherwise one risks perpetuating or even exacerbating the tendency to underestimate, to a greater or lesser degree, local factors and conditions, which do not disappear or lose (but maybe readjust) their capacity to make an impact simply because they are in turn exposed to the impact of globalization streams.

In actual fact, it is precisely such an assumption that elicits the sense of commitment to granting visibility to locally situated instances of invisible TV. This would not really be worth doing if it were merely a question of competing for a place in the international shop window of media studies. It is rather a question of helping, insofar as it is possible, to throw light on the opaque zones in the map of televisual landscapes in the western and non-western world, thus providing knowledge about previously (wholly or partially) uncharted territories: which benefits, among other things, the indispensable but all too infrequently performed task of identifying, comparing and assessing the similarities and differences between diverse localities.

We are obviously well aware that the maps do no coincide with territories (unless in Borges's fictional science of cartography). Instead they are representational tools that call into play practices of selection and exclusion. This work is not exception, indeed it is the outcome of a purposeful selection of subjects, drawn from the superabundant material that has accumulated in more than half a century of Italian TV drama history. Although this long time span is completely retraced within and through the eight preceding chapters, I have based both the reconstruction of the historical evolution of TV drama (provided in the first half of the book) and the account of the present-day dramatic landscape (provided in the second) on the identification of certain key moments and processes and a targeted choice of specific genres, texts and case studies. I freely admit that there is more in past and present of Italian TV fiction than meets the eye (to repeat the maxim quoted in the introduction), that is to say more than one can find in these pages. But it was never my intention to relate an exhaustive history or conduct a complete investigation on the whole field of TV drama; nor would these have been appropriate for my purpose. As a native Italian scholar, I have singled out the subject matter from an insider's perspective, wishing to bring together a number of aspects and characteristics that could prove more conducive to grasping and understanding the historical, cultural and generic specificities of Italian TV drama.

Conclusion

We have witnessed over the years the pluralization of co-existing and overlapping, to different extents, televisual spaces, on global, transnational, regional, local scale (Straubhaar, 2007). This re-configuration has not undermined the conception and reality of televisual space as being pre-eminently (although not exclusively) national; and the paraphrase of one of Mark Twain's famous quips – 'rumours of the death of the nation have been greatly exaggerated' – has echoed in many authoritative statements in support of the lasting importance and even the central position of the nation for today's media world and hence for TV studies (Curran and Park, 2000; Morris and Waisbord, 2001; Turner and Tay, 2009; Thussu, 2009).

The history of Italian TV drama is closely interwoven with the relationship that home-grown storytelling, especially that which emanates from public broadcasting, has maintained with national culture and history, as I have also recalled in the first part of this conclusion. It would however be impossible to take full account of such relationships within the framework of a 'territorial essentialism' (Hepp and Couldry, 2009) that claimed to include the production and consumption of home-grown cultural forms within an inward-looking, bordered national space, impervious to any intrusion or influence from outside. Indeed Italian TV drama has from its beginnings taken shape and developed within a national cultural space (relatively) open and porous with respect to non-national media cultures; constant interactions have been established with the latter, although differently articulated at different times according to diverse situations and purposes. The non-national 'other' has been intensively exploited as a source of narrative inspiration (Chapter 1) as well as a programming resource and a Trojan horse in changes of systems (Chapter 2); it has been the compelling trigger for an identity-related reaction 'with a vengeance', destined to have a deep and lasting impact on the national imagination (Chapters 3 and 6); it has made possible the re-launch of the Italian televisual industry (Chapter 4); and it has become permanently entwined with the genesis and evolution of the domestic police drama (Chapter 5).

I am not concerned with establishing, even hypothetically, the possible anomaly or by contrast the ordinariness of the long-lasting experience of Italian televisual storytelling: which over the course of its history has often negotiated with elements of foreignness the construction and even the strengthening of its own identity, unmistakably embedded into the national cultural space, and its vocation to narrate and address the nation.

But if I have made this thread of discourse into something of a 'running plot' in most chapters of this book, it is because I think that the intriguing articulation between stories from the soil and stories from the sea that we encounter along the historical trail of Italian TV drama lends itself to introducing into the field of TV studies an issue for discussion, whose interest goes far beyond Italy.

References

Abbott, Stacey (2009), *How Lost Found Its Audience: The Making of a Cult Blockbuster*, pp. 9–26 in Roberta Pearson (ed.), *Reading Lost*, London: I.B. Tauris.

Adam, Barbara (1995), *Timewatch: Social Analysis of Time*, Cambridge: Polity Press.

AIE (2010), *Rapporto sullo stato dell'editoria in Italia*, Milano: Associazione Italiana Editori.

Alessandrini, Ludovico (1988) *Una testimonianza*, pp. 83–91 in F. Pinto, G. Barlozzetti, C.Salizzato (eds), *La televisione presenta: La produzione cinematografica della RAI 1965–1975*, Venezia: Marsilio.

Allen, Robert C. (1985), *Speaking of Soap Opera*, Chapel Hill: University of North Carolina Press.

Amurri, Sandra (1992), '*Piovra*. L'abbiamo vista con Ayala/*Piovra*. We Watched It with Ayala', *Epoca*, 2 December.

Anania, Francesca (2003), *Immagini di storia: La televisione racconta il Novecento*, Roma: ERI.

Anderson, Carolyn and Lupo, Jonathan (2008), 'Introduction to the Special Issues', *Journal of Popular Film and Television*, vol. 36,2, pp. 50-51.

Arlacchi, Pino (2009), *Gli uomini del disonore*, Milan: il Saggiatore.

Baransky, Zygmunt G. and Robert Lumley (eds) (1990), *Culture and Conflict in Post-war Italy*, New York: St. Martin's Press.

Bauman, Zygmunt (2001), *Community*, Cambridge: Polity.

Bauman, Zygmunt (2002), 'Violence in the Age of Uncertainty', pp. 52–73 in Adam Crawford (ed.), *Crime and Insecurity: The Governance of Safety in Europe*, Uffculme: Willan Publishing.

Bechelloni, Giovanni (2010), *I nostri eroi: La funzione bardica della televisione*, Napoli: Liguori.

Beck, Ulrich (2003), *La società cosmopolita*, Bologna: il Mulino.

Benjamin, Walter (1999), *Illuminations*, London: Pimlico.

Bennett, Tony and Woollacott, Janet (1983), *Bond and Beyond: The Political Career of a Popular Hero*, London: Macmillan Education.

Bentivegna, Calogero (1995), *Storia della mafia dalle origini ai nostri giorni*, Milan: Hobby & Work.

Berbenni, Stefania (1995), 'Telemafia in chiave politica/A Political Mafia Story on Television', *Panorama*, 7 April.

Berger, Peter L. (ed.) (1999), *The Desecularization of the World: Resurgent Religion and Worlds Politics*, Grand Rapids: Wm. B. Eerdmans Publishing Co.

Bettetini, Gianfranco (ed.) (1985), *Televisione: la provvisoria identità italiana*, Torino: Edizioni della Fondazione Agnelli.

Bianchini, Angela (1968), *Il romanzo d'appendice*, Torino: ERI.

Bidussa, David (1994), *Il mito del bravo italiano*, Milano: Il Saggiatore.

Bidussa, David (2005), 'Le *foibe* e l'illusione della storia coerente/The *foibe* and the Illusion of Consistent History', *Riformista*, 9 February, p. 4.

Bignell, Jonathan and Fickers Andreas (eds) (2008), *A European Television History*, Malden and Oxford: Wiley-Blackwell.

Bingham, Dennis (2010), *Whose Lives Are They Anyway? The Biopic as Contemporary Film Genre*, New Brunswick: Rutgers University Press.

References

Blumler, Jay G., Gurevitch Michael and Katz Elihu (1985), *Reaching Out: A Future for Gratifications Research*, in Karl Rosengren, Lawrence A. Wenner and Philip Palmgree (eds), *Media Gratifications Research*, London: Sage.

Bocca, Giorgio (1994), 'Cavaliere, *La Piovra* non è solo in tv/The Mafia is not only on TV', *La Repubblica*, 18 October, p. 1.

Bocca, Giorgio (1995), 'Per favore non toccateci *La Piovra*/Please, Don't Touch *La Piovra*', *Venerdì di Repubblica*, 24 March, p. 7.

Bolzoni, Attilio (1989), 'Cattani ucciso come Cassarà/Cattani Has Been Murdered like Cassarà', *La Repubblica*, 21 March, p.1.

Boorstin, Daniel (1992), *The Image: A Guide to Pseudo-Events in America*, New York: Vintage Books, New York.

Bosseno, Christian (ed.), (2010), *Télévision française: la saison 2010*, Paris: L'Harmattan.

Bourdieu, Pierre (2007), *Distinction: A Social Critique of Judgement and Taste*, Harvard: Harvard University Press.

Bourdon, Jerome (2004a), '*Shakespeare, Dallas et le commissaire: Une histoire de la fiction Téléviseé en Europe*', *Les Temps des Médias*, 2, pp. 176–197.

Bourdon, Jerome (2004b), 'Old and New Ghosts: Public Service Television and the Popular: A History', *European Journal of Cultural Studies*, 7: 3, pp. 283–304.

Brancato, Sergio (2007), *Senza fine*, Napoli: Liguori.

Brecht, Bertolt and Bentley, E. (1994), *Galileo*, New York: Grove Press.

Brooks, Peter (1996), *The Melodramatic Imagination*, Yale: Yale University Press.

Brundson, Charlotte (1997), *Screen Tastes: Soap Opera to Satellite Dishes*, London: Routledge.

Brundson, Charlotte (1998), 'Structure of Anxiety: Recent British Television Crime Fiction', *Screen*, 3, pp. 223–243.

Brunetta, Giampiero (1991), *Cent'anni di cinema italiano*, Torino: Einaudi.

Brunetta, Gian Piero (2009), *The History of Italian Cinema: A Guide to Italian Film from Its Origin to the Twenty-First Century*, Princeton: Princeton University Press.

Bucci, Tonino (2005), '*Foibe*, il tranello del buonismo/*Foibe*, the Do-Goodery Trap' *Liberazione*, 3 February, p. 15.

Buonanno, Milly (1994), *Narrami o diva. Studi sull'immaginario televisivo*, Napoli: Liguori.

Buonanno, Milly (1999), *Indigeni si diventa*, Milano: Sansoni.

Buonanno, Milly (2000), *Il Maresciallo Rocca. The Italian Way to the Police Series*, pp. 266—281, in Horace Newcomb (ed.), *Television, the Critical View*, Oxford: Oxford University Press.

Buonanno, Milly (2002), *Le formule del racconto televisivo*, Milano: Sansoni.

Buonanno, Milly (2004), *Italian Television*, pp. 77–80 in John Sinclair, (ed.), *Contemporary World Television*, London: BFI.

Buonanno Milly (2007), *Sulla scena del rimosso: Il dramma televisivo e il senso della storia*, Napoli: IperMedium.

Buonanno, Milly (2008), *The Age of Television: Experiences and Theories*, Bristol: Intellect.

C.S. (1984), 'Di grande attualità il tema della mafia/The Mafia is a Hot Topic', *l'Avanti*, 23 March.

Calvini, Angela (1999), '*Jesus*, il pubblico lo giudica/*Jesus*, the Reaction of the Public', *Avvenire*, 8 December, p. 23.

Campbell, Joseph (1993), *The Hero with a Thousand Faces*, New York: Fontana Press (Italian translation *L'eroe dai mille volti*, Milano: Guanda).

Capecchi, Saveria (2000), *Ridendo e sognando con la soap*, Roma: RAI-ERI.

Cappelli, Valerio (1995), 'Stavolta la realtà ha superato *La piovra*/This Time Reality Has Gone Beyond *La piovra*', *Corriere della Sera*, 5 March, p. 33.

Cappello, Gianna (2003), *Cronaca di un successo annunciato. Il pubblico della fiction religiosa nel periodo giubilare*, pp. 101–131, in Stefano Martelli, *Il Giubileo mediato*, Milano: Franco Angeli.

Caprara, Fulvia (1992), '*Piovra*, scende in campo la DIA/*Piovra*, the DIA Takes Action', *La Stampa*, 15 October, p. 22.

Caprara, Fulvia (1995), '*La Piovra* televisiva? E' uno choc necessario/*La Piovra* on TV is a Necessary Choc', *La Stampa*, 3 March, p. 11.

Cardinal, Marie (2000), *The Words to Say It*, London: Women's Press Ltd.

Cassirer, Ernst (1973), *La filosofia dell'illuminismo*, Firenze: Sansoni.

Caughie, John (2000), *Television Drama. Realism, Modernism and British Culture.* Oxford: Oxford University Press.

Cavicchia Scalamonti, Antonio (2001), *Introduzione*, pp. 9–26 in Zvetan Todorov, *Gli abusi della memoria*, Napoli: Ipermedium.

Cawelti, John G. (1976), *Adventure, Mystery and Romance*, Chicago: The University of Chicago Press.

Cervi, Mario (2005), 'Menzogne coperte da silenzi'/Lies, Concealed by Silence' *Il Giornale*, 29 January, p.1.

Cervone, Paolo (1993), 'La Rai atterra nel deserto, ed è la Bibbia/The Rai Lands in the Desert, and It Is Bible', *Corriere della Sera*, 29 April, p. 33.

Cesarale, Sandra (1999), 'Poupard: Gesù in tv, coraggioso e controcorrente/Jesus on TV, Courageous and Cutting-Edge', *Corriere della Sera*, 6 December, p. 30.

Chaniac, Régine (1996), 'Littérature et télévision', *Cinémaction*, 79, pp. 28–36.

Chesebro, James W. (1987), *Communication, Values, Popular TV Series*, pp. 17–51 in Horace Newcomb (ed.), *Television, the Critical View*, Oxford: Oxford University Press.

Chesterton, Gilbert K. (2008), *The Defendant*, Sioux Falls: NuVision Publications.

Ciambricco, Alberto (1975), *Il tenente Sheridan: Piccola storia di un grande successo*, pp. 193–206 in AA.VV. *Televisione, la provvisoria identità italiana*, Torino: Edizioni della Fondazione Agnelli.

Cocchiara, Giuseppe (1981), *Il mondo alla rovescia*, Torino: Bollati-Boringhieri.

Colombo, Fausto and Aroldi, P. (2003), *Le età della TV*, Milano: Vita e Pensiero.

Conti, P. (1992), 'L'ultima *Piovra*/The Last *Piovra*', *L'Europeo*, 2 November.

Corbi, Maria (1994), 'Cosa nostra uccide, non è una telenovela/The Mafia Kills, It is not a Telenovela', *La Stampa*, 16 October, p. 3.

Creeber, Glen (2001a), 'Cigarettes and Alcohol. Investigating Gender, Genre and Gratifications in Prime Suspect', *Television & New Media*, 2, pp. 149-166.

Creeber, Glen (2001b), 'Taking Our Personal Lives Seriously: Intimacy, Continuity and Memory in the Television Drama Serial', *Media Culture and Society*, 23, pp. 439-455.

Croft, Stephen (1995), *Global Neighbours?* pp. 98-121 in Robert C. Allen (ed.) *To Be Continued ...* , London: Routledge.

Curran, James and Park M. (eds.) (2000), *De-westernizing Media Studies*, London: Routledge.

Curti, Lidia (1990), *Imported Utopias*, pp. 320-336 in Zygmunt G. Baransky and Robert Lumley (eds), *Culture and Conflict in Postwar Italy*, New York: St. Martin's Press.

Custen, George (1992), *Bio/Pics: How Hollywood Constructed Public History*, New Brunswick: Rutgers University.

D'Avanzo, Giuseppe (1995), 'Ma la vera *Piovra* è molto più crudele/The Real *Piovra* is Much Ferocious' , *La Repubblica*, 6 March, p. 6 extra.

Dayan, Daniel and Katz, Elihu (1992), *Media Events: The Life Broadcasting of History*, Cambridge: Harvard University Press.

De Fornari, Oreste (1990), *Teleromanza: Storia indiscreta dello sceneggiato TV*, Milano: Mondadori.

De Mauro, Tullio (1991), *Storia linguistica dell'Italia unita*, Bari: Laterza.

De Rita, Lidia (1964), *I contadini e la televisione*, Bologna: il Mulino.

Deaglio, Enrico (1991), *La banalità del bene: Storia di Giorgio Perlasca*, Milano: Feltrinelli.

Deaglio, Enrico (1992), *Il figlio della professoressa Colomba/The Son of Professor Colomba*, Palermo: Sellerio Editore.

Deaglio, Enrico (1995), 'Nel nome del padrino/In the Name of the Godfather', *Effe*, 1, p. 8.

Del Boca, Angelo (2005), *Italiani brava gente? Un mito duro a morire*, Vicenza: Neri Pozza.

Delavaud, Gilles et Maréchal, Denis (eds) (2011), *Télévision: le moment expérimental*, Paris: Editions Apogée.

Di Lello, Aldo (2005), 'Foibe, la Rai rompe la congiura del silenzio/Foibe, the Rai Ends the Conspiracy of Silence' *Secolo d'Italia*, 29 January, p. 1.

Drucker, Susan and Cathcart, Robert (eds) (1994), *American Heroes in a Media Age*, Cresskill: Hampton Press.

Eco, Umberto (1984), *Tipologia della ripetizione*, pp. 19–36 in Casetti, F. (ed.), *L'immagine al plurale*, Venezia: Marsilio.

Edgerton, Gary (1985), *The American Made-for-TV Movie*, pp. 151–180 in Brian Rose (ed.), *TV Genres*, Westport: Greenwood Press.

Edgerton, Gary (1991), 'High Concept Small Screen: Reperceiving the Industrial and Stylistic Origins of the American Made-for-TV Movie', *Journal of Popular Film and Television*, 19: 3, 114–127.

Edgerton, Gary (2001), *Television as Historian*, pp. 1–16 in Gary Edgerton and Peter Rollins (eds) *Television Histories*, Lexington: The University Press of Kentucky.

Eisenstein, Elisabeth (1993), *The Printing Revolution in Early Modern Europe*, Cambridge: Cambridge University Press (Italian translation: *Le rivoluzioni del libro*, Bologna: il Mulino, 1997).

Ellis, John (1992), *Visible Fictions*, London: Routledge.

Ellis, John (2000), *Seeing Things: Television in the Age of Uncertainty*, London: I.B. Tauris.

Enzensberger, Hans Magnus (1992), *Mediocrity and Delusion: Collected Diversions*, London: Verso.

Featherstone, Michael (1992), 'The Heroic Life and Everyday Life', *Theory Culture Society*, 9, pp. 159–182.

Fiandaca, Giovanni (ed.) (2007), *Women and the Mafia*, New York: Springer.

Fiske, John (1987), *Television Culture*, London: Methuen.

Fogu, Claudio (2006), *Italiani brava gente: The Legacy of Fascist Historical Culture on Italian Politics of Memory*, pp. 147–176 in R. Ned Lebow, W. Kansteiner and C. Fogu (eds), *The Politics of Memory in Postwar Europe*, Durham: Duke University Press.

Foot, John (2009), *Italy's Divided Memory*, New York: Palgrave Macmillan.

Forgacs, David (1990), *Italian Culture in the Industrial Era, 1910–80*, Manchester: Manchester University Press.

Forgacs, David and Gundle, Stephen (2007), *Mass Culture and Italian Society from Fascism to the Cold War*, Bloomington: Indiana University Press.

Fragalà, Girolamo (2005), 'Record di ascolti e voglia di conoscere/Record Ratings and the Need to Know', *Il Mattino*, 9 February, p. 21.

Freccero, Carlo (1986), *Il palinsesto della televisione commerciale*, pp. 136–145 in Guido Barlozzetti (ed.) *Il palinsesto*, Milano: Franco Angeli.

Frye, Northrop (1957), *Anatomy of Criticism*, Princeton: Princeton University Press.

Fumarola, Silvia (1992), 'Il ritorno della *Piovra*, la battaglia continua/The *Piovra* Comes Back, the Battle Goes On', *La Repubblica*, 15 October, p. 41.

Fumarola, Silvia (1995), 'Fermate *La Piovra*!/Stop *La Piovra*!' *La Repubblica*, March 1, p. 31.

Fumarola, Silvia (2000), 'In 11 milioni con Padre Pio/11 Millions with Father Pius', *La Repubblica*, 19 April, p. 57.

Gabrielli, Aldo (1989), *Grande dizionario illustrato della lingua italiana*, Milan: Mondadori.

Gallozzi, Gabriella (2005), 'Fiction sulle foibe, comparse maltrattate?' *L'Unità*, January 30, p. 21.

Garambois, Silvia (1995), 'E Zeffirelli protesta contro *La Piovra* tv/Zeffirelli protests against *La Piovra*', *l'Unità*, 1 March.

Garbesi, Marina (1995), 'I vescovi siciliani attaccano: *La Piovra* è una vergogna/The Sicilian Bishops Criticize *La Piovra*', *La Repubblica*, 22 March, p. 19.

Garelli, Francesco (1991), 'Le diverse italie della fede', *il Mulino*, 5, pp. 859–871.

Garelli, Francesco (2003), 'Il sentimento religioso in Italia', *il Mulino*, 5, pp. 814–822.

Gates, Anita (2001), 'Devout, Wise and Loves to Dance at Weddings', pp. 218–219, in Staff of the NYT, *The NYT Television Reviews 2000*, Chicago: Fitzroy Dearborn Publishers.

Gavioli, Orazio (1984), 'La fiction che aiuta a sapere/This Fiction Helps Us to Know', *La Repubblica*, 21 March, p. 15 extra.

Geraghty, Christine (1991), *Women and Soap Opera*, Cambridge: Polity Press.

Germani, Sergio G. (2005), 'Un falso storico la prima volta in tv delle foibe/History Feigned, the First Time for the *foibe* in TV', *Il manifesto*, 5 February, p. 16.

Giddens, Anthony (1991), *Modernity and Self-Identity*, Cambridge: Polity Press.

Gouldner, Alvin (1975), *Sociology and the Everyday Life*, in Lewis Coser (ed.), *The Idea of Social Structure*, New York: Harcourt Brace.

Grace, Pamela (2009), *The Religious Film*, Malden: Wiley-Blackwell.

Gramsci, Antonio (1985), *Selections from Cultural Writings*, London: Lawrence and Wishart.

Grasso, Aldo (1992), *Storia della televisione italiana*, Milano: Garzanti.

Grasso, Aldo (1999), 'Quel Cristo televisivo, tra gadget e modelle/The Televisual Christ, Among Gadgets and Top-Models', *Corriere della Sera*, 6 December, p. 1.

Grasso, Aldo (2000), *Radio e televisione: Teorie, analisi, storie, esercizi*, Milano: Vita e Pensiero.

Grasso, Aldo (2005), 'La tragedia delle foibe in tv diventa piccola'/The Tragedy of the *foibe* Diminished in TV, *Il Corriere della Sera*, 6 February, p. 33.

Grasso, Aldo (2007), *Buona maestra*, Milan: Mondadori.

Gripsrud, Jostein (1995), *The Dynasty Years*, London: Routledge.

Gumpert, Gary (1994), *The Wrinkle Theory: The Deconsecration of the Hero*, pp. 47-61 in Drucker, Susan and Cathcart, Robert (eds.), *American Heroes in a Media Age*, Cresskill: Hampton Press.

Gundle, Stephen (1990), *From Neo-Realism to Luci Rosse: Cinema, Politics, Society, 1945–1985*, pp. 195–224 in Zygmunt Baransky G. and Robert Lumley (eds), *Culture and Conflict in Postwar Italy*, New York: St. Martin's Press.

Gundle, Stephen (2000), *Between Hollywood and Moscow: The Italian Communists and the Challenge of Mass Culture*, Durham: Duke University Press.

Henderson, Lesley (2007) *Social Issues in Television Fiction*, Edinburgh: Edinburgh University Press.

Hepp, Andreas and Couldry, Nick (2009), *What Should Comparative Media Research Be Comparing?*, pp.32-47 in Thussu Daya K (ed.), *Internationalizing Media Studies*, London: Routledge.

Hills, Matt (2010), 'When Television Doesn't Overflow beyond the Box: The Invisibility of Momentary Fandom', *Critical Studies in Television*, 5: 1, pp. 97–110.

Hobsbawm, Eric J. (1995), *Age of Extremes: The Short Twentieth Century*, London: Abacus.

Hobson, Dorothy (2003), *Soap Opera*, Cambridge: Polity Press.

Ingrascì, Ombretta (2007), *Donne d'onore: Storie di mafia al femminile*, Milano: Bruno Mondadori.

Jacobs, Jason (2000), *The Intimate Screen: Early British Television Drama*, Oxford: Oxford University Press.

Jancovich, Mark and Lyons, James (eds) (2003), *Quality Popular TV*, London: BFI.

Jedlowski, Paolo (2005), *Media e memoria: Costruzione sociale del passato e mezzi di comunicazione di massa*, pp. 31–44, in M. Rampazi, A. L. Tota (eds), *Il linguaggio del passato: Memoria collettiva, mass media e discorso pubblico*, Roma: Carocci.

Kattan, Emmanuel (2002), *Penser le devoir de mémoire*, Paris: Presses Universitaires de France.

Katz, Elihu and Liebes, Tamar (1991), *The Export of Meanings: Cross-Cultural Readings of Dallas*, Oxford: Oxford University Press.

Kerr, Paul (1982), 'Classic Serials: To Be Continued', *Screen*, 23: 1, pp. 6–19.

La Spina, Antonio (2009), 'L'analisi sociologica della mafia oggi', *Rassegna italiana di sociologia*, 2, pp. 301–335.

Levi, Roberto (2005), 'Un cuore nel pozzo riscattato dagli attori/Heart in the Pit Redeemed by the Actors', *il Giornale*, 9 February, p. 36.

Lombezzi, Mimmo (1980), *Un binocolo per il loggione*, pp. 37–58 in Gianfranco Bettetini (ed.), *American Way of Television: Le origini della tv in Italia*, Milano: Sansoni.

Lotz, Amanda D. (ed.) (2009), *Beyond Prime Time*, London: Routledge.

Lowenthal, Leo (1944), *The Triumph of Mass Idols*, pp. 109–140 in Leo Lowenthal (ed.), *Literature, Popular Culture and Society*, Englewood Cliff: Prentice-Hall.

Mammì, Alessandra (1994), 'Senza mafia né patria/No Mafia nor Country', *L'Espresso*, 21 October.

Marill, Alvin H. (2007), *Big Pictures on the Small Screen*, Westport: Praeger.

Martelli, Stefano (1990), *La religione nella società post-moderna: Tra secolarizzazione e de-secolarizzazione*, Bologna: Dehoniane.

Martelli, Stefano (2003), *Il Giubileo mediato. Audience dei programmi televisivi e religiosità in Italia*, Milano: Franco Angeli.

Mazziotti, Nora (1996), *La industria de la telenovela*, Buenos Aires: Paidos.

McCabe, Janet and Akass, Kim (eds) (2007), *Quality TV: Contemporary American Television and Beyond*, London: I.B. Tauris.

McQuail, Denis (1997), *Audience Analysis*, London: Sage.

MEDIA Salles (1994), *European Cinema Yearbook*, Milan: MEDIA Salles.

Messina, Sebastiano (2005), 'La storia divisa tra fiction e documentario/History Divided Between Fiction and Documentary', *La Repubblica*, 7 February, p. 53.

Miller, Daniel (1992), *The Young and Restless in Trinidad: A Case of the Local and the Global in Mass Consumption*, pp. 163–182 in Roger Silverstone and Eric Hirsch (eds), *Consuming Technologies*, London: Routledge.

Miller, Jeffrey S. (2000), *Something Completely Different*, Minneapolis: University of Minnesota Press.

Mills, Brett (2010), 'Invisible Television: The Programmes No One Talks About Even Though Lots of People Watch Them', *Critical Studies in Television*, 5: 1, pp. 1–16.

Mittel, Jason (2009), *Lost in a Great Story: Evaluation in Narrative Television (And Television Studies)*, pp. 119–138 in Roberta Pearson (ed.), *Reading Lost*, London: I.B. Tauris.

Montanari, Arianna (1995), *Eroi immaginari: L'identità nazionale nei romanzi, film, telefilm polizieschi*, Napoli: Liguori.

Monteleone, Franco (1992) *Storia della radio e della televisione in Italia*, Venezia: Marsilio.

Moran, Albert (1998), *Copycat TV*, Luton: University of Luton Press.

Morris, Nancy and Waisbord, Silvia (eds.) (2001), *Media and Globalizazion. Why the State Matters*, New York: Rowman & Littlefield.

Mulvey, Laura (1975), 'Visual Pleasure and Narrative Cinema', *Screen*, 16: 3, pp. 6–18.

Neale, Stephen (ed.) (2002): *Genre and Contemporary Hollywood*, London: British Film Institute.

Neale, Stephen (2000), *Genre and Hollywood*, London: Routledge.

Nelson, Robin (2008), *Costume Drama*, pp. 49–52 in Creeber, G. (ed.), *Television Genre Book*, London: British Film Institute.

Newcomb, Horace (1974), *TV: The Most Popular Art*. New York: Doubleday.

Newcomb, Horace (1988), *One Night of Prime Time*, pp. 88–112 in James W. Carey (ed.) *Media, Myths and Narrative*, London: Sage.

Newcomb, Horace and Robert S. Alley (1983), *The Producer's Medium*, Oxford: Oxford University Press.

Nove, Aldo (2005), 'Le *foibe* e il linguaggio inconscio/The *Foibe* and the Unconscious Language', *Liberazione*, 3 February, p. 1.

O'Connor, John (1983), 'TV: Italian "Life of Verdi" in 6 parts', *The New York Times*, October 24. (http://query.nytimes.com/gst/fullpage.html?res=9C02E7DF133BF93 7A15753C1A965948260. Accessed 20 December 2010).

O'Donnell, Hugh (1999), *Good Times Bad Times*, London: Leicester University Press.

Ong, Walter (1982), *Orality and Literacy*, Routledge: London (Italian translation: *Oralità e scrittura*, Bologna: il Mulino, 1986).

Pace, Enzo (2003), 'La modernizzazione religiosa del cattolicesimo italiano', *il Mulino*, 5, pp. 823–831.

Palombelli, Barbara (1994), 'Tre milioni in piazza? Nelle case erano di più/Three Million on the Streets? There Were More at Home', *La Repubblica*, October 16, p.2.

Patruno, Franco (1999), 'Riflessioni su Jesus/Reflections about Jesus', *L'Osservatore romano*, 13–14 December, p.14.

Pearson, Roberta (2007), *Anatomising Gilbert Grissom*, pp. 39–56 in Michael Allen, *Reading CSI*, London: I.B. Tauris.

Peirce, Gualtiero (1995), 'E' una Sicilia davvero Beautiful/A Very Beautiful Sicily', *La Repubblica*, 6 March, p. 7.

Peresson, Giovanni (2008), *Lettura sotto inchiesta: Leggere, comprare*, pp. 205–224 in Spinazzola, V. (ed.), *Tirature 2008*, Milano: Il Saggiatore.

Perra Emiliano (2010a), 'Legitimizing Fascism through the Holocaust? The Reception of the Miniseries *Perlasca: Un eroe italiano* in Italy', *Memory Studies*, 3: 2, pp. 95–109.

Perra, Emiliano (2010b), *Conflicts of Memory*, Bern: Peter Lang.

Peters, John Durham (1999), *Speaking into the Air*, Chicago: University of Chicago Press.

Petraglia, Sandro e Rulli, Stefano (1992), 'La nostra *Piovra* era bella, E sarà l'ultima/Our *Piovra* was Fine, and Will Be the Last', *Il Manifesto*, 24 December.

Petraglia, Sandro, Rulli Stefano e Purgatori Andrea (1990), *La Piovra 5, Il cuore del problema*, Milan: Rizzoli.

Piccinini, Alessandra (1995) 'Scandalosamente *Piovra*/The Scandalous *Piovra*', *Il Manifesto*, 4 March.

Pickering, Michael and Emily Keightley (2006) 'The Modalities of Nostalgia', *Current Sociology*, 54: 6, pp. 919—941.

Pinto Francesco, Barlozzetti Guido and Salizzato Claver (eds) (1988), *La televisione presenta. La produzione cinematografia della RAI 1965-1975*, Venezia: Marsilio.

Pischedda, Bruno (2007), *Maturità del poliziesco classico*, pp. 10–20 in Vittorio Spinazzola (ed.), *Tirature 2007*, Milan: il Saggiatore.

Placido, Beniamino (1994), 'Virtuale ma non virtuosa/Virtual not Virtuous', *La Repubblica*, 17 October, p. 25.

Pugliese, Sergio (1964), 'Un mestiere difficile', pp. 72–75 in Anon, *Dieci anni di televisione in Italia*, Roma: RAI-Servizio di Documentazione e Studi.

Putnam, Robert D. (1994), *Making Democracy Work*, Princeton: Princeton University Press.

Rapping, Elayne (1992), *The Movie of the Week: Private Stories, Public Events*, Minneapolis: University of Minnesota Press.

Ricoeur, Paul (2004), *Ricordare, dimenticare, perdonare*, Bologna: il Mulino

Rixon, Paul (2006), *American Television on British Screens*, London: Palgrave MacMillan.

Roche, George (1987), *A World without Heroes: The Modern Tragedy*, Hillsdale: The Hillsdale College Press.

Rowlands, Mark (2008), *Fame*, Stocksfield: Acumen.

Rueda Laffond, José C. (2011), *Televising the Sixties in Spain: Memories and Historical Constructions*, pp.174–188, in M. Neiger, O. Meyers and E. Zandberg (eds), *On Media Memory. Collective Memory in a New Media Age*, New York: Palgrave Macmillan.

s.gar. (1984), '*La Piovra* mafiosa sotto accusa in tv/The Octopus-Mafia Under Accusation on TV', *L'Unità*, 19 March.

Sanguineti, Tatti (1980), *Televisione e cinema negli anni cinquanta*, pp. 83–118 in Gianfranco Bettetini (ed.), *American Way of Television: Le origini della TV in Italia*, Firenze: Sansoni.

Sassen, Saskia (2007), *Going Digging in the Shadow of Master Categories*, pp. 85–100 in M. Deflem, *Sociologists in a Global Age: Biographical Perspectives*, Aldershot: Ashgate.

Saviano, Roberto (2006), *Gomorra: Viaggio nell'impero economico e nel sogno di potere della camorra*, Milano: Mondadori (English Translation: *Gomorrah: Italy's other Mafia*, New York: Macmillan, 2007).

Schiller, Herbert (1969), *Mass Communication and the American Empire*, New York: Augustus M. Kelley.

Schiller, Herbert (1976), *Communication and Cultural Domination*, New York: White Plains.

Schiller, Herbert (1991), 'Not yet the Post-Imperialist Era', *Critical Studies in Mass Communication*, 8: 1, pp. 13–28.

Schlesinger, Philip (1990), *The Berlusconi Phenomenon*, pp. 270–285 in Zygmunt G. Baransky and Robert Lumley (eds), *Culture and Conflict in Postwar Italy*, New York: St Martins Press.

Seagrave, Kerry (1998), *American Television Abroad: Hollywood's Attempt to Dominate World Television*, Jefferson: McFarland.

Selznick, Barbara (2008), *Global Television: Coproducing Culture*, Temple: Temple University Press.

Sheehan, James. J. (2008), *Where Have All the Soldiers Gone?*, New York: Mariner Books (Italian translation: *L'età post-eroica*, Rome: Laterza, 2009).

Silj, Alessandro (1988), *East of Dallas*, London: British Film Institute.

Silj, Alessandro (ed.) (1992), *La nuova televisione in Europa*, vol. II, Milano: Gruppo Fininvest.

Silva, Sergio (1992), 'Ma David Licata sopravviverà/Davide Licata Will Survive', *L'Unità*, 23 October, p. 19.

Silverstone, Roger (1999), *Why Study the Media?*, London: Sage.

Sorlin, Pierre (1991), *European Cinemas European Societies 1939–1990*, London: Routledge.

Sparks, Richard (1992), *Television and the Drama of Crime*, Buckingham: Open University Press.

Spigel, Lynn (2001), *Welcome to the Dreamhouse*, Durham: Duke University Press.

Strate, Lance (1994), *Heroes: A Communication Perspective*, pp. 15–24 in Susan Drucker and Robert Cathcart (eds), *American Heroes in a Media Age*, Cresskill: Hampton Press.

Straubhaar, Joe (1991), 'Beyond Media Imperialism: Asymmetrical Interdependence and Cultural Proximity', *Critical Studies in Mass Communication*, 8, pp. 1–11.

Straubhaar, Joe (2007), *World Television. From Global to Local*, London: Sage.

Surchi, S. (1984), 'La grande "bestia" e la giustizia/The Great Beast and the Justice', *Il Popolo*, 18 March.

Taylor, Ella (1991), *Prime-Time Families: Television Culture in Post-War America*, Berkeley: University of California Press.

Thompson, Robert J. (1997), *Television's Second Golden Age*, Syracuse: Syracuse University Press.

Thussu, Daya K. (ed.) (2009), *Internazionalizing Media Studies*, London: Routledge.

References

Todorov, Zvetan (2001), *Gli abusi della memoria,* Napoli: Ipermedium.

Tranfaglia, Nicola (1994), *Introduzione* in Angela Bedotto, (ed.), *Mafie: Panorama Bibliografico (1945–1993),* Milan: Franco Angeli.

Treveri Gennari, Daniela (2009), *Post-War Italian Cinema: American Intervention, Vatican Interest,* London: Routledge.

Trupia, Piero (2002), *Il potere di convocazione: Manuale per una comunicazione efficace,* Napoli: Liguori.

Turnbull, Sue (2010), 'Missing in Action: On the Invisibility of (Most) Australian Television', *Critical Studies in Television,* 5: 1, pp. 111–121.

Turner, Graeme (2010), *Ordinary People and the Media: The Demotic Turn,* London: Sage.

Turner, Graeme and Tay, Jinna (eds.) (2009), *Television Studies After TV,* London: Routledge.

Turner, Graeme and Tay, Jinna (2010), 'Not the Apocalypse: Television Futures in the Digital Age', *International Journal of Digital Television,* 1, pp. 31-50

Van Zoonen, Liesbet (2005), *Entertaining the Citizen,* Lanham: Rowman & Littlefield.

Veneziani, Marcello (2005), 'Foibe crimine comunista, Ma in tv è vietato dirlo/*Foibe* – A Communist Crime.but in TV It's Forbidden to Say It, *Libero quotidiano,* 30 January, p. 1.

Wagstaff, Christopher (2007), *Italian Neo-Realist Cinema: An Aesthetic Approach,* Toronto: University of Toronto Press.

Warshow, Robert (2001), *The Immediate Experience,* Cambridge: Harvard University Press.

Weissmann, Elke (2009), 'Travelling Cultures: The Development of the American Mini Serial and its Import to Britain,' in *Journal of British Cinema and Television,* 6: 1, pp. 41–57.

White, Mimi (1994), 'Women, Memory and Serial Melodrama', *Screen,* 35: 4, pp. 336–353.

Williams, Raymond (1974), *Television: Technology and Cultural Form*, London: Fontana.

Winston, Diane (ed.) (2009), *Small Screen, Big Picture: Television and Lived Religion*, Waco: Baylor University Press.

Wood, Mary (2005), *Italian Cinema*, Oxford: Berg.

Zerubavel, Eviatar (1981), *Hidden Rhythms: Schedules and Calendars in Social Life*, Chicago: University of Chicago Press.

Index

A&E, 173
Abatantuono, Diego, 116
Abbott, Stacey, 51
ABC, 38-41, 142, 175
Abraham, 184
Abraham, Fahrid Murray, 184
Abramo/Abraham, 179, 185, 195n
Achtung!Bandit, 46n
Adam, Barbara, 21-22
Addams Family, The, 40
Aeneid, 37
Agostino d'Ippona/St. Augustine of Hippo, 167, 195n
Agrodolce/Bittersweet, 103
AIE, 17
Akass, Kim, 143
Al di là delle frontiere/Beyond Frontiers, 211, 214
Alcott, Louisa May, 23
Alessandrini, Ludovico, 30
Alfiere, lo/The Ensign, 24-25n
Alfred Hitchcock Presents, 40, 114
Alianello, Carlo, 25n
Alias, 129
Allasio, Marisa, 30
Allen, Robert C., 76, 79, 126, 235
Alley, Robert S., 228
Alt, Carol, 150
Amadeus, 173
Amenta, Marco, 164n

American Idol, 175
Amurri, Sandra, 83
Amy Fisher Story, The, 175, 194n
Anania, Francesca, 210
Anderson, Carolyn, 167
Andreotti, Giulio, 84-87n
Antonioni, Michelangelo, 46n
Arcuti, captain Antonio, 87n
Aristotle, 119
Arlacchi, Pino, 58, 162
Arnaudi, marshal Gigi, 113
Aroldi, Piermarco, 14-15
Assunta Spina, 202-203
Attenborough, Richard, 172
Attentatuni, lo/The Big Assassination, 151
August, 202
Augustus, 177
Austen, Jane, 23
Avvenire, 187, 238
Ayala, judge Giuseppe, 83, 87n

Badalmenti, Tano, 86
Badalucco, Nicola, 55
Balzac, Honoré de, 23
Bambino in fuga, un/A Child on the Run, 160
Baransky, Zygmunt G., 39
Barney Miller, 114
Bartali, Gino, 177, 195n
Battlestar Galactica, 181
Bauman, Zygmunt, 110, 126

BBC, 17, 21-22, 38, 173, ; BBC3, 173 ; BBC4, 173
*Beautiful Mind, A,*173,
Bechelloni, Giovanni, 172, 193, 222
Beck, Ulrich, 136
Bella Mafia/Beautiful Mafia, 144
Bellissima, 46n
Ben Hur, 33
Benjamin, Walter, 7-8, 110, 138
Bennett, Tony, 7, 52, 54-55, 62-63
Bentivegna, Calogero, 62
Bentley, Eric, 170
Berbenni, Stefania, 83
Berger, Peter, 189
Berlusconi, Silvio, 3-4, 40, 84-85, 105n, 218, 220
Bernabei, Ettore, 35, 184, 186
Bertelsmann-Stiftung, 195n
Bettetini, Gianfranco, 15
Bianchini, Angela, 66, 97
Bidussa, David, 221, 223
Big Brother, 208
Big Love, 181
Bignell, Jonathan, 14
Bill, The, 125
Bingham, Dennis, 172
Bisbetica domata, la/ The Taming of the Shrew, 38
Bisset, Jacqueline, 182-184
Black Donnellys, The, 144
Blaise Pascal, 167
Blumler, Jay G., 53
Boardwalk Empire, 144
Bocca, Giorgio, 60, 85
Bogart, Humphrey, 112
Bolchi, Sandro, 45n-46n
Bold and the Beautiful, The, 96
Bolkonskij, prince Andrej, 204
Bolzoni, Attilio, 68
Bonanno: A Godfather's Story, 144
Bonanza, 40
Bond and Beyond: The Political Career of a Popular Hero, 7, 52
Bond, James, 52-53, 55, 57, 63, 123
Boni, Alessio, 168, 204

Bonicelli, Vittorio, 38
Bonnard, Mario, 46n
Boorstin, Daniel, 170, 172, 175
Borsellino, judge Paolo, 73, 87n, 151, 157, 160, 164n, 177
Bosseno, Christian, 200
Bourdieu, Pierre, 21
Bourdon, Jerome, 13, 15, 21-22
Brancaccio, 151-152,
Brancato, Sergio, 92
Brecht, Bertold, 170
Brigada, 144
Bronta, Saverio, 86
Brontë, Emily, 23; Brontë sisters, 23
Brooks, Peter, 67-68
Brotherhood, 144
Brundson, Charlotte, 17, 110
Brunetta, Giampiero, 30-31, 36, 40, 114, 118
Bucci, Tonino, 220
Buona battaglia di don Pietro Pappagallo, la/The Good Battle of Don Peter Pappagallo, 211, 216, 222
Buonanno, Milly, 14, 19, 39, 54, 78, 100, 104, 116, 118, 137, 152, 228
Burgess, Anthony, 38
Burning Bed, The, 175
Buscetta, Tommaso, 82, 86
Buttafuoco, Joey, 194n

Caccia al ladro d'autore/Hunt for the Author's Thief, 115
Caesar, 177
Callaghan, Inspector, 114
Calvini, Angela, 187
Camerini, Mario, 37, 46n
Camilla, 95
Camilleri, Andrea, 123
Camorrista, il/The Camorrist, 162
Campbell, Joseph, 170
Canal Plus, 145, 158
Canale 5, 5, 101, 103, 125-127, 131, 134, 136-137, 141, 148, 150, 152, 154-155, 157-158, 164n, 178, 190, 191, 193-194, 201-202, 205, 2011, 215
Canne al vento/Reeds in the Wind, 24

Index

Cannon, 114
Capecchi, Saveria, 100
Capo dei capi, il/The Boss of Bosses, 141-142, 148, 152, 154-155
Capote, 173
Cappelli, Valerio, 86
Cappello, Gianna, 190-191
Caprara, Fulvia, 67, 86
Captain Corelli's Mandolin, 214
Caravaggio (Michelangelo Merisi), 168, 177
Caravaggio, 168,
Cariddi, Tano, 67-68, 70-71, 79
Cardinal, Marie, 13
Carnera, Primo, 177, 195n
Cartesius/Descartes, 167
Casacci, Mario, 112
Caselli, judge Gian Carlo, 86
Casino, 143
Cassarà, Antonino, 68, 87n
Cassirer, Ernst, 194n
Castellani, Renato, 37, 43
Castellitto, Sergio, 190, 193
Castello, Enric, 9
Casualties of Love, 175
Cathcart, Robert, 169, 172
Cattani, Inspector Corrado, 45, 52, 56, 59, 61, 68-73, 76-77, 80-82, 86-87n, 141, 149, 157
Caughie, John, 17, 29, 208, 213
Cavicchia Scalamonti, Antonio, 207
Cawelti, John G., 65, 111, 142
CBS, 37-38, 40, 42, 101, 118, 137, 143-144, 175, 184,
Cefalonia, 211, 214, 216, 222, 224
Cento giorni a Palermo/100 Days in Palermo, 162
Cento passi, i/One Hundred Steps, 164n
Centovetrine/The Shopping Centre, 103
Centro Cattolico Cinematografico (CCC) / Catholic Film Centre, 32, 46n
Cervi, Mario, 220
Cervone, Paolo, 195n
Cesarale, Sandra, 187-188
Chaniac, Régine, 17, 22
Channel 4, 52

Channel 5, 43
Charlemagne, 177
Charlie's Angels, 41
Chesebro, James W., 119-121
Chesterton, Gilbert Keith, 113, 135
CHIPS, 114
Christ (Jesus), 9, 181-184, 186-188, 195n, 199
Ciambricco, Alberto, 112
Ciano, Galeazzo, 212, 215,
Cime tempestose/Wuthering Heights, 23, 201-202
Cinque inchieste per un commissario/Five Investigations for an Inspector, 115
Cittadella, la/The Citadel, 202
Cocchiara, Giuseppe, 138n, 161
Coco Chanel, 177
Cold Case, 137
Collins, Wilkie, 66
Colombo, Fausto, 14-15
Colombo, 114
Columbo, 40
Columbus, Christopher, 44
Come l'America/ Like America, 211
Commissario a Roma, un/An Inspector in Rome, 116
Commissario Corso/Inspector Corso, 116
Commissario De Vincenzi, il/Inspector De Vincenzi, 114
Commissario Montalbano, il/Inspector Montalbano, 123-125
Conan Doyle, Arthur, 111
Confessioni di un italiano, le/ The Castle of Fratta, 24-25n
Conseguenze dell'amore, le/The Consequences of Love, 163-164n
Conti, judge Silvia, 71-72, 76
Conti, P., 64
Contorno, Totuccio, 85
Coppi, Fausto, 177, 195n
Coppola, Francis Ford, 87n, 142-144
Coraggio di Angela, il/The Bravery of Angela, 152, 158-160
Coraggio di parlare, il/The Courage to Speak, 158
Corbi, Maria, 84

Corleone, Michael, 145
Coronation Street, 99
Corriere della Sera, 187, 221
Cortellesi, Paola, 178
Couldry, Nick, 233
Creeber, Glen, 38, 132
Crime Stories, 143
Criminal Minds, 137
Cristoforo Colombo/Christopher Columbus, 43
Critical Studies in Television, 4-5, 9
Croft, Stephen, 96
Cronaca di un amore/ Story of a Love Affair, 46n
CSI: Crime Scene Investigation, 137, 181
CSI: New York, 137
Cuéntame como pasó /Tell Me What Happened, 105, 200
Cuore/Heart: a School-boy's Journal, 24, 202
Cuore nel pozzo, il/The Heart in the Pit, 211, 214, 216, 218-221
Cuori rubati/Stolen Hearts, 103
Curran, James, 231
Curti, Lidia, 41
Custen, George F., 146, 172-176

D'Acquisto, Salvo, 177, 195n
D'Avanzo, Giuseppe, 82
Dahan, Olivier, 173
Dalida, 177, 195n
Dalla Chiesa, general Carlo Alberto, 151, 157, 164n, 177
Dallas, 8, 42-45, 51, 53, 58-59, 74, 94, 106, 149
Damiani, Damiano, 55-56, 75, 162
Dapporto, Massimo, 150
David, 185,
Dayan, Daniel, 81-84
De Amicis, Edmondo, 25n,
De Angelis, Augusto, 113
de Bernières, Louis, 214
De Biase, Francesca, 136
De Bosio, Giancarlo, 38,
De Caprio, Sergio, 164n
De Concini, Ennio, 56-57
De Fornari, Oreste, 16
De Gasperi, Alcide, 177, 194
De Laurentiis, Dino, 37, 47n

De Mauro, Tullio, 17-18
De Mille, Cecil, 38
De Palma, Brian, 56, 143
De Rita, Lidia, 15
De Santis, Giuseppe, 46n
De Sica, Vittorio, 46n, 84
Deaglio, Enrico, 61, 80-81, 216
Débats, 66,
Del Boca, Angelo, 223
Delavaud, Gilles, 9, 14
Deledda, Grazia, 24
Dhoest, Alexander, 9
Di Lello, Aldo, 220
Di Vittorio, Giuseppe, 177, 194
Dickens, Charles, 23, 66
Dimenticare Palermo/Forget Palermo, 162,
Distretto di polizia/Police District, 125-127, 131-135, 137
Divo, il, 87n
Divorzio all'Italiana/ Divorce Italian Style, 56
Dolce vita, la/ The sweet life, 36
Don Matteo, 121-125
Donna d'onore/Woman of Honour, 150
Donna detective/Woman detective, 131
Donne di Mafia/Mafia Women, 160
Dostoevsky, Fyodor, 23
Dottor Antonio, il/ Doctor Antonio, 24-25n
Douglas, Kirk, 37
Doyle, Wayne, 98
Dr. Kildare, 40
Dreiser, Theodore, 65
Drucker, Susan, 169, 172
Due soldi di speranza/ Two Cents Worth of Hope, 37
Dumas, Alexandre, 23

Eco, Umberto, 19
Edda, 211-212, 215
Edera/Ivy, 95
Edgerton, Gary, 38-39, 200, 208, 210, 213
EEC, 36
Einstein, Albert, 177
Eisenstein, Elisabeth, 169
Elisa di Rivombrosa/Elisa from Rivombrosa, 201, 205

Elisa, 205
Ellery Quinn, 114
Ellis, John, 3, 39, 111, 167, 209
Emerson, Ralph Waldo, 170
Enzensberger, Hans Magnus, 29
Epoca, 235
Equalizer, The, 114
Erin Brockovich, 173
Espinosa, 67, 71
Esther, 184-185
Ettore, 220
Exodus: il sogno di Ada/Exodus:Ada's dream, 211, 214, 221

Fabbri, Paolo, 97
Falcone, judge Giovanni, 66, 73, 87n, 150-151, 157, 164n, 177
Fantasia Barrino Story: Life is not a Fairy Tale, The, 175
Fantastichini, Ennio, 86
Fawcett, Farrah, 175
FBI Francesco Bertolazzi Investigatore/FBI, Francesco Bertolazzi Private Eye, 113, 118
Featherstone, Mike, 171
Fellini, Federico, 36
Femme d'honneur, une/A Woman of Honour, 128
Femmes de loi/Women of the Law, 128
Ferrara, Abel, 143
Ferrara, Giuseppe, 162
Ferrari, Enzo Anselmo, 177, 194n
Ferrari, Isabella, 127, 132
Feuillet, Octave, 23
Fiandaca, Giovanni, 161
Fichera, Massimo, 92
Fickers, Andreas, 14
Fielding, Henry, 23
Figli strappati, i/Abducted Children, 211
Figlio della professoressa Colomba, il/ The Son of the Teacher Colomba, 80
Fininvest, 40, 42
Fiorello, Giuseppe, 220
Fisher, Amy, 194
Fiske, John, 54-55

Flaubert, Gustave, 23
Fogazzaro, Antonio, 25n
Fogliani, inspector Linda, 130
Fogu, Claudio, 215
Foot, John, 213, 216
Forgacs, David, 17, 21, 23, 31, 46
Forman, Miloš, 173
Forsyte Saga, The, 38
Fort Apasc, 164n
Fortebracci, Tonio, 155-156
Fragalà, Girolamo, 221
Francesca e Nunziata, 202
Francesco d'Assisi/Francis of Assisi, 195
Francesco/Francis, 192
Franco, Francisco, 200
Frears, Stephen, 173
Freccero, Carlo, 42
Frederick II of Prussia, 194n
Fremantle, 97
Frye, Northrop, 119-120
Füssli, Johann Heinrich, 4
Fuga degli innocenti, la/Hidden Children, 211, 214, 216, 221
Fuga per la libertà/Escape to Freedom, 211
Fumarola, Silvia, 63, 84, 193

Gabrielli, Aldo, 62
Gaetano, Rino, 177, 195n
Galileo, 170
Gallozzi, Gabriella, 220
Gandhi, 172
Garambois, Silvia, 84
Garbesi, Marina, 84
Garelli, Francesco, 188-189
Garko, Gabriel, 148, 155
Garrone, Matteo, 164n
Gates, Anita, 186
Gattopardo, il/ The Leopard, 24
Gavioli, Orazio, 59-60
General Hospital, 41
Genesis, 184-185
Georgia O'Keeffe, 173
Geraghty, Christine, 79
Germani, Sergio, 221
Germi, Pietro, 56, 162

Gesù di Nazareth/Jesus of Nazareth, 98, 195n
Ghini, Massimo, 212
Giallo Club/Detection Club, 112-113
Giallo di sera/ Evening Mystery, 113
Giallosera, 115
Gibson, Mel, 181
Giddens, Anthony, 148
Gioè, Claudio, 154
Giordana, Marco Tullio, 164n
Giorno della civetta, il/ The Day of the Owl, 56, 162
Giovanni Falcone, 150-152
Giovanni Paolo II/John Paul II, 179, 191
Girotti, Massimo, 47n
Giulietta e Romeo/ Romeo and Juliet, 37-38
Giuseppe/Joseph, 179, 184-185
Glen, John, 57
Godfather, The, 8, 142-146; Godfather 3, The, 87
Godfather's Story, A, 144
Gogol, Nikolai, 23
Goldoni, Carlo, 15
Gomorra. Viaggio nell'impero economico e nel sogno di dominio della camorra/ Gomorrah. Italy's Other Mafia, 142, 162, 164n
Gone with the Wind, 66
Gotta, Salvator, 25n
Gouldner, Alvin, 171
Grace, Pamela, 181, 187
Gramsci, Antonio, 23
Grande Torino, il/The Great Torino, 202, 210-211
Grasso, Aldo, 15, 17, 29, 34, 137, 187, 221
Gripsrud, Jostein, 54
Grissom, Gil, 137
Grundy International, 93, 96-98
Guaccero, Bianca, 203
Guerra è finita, la/The War is Over, 211, 223
Guiding Light, 96
Gumpert, Gary, 170
Gundle, Stephen, 15, 17, 23, 30-33, 36
Gunsmoke, 40

Haggis, Paul, 144
Happy Days, 41
Harris, Richard, 184

Hart to Hart, 114
HBO, 143-144, 148, 173
Henderson, Lesley, 103
Hepp, Andreas, 233
Hero with a Thousand Faces, The, 170
Hershey, Barbara, 195n
High Chaparral, The, 40
Hill Street Blues, 114, 137
Hill, Terence, 122
Hills, Matt, 5
History Channel, 212
Hitler, Adolf, 200
Ho sposato uno sbirro/I Married a Cop, 131
Hobsbawm, Eric J., 199
Hobson, Dorothy, 96
Hodgson Burnett, Frances, 23
Holocaust, 39, 41, 194n
Homer, 37
Hooper, Tom, 173
House of Saddam, 173
Howard, Ron, 173
Hugo, Victor, 23, 65-66
Humiliated and Insulted, 23
Hunter, 114

I love Lucy, 40
I, Claudius, 173
Il giornale di Sicilia, 55
Il Manifesto, 85-86
Il Messaggero, 56
Il Popolo, 58
Iliad, 135
Incantesimo/Enchantment, 103
Ingrascì, Ombretta, 161
International Herald Tribune, 142
International Journal of Cultural Studies, 4
Into the storm: Churchill at War, 173
Ironside, 114
Ispettore Sarti, lo/Inspector Sarti, 116
It's Now or Never, 98
Jacob, 185
Jacobs, Jason, 14
Jancovich, Mark, 143
Jedlowski, Paolo, 216
Jeremiah, 185

Jeremiah, 184
Jesus, 181-188, 191
Joe Petrosino, 146, 151, 164n
Joffé, Roland, 56
John Paul II, 193, 201
John XXIII, 193, 201
Johnny Cash, 173
Joseph, 184
Julie Lescaut, 128

Karamazov, 45n
Karol un uomo diventato Papa/Karol a Man who Become Pope, 179, 191-192
Kattan, Emmanuel, 200-201
Katz, Elihu, 42, 81-84
Keightley, Emily, 206, 210
Kerr, Paul, 17, 38, 47n
King's Speech, The, 173
Kingdom of Heaven, 181
Kingsley, Ben, 184
Kojak, 40, 114
Kristeva, Julia, 55

L'Avanti, 58
L'Espresso, 82
L'Osservatore romano, 187
L'Unità, 58, 63
La Plante, Lynda, 144
La Repubblica, 59, 98, 85-86
La Spina, Antonio, 147
Ladri di biciclette/Bicycle Thief, 46n, 84
Lancaster, Burt, 38
Lattuada, Alberto, 43
Law & Order: SVU, 137
Law, The, 38
Lawless Years, The, 142
Lawrence of Arabia, 172
Lay, Ubaldo, 112
Lean, David, 172
Legend of Tennessee Moltisanti, The, 164n
Leone, Sergio, 36, 56
LeRoy, Melvin, 33
Levi, Roberto, 221
Liberate mio figlio/Set my Son Free, 160

Licata, Davide, 69, 76, 87n
Liebes, Tamar, 42
Lifetime, 173, 175
Linda e il brigadiere/Linda and the Brigadier, 130-131
Lindenstrasse, 99
Little Lord Fauntleroy, 23
Little Women, 23
Lizzani, Carlo, 46n
Lollobrigida, Gina, 30
Lombezzi, Mimmo, 15-16
Loren, Sofia, 30
Lost, 51, 181
Lotz, Amanda D., 173
Lourdes, 191
Loving, 96
Lowenthal, Leo, 172-174, 177, 194n
Lucchesi, Licio, 87n
Lucky Luciano, 162
Lui e lei/He and She, 131-133
Lumley, Robert, 39
Lupo, Jonathan, 167
Lux Vide, 184, 193
Lyons, James, 143
Macchiavelli, Loriano, 113, 116
Madden, Jon, 214
Madre Teresa/Mother Teresa, 181, 191
Mafalda di Savoia/Mafalda of Savoy, 211, 215
Maffei, Mario, 46n
Mafia Wives, 144
Mafiosa/The Mafia Woman, 145, 158
Magnum PI, 114
Maigret, inspector Jules, 111
Maigret, Madame, 111
Malone, Jack, 118
Mammì, Alessandra, 82, 92
Manfredi, Nino, 116
Mangano, Silvana, 30
Mangold, Jane, 173,
Mani sulla città, le/Hands on the City, 162
Manzoni, Alessandro, 19, 34, 46n, 202
Marcinelle, 202, 211
Marco Polo, 43-44
Maréchal, Denis, 9, 14

Mares, Claudia, 164n
Maresciallo Rocca, il/Marshal Rocca, 116-119, 121, 123-125
Maria Goretti, 181, 191
Maria Josè, 211, 215
Maria Josè, 215
Marill, Alvin H., 38
Martelli, Stefano, 187, 189
Martines, Alessandra, 212
Mary of Bethany, 187
Mash, 40
Mastro don Gesualdo, 35
Mattei, Enrico, 177, 194n
Mazziotti, Nora, 95
McCabe, Janet, 143
McCloud, 114
McQuail, Denis, 229
Media International Australia, 9
Mediaset, 5, 39, 42, 95, 103, 105n-106n, 127, 134, 136, 149-152, 154-155, 157, 176, 178, 190, 193, 205
Médico de familia, 105,106n
Medico in famiglia, un/A Doctor in the Family, 204
Mercurio, Paul, 184
Messina, Sebastiano, 221
Meucci, Antonio, 177, 195n
Mi ricordo di Anna Frank/ I Remember Anna Frank, 211
Miami Vice, 114
Michelangelo, 177, 183
Michelini, Giulia, 136
Milano violenta/Violent Milan,114
Milk, 173
Millardet, Patricia, 72
Miller, Daniel, 74
Miller, Jeffrey S., 13, 105
Miller, Bennett, 173
Mills, Brett, 4
Misérables, Les, 65-66
Miss Austen Regrets, 173
Mission, The, 56
Mitchell, Margaret, 66
Mittel, Jason, 51, 60
Moltisanti, Christopher, 142, 164n

Montalbano/ Inspector Montalbano, 123-125, 128
Montaldo, Giuliano, 43
Montanari, Arianna, 73, 246
Monteleone, Franco, 15, 30, 35
Montessori, Maria, 177-178, 195n
Montessori, Maria, 178
Moran, Albert, 9, 96
Mordecai, 184
Moro, Aldo, 177, 194n
Morricone, Ennio, 38, 56
Morris, Nancy, 223
Mosè/Moses the Lawgiver, 38, 179, 185, 195n
Moses, 184
Mulvey, Laura, 128
Murder She Wrote, 114
Mussolini, Benito, 46, 210, 215, 223
Mussolini, Edda, 212, 215
Mystères de Paris, Les/The Mysteries of Paris, 65-66

Napoli spara /Naples shoots, 114
Napoli violenta/Violent Naples, 114
Natalee Holloway, 175
NBC, 38-41, 137, 142-145, 175
NCIS, 137
Neale, Stephen, 153, 172
Negrin, Alberto, 218
Neighbours, 96-99
Nelson, Robin, 22, 200
Nero Wolfe, 111
Nerone, 202
New York Times, 47n, 164
Newcomb, Horace, 93, 199, 228
Newman Paul, 47n
Nibelungen, The, 200
Nicholas, Patrick, 4
Nievo, Ippolito, 24-25n
Nightmare, 4
Nikita, 129
Nine Networks, 144
Niola, Marino, 97
Nome della legge, in/In the Name of the Law, 162
Non parlo più/I Shall Say No More, 160
Nove, Aldo, 219

Index

O sole mio, 98
O'Connor, John, 47n
O'Donnell, Hugh, 9, 95-96, 98
Octopussy, 57
Odissea/ The Odyssey, 34, 37
Oldman, Gary, 184
Olmi, Ermanno, 184
Once Upon a Time in America, 56
Ong, Walter, 169
Onore e il rispetto, lo/Honour and Respect, 148, 155-156
Opera Vigilanza Repressione Antifascismo (OVRA), 56
Origini della mafia, alle/The Origins of the Mafia, 146
Ossessione, 47n
Ottocento/Nineteenth Century, 24

Pace, Enzo, 189
Padre Pio da Pietrelcina, 193-194, 199
Padre Pio tra cielo e terra/Father Pius between Heaven and Earth, 191-192
Padre Pio/Father Pius, 179, 190-191
Paisà, 46n
Palatucci, Giovanni, 216, 222
Palombelli, Barbara, 84
Paolo Borsellino, 152, 157
Papa buono, il/The Good Pope, 179, 191-192
Papa Giovanni/Pope Giovanni, 179, 191
Papa Luciani. Il sorriso di Dio/Pope Luciani, the Smile of God, 191
Papa Luciani/Pope Luciani, 179
Pappagallo, Don Pietro, 216
Park, Myung-Jin, 231
Passion of the Christ, The, 181
Passioni /Passions, 84, 95
Patruno, Franco, 187
Pearson, Roberta, 137
Peirce, Gualtiero, 74
Perelli, Luigi, 63, 67
Peresson, Giovanni, 17
Perlasca, Giorgio, 177, 194n, 201, 216-217, 222, 224
Perlasca. Un eroe italiano/Perlasca: An Italian Hero, 194n, 211, 214, 217, 221-222

Perra, Emiliano, 216, 222-223
Perry Como Show, 21
Perry Mason, 40, 114
Peters, John Durham, 230
Petraglia, Sandro, 61, 64
Philo Vance, 113
Piccinini, Alessandra, 64, 85
Piccolo mondo antico/The Patriot, 24-25n, 202
Pickering, Michael, 206, 210
Pinto, Francesco, 45n
Piovra, la/The Octopus. Power of the Mafia, 8, 44-45, 49, 51-87n, 91, 118, 139, 141, 145-146, 149, 151-152, 156-157, 163
Pirandello, Luigi, 55
Pisana, la/ The Woman of Pisa, 24
Pischedda, Bruno, 109
Placido Rizzotto, 164n
Placido, Beniamino, 84
Placido, Michele, 68-69, 72, 81, 149, 192, 194
Police Woman, 114
Polo, Marco, 44
Pontificio Consiglio della Cultura, 187
Posto al sole, un/ A Place in the Sun, 8, 89, 91, 93, 96-105
Poupard, cardinal Paul, 187-188
Powell Robert, 38
Pravda, 52
Presley, Elvis, 98
Preziosi, Alessandro, 205
Prime Suspect, 132, 144
Prodi, Romano, 100
Proietti, Gigi, 117
Promessi sposi, i/The Betrothed, 19, 33-35, 37, 46n, 201-202
Provenzano, Bernardo, 147, 150-151
Puccini, Giacomo, 177
Puccini, Vittoria, 205
Pugliese, Sergio, 15, 18, 24
Puglisi, Don Giuseppe (Pino), 151, 164n, 177
Pushkin, Alexander Sergeyevich, 23
Putnam, Robert D., 120
Puzo, Mario, 142

Queen, The, 173
Questa è la mia terra/This Is My Land, 211
Qui squadra mobile/Here, the Mobile Squad, 113
Quo Vadis?, 33, 43

Raccontami/Tell Me, 202
Racconti del maresciallo, i/The Marshal's Tales, 113, 115
Racconti di Padre Brown, i /The Father Brown Stories, 113
Ragazze di Sanfrediano, le/The Girls of Sanfrediano, 202
Rai, 14-16, 21, 24, 30, 34-40, 42-45n, 52, 58, 69, 72, 80-81, 92-93, 96-97, 99, 101-102, 105n-106n, 117, 122, 124, 146, 149-151, 159, 176, 179-180, 182-184, 187, 192-193. 203-204, 212, 217, 219-220; Rai 1 (Raiuno/first channel), 5, 51, 69, 72, 81, 101-103, 113-118, 121-124, 130-131, 146, 150, 152, 154, 158-160, 168, 180, 182-184, 191-194n, 201-204, 211-212, 214-217, 219-220, 223; Rai 2 (Raidue), 103, 113-116, 118, 123, 146, 154, 158, 160; Rai 3 (third channel), 93, 97, 99, 103, 125, 210
Rambaldi, Carlo, 37
Rapping, Elayne, 175
Reagan, The, 173
Rebecca la prima moglie/Rebecca, 202
Red Brigades, 194n
Reed, Oliver, 184
Resurrezione/Resurrection, 202
Rete 4, 95
Rich Man Poor Man, 38, 41
Ricoeur, Paul, 200, 207
Riina, Totò, 87n, 141, 142, 147-148, 151, 154-155, 164n
RIS Roma/RIS Rome, 134
RIS: Imperfect Crimes, 137
Risi, Marco, 164n
Riso amaro/Bitter Rice, 46n
Rispo, Patrizio, 101
Ristori, count Fabrizio, 205
Rita da Cascia, 192
Rixon, Paul, 20

Rizzoli, Angelo, 193
Rocca, marshal Giovanni, 125, 128, 131
Roche, George, 169
Roeg, Nicolas, 184
Rojek, Chris, 175
Roma città aperta/ Rome, Open City, 46n
Roma violenta/Violent Rome, 114
Roman Holiday, 33
Romance of a Poor Young Man, The, 23
Romano, Giulia, 131-132
Romanzo di Loris, il/Loris's Novel, 55
Romanzo di un maestro, il/ The Novel of a Teacher, 24
Roots, 39, 41
Rosi, Fracesco, 162
Rossellini, Roberto, 46n, 167
Rossi, Franco, 37, 43
Rowlands, Mark, 171-173
RTR TV, 144
Rueda Laffond, José Carlos, 200
Ruffini, Paolo, 25n
Ruffo, Claudia, 101
Rulli, Stefano, 64

S. S. Van Dine, 113
Salomon, 185
Salvatore Giuliano, 162
Salvo D'Acquisto, 211, 214, 222
Samson and Delilah, 185
San Filippo Neri, 195n
San Giovanni. L'apocalisse/Saint John. The Apocalypse, 181, 185
San Paolo/ Saint Paul, 181, 185, 191
San Pietro/Saint Peter, 181
Sangue dei vinti, il/The Blood of the Defeated, 211
Sanguineti, Tatti, 16
Sant'Antonio/Saint Antony, 192
Sarah, 195n
Sargent, Joseph, 184
Sassen, Saskia, 20
Sasso in bocca, il/Stone in the Mouth, 162
Saviano, Roberto, 142, 164n
Savino, Lunetta, 159
Scalise, inspector Giovanna, 127, 131-134
Schiller, Herbert, 13

Schindler's List, 172
Schindler, Oskar, 194n, 201
Schlesinger, Philip, 43
Siciliana ribelle, la/The Rebel Sicilian Girl, 164n
Scimeca, Pasquale, 164n
Scorsese, Martin, 143-144
Scott, Ridley, 130, 181
Seagrave, Kerry, 40-41, 46n
Segreto di Thomas, il/Thomas's Secret, 211
Selznick, Barbara, 44
Senza confini/No Boundaries, 211, 216, 221-222
Sereni, Ada, 177, 195n, 214
Serranos, Los/The Serranos, 105
Shakespeare, William, 38
Sheehan, James. J., 169
Sheridan, lieutenant Ezechiele, 112-113
Sherlock Holmes, 111
Showtime, 144, 173
Silj, Alessandro, 23, 42, 92, 94
Silva, Sergio, 56, 63-64, 87n
Silverstone, Roger, 206, 210, 213
Simenon, George, 111
Sinclair, Upton, 65
Sisto, Jeremy, 182-183, 195n
Socrate/Socrates, 167
Soderbergh, Steven, 173
Sola debole voce, una/A Lone Weak Voice, 158, 160
Soldati, Mario, 113
Sopranos, The, 8, 142-144, 147-148, 153
Sorlin, Pierre, 32-33
Sorrentino, Paolo, 87n, 163-164n
Sorrisi e canzoni, 80, 87n
Sotto il sole di Roma/ Under the Roman Sun, 37
Sottocasa/Downhome, 103
Spada, Gianluca, 115
Sparks, Richard, 44, 52
Speer, Albert, 200
Spielberg, Steven, 172
Spigel, Lynn, 210
Squadra antimafia/Anti-Mafia Squad, 134, 164n
Squadra, la/The Squad, 125
St. John the Evangelist, 184
Starsky and Hutch, 41, 114

State buoni se potete/Be Quiet if You Can, 195n
Stevenson, Robert Louis, 23
Storia della camorra/History of the Camorra, 146
Storia di Anna/ The Story of Anna, 44
Storia di guerra e d'amicizia/Story of War and Friendship, 211
Storyteller, The, 110
Stout, Rex, 111
Stowe, Harriet Beecher, 66
Strate, Lance, 169
Straubhaar, Joe, 23, 94, 228, 233
Stream, 94
Streets of San Francisco, The, 114
Stromboli, 46n
Sue, Eugène, 65-66
Surchi, Sergio, 58
Susman, Warren, 213

Tangentopoli/Bribesville, 105n
Tano da morire/Tano Is to Die, 163
Tarantino, Quentin, 142
Tay, Jinna, 231, 233
Taylor, Ella, 126
Telecinco, 105
Telepiù, 94
Temple Grandin, 173
Ten Commandments, The, 38
Tennison, Jane, 132, 144
Terrasini, lawyer, 67
Terra trema, la/ The Earth Trembles, 46n
Thackeray, William Makepeace, 23
The Independent, 194n
Thelma e Louise, 130, 133
The Wall Street Journal, 100
Thomas, Louis C., 113
Thompson, Robert J., 93
Thussu, Daya, 233
Time Europe Magazine, 87, 160
Tirabassi, Giorgio, 157
Tito, Josip Broz, 220
TNT, 184
Todorov, Zvetan, 201, 207
Tolstoy, Lev, 23
Tom Jones, 23
Tomasi di Lampedusa, Giuseppe, 24

Tornatore, Giuseppe, 162
Torre, Roberta, 163
Tranfaglia, Nicola, 62
Treveri Gennari, Daniela, 32
Trupia, Piero, 227
Turgenev, Ivan Sergeyevich, 23
Turnbull, Sue, 4
Turner, Graeme, 175-176, 231, 233
TVE, 200
Twain, Mark, 233
Twenty Thousand Leagues Under the Sea, 57
Twilight Zone, 40

Ulisse/Ulysses, 37
Ultimo dei corleonesi, lo/The Last of the Corleonesi, 151-152, 154
Ultimo padrino, lo/The Last Godfather, 150, 152, 154
Ultimo/The Last, 152, 157
Umberto D, 46n
Umberto di Savoia, 215
Uncle Tom's Cabin, 66
Underbelly, 144
Unter uns, 98
Untouchables, The, 56, 142-143, 153
Uomo di rispetto, un/Man of Respect, 150, 154

Vaccari Giacomo, 47n
Valeria medico legale/Valeria the Forensic Doctor, 131
Van Sant, Gus, 173
Van Zoonen, Liesbet, 53
Veneziani, Marcello, 220
Ventriglia, Gino, 98
Venturi, captain Riccardo, 137
Verdi/ The Life of Verdi, 43, 47n
Verga, Giovanni, 47n
Verne, Jules, 57
Victor Emanuel III, King, 215
Vidor, King, 37
Vie en rose, La, 173
Vigata, 123
Virgil, 37
Virginia, la monaca di Monza/Virginia, the Nun of Monza, 201-202

Visconti, Luchino, 38, 46n-47n
Vita di Cavour/Life of Cavour, 167
Vita di Dante/Life of Dante, 167
Vita di Leonardo da Vinci, la /The life of Leonardo da Vinci, 37, 167
Vita di Michelangelo/Life of Michelangelo, 167
Vita rubata, la/Stolen Life, 152
Vivere/Living, 103
Voce alta, a/Out Loud, 158
Voight, John, 180
Voltaire, 170, 194n

Wagstaff, Christopher, 31, 46n
Waisbord, Silvio, 233
Walk the Line, 173
Wallace, Irving, 66
Walsh, Raoul, 153
War and Peace, 37, 204
Warhol, Andy, 174
Warshow, Robert, 145-146, 148
Weissmann, Elke, 38-39
White Heat, 153
White, Mimi, 77, 104
Why I Wore Lipstick to My Mastectomy, 175
Williams, Raymond, 42
Winston, Diane, 181
Winter, Jay, 213
Wiseguy, 143
Without a Trace, 118, 137
Wojtyla, Karol, 180
Wood, Mary, 33
Woollacott, Janet, 7, 52, 54-55, 62-63
Wyler, William, 33

Xena, 129

Yad VaShem – Holocaust Martyrs and Heroes Remembrance Authority, 194n
Young, Roger, 184

Zeffirelli, Franco, 38, 84-85
Zerubavel, Eviatar, 111
Zingaretti, Luca, 123-124, 217
Zola, Émile, 23

www.ingramcontent.com/pod-product-compliance
Ingram Content Group UK Ltd.
Pitfield, Milton Keynes, MK11 3LW, UK
UKHW051849210426
5322IPUK00025B/629